SISTER SOCIETIES

SISTER

 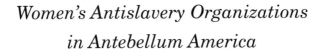

SOCIETIES

Women's Antislavery Organizations
in Antebellum America

BETH A. SALERNO

NORTHERN ILLINOIS

UNIVERSITY

PRESS

DeKalb

© 2005, 2008 by Northern Illinois University Press

Published by the Northern Illinois University Press, DeKalb, Illinois   60115

Manufactured in the United States using acid-free, postconsumer recycled paper

First printing in paperback, 2008

ISBN-13: 978-0-87580-619-8 (paperback : alk. paper)

Design by Julia Fauci

Library of Congress Cataloging-in-Publication Data

Salerno, Beth A.

Sister societies : women's antislavery organizations in antebellum

America / Beth A. Salerno.

p.   cm.

Includes bibliographical references and index.

ISBN-13: 978-0-87580-338-8 (clothbound : alk. paper)

ISBN-10: 0-87580-338-5 (clothbound : alk. paper)

1. Antislavery movements—United States—History—19th century.

2. Women abolitionists—United States—History—19th century.

3. Women—United States—Societies, etc. 4. Women in politics—

United States—History—19th century. I. Title.

E449.S167 2005

973.7'114'082—dc22

2004030004

Dedicated to my husband, Tod F. Ramseyer, with love,

to my parents, Mario Salerno, Jr., and Sandra M. Salerno, with thanks,

and to the women about whom this book is written, with admiration.

Contents

Acknowledgments

This book is the product of a wonderfully collegial process in which graduate advisors, colleagues, editors, referees, and friends all provided extensive comment on versions of the manuscript. I am deeply grateful for their help, and for their understanding. It is a better book for their having read it; the errors that remain are my own.

The research for this book began at the University of Minnesota–Twin Cities History Department. It would not have happened without the guidance of my graduate advisor, Sara Evans, who was willing to accept me into the program and regularly remind me what I was doing there. She helped me create the "free space" I needed to find my own voice. Lisa Norling and Roland Delattre provided their own insights and support, while John Howe provided so many comments on the manuscript it took me six years to address them all.

Archivists across the country have provided help with this work. I am particularly grateful to the staffs of the Boston Public Library Rare Books and Manuscripts Department, the American Antiquarian Society, the Historical Society of Pennsylvania, the Research Library at Old Sturbridge Village, the New York Public Library, the New York Historical Association, the Rochester University Library, the New Hampshire Historical Society, the Haverford College Library Special Collections, the Swarthmore College Friends Historical Library, and the Phillips Library of the Peabody Essex Museum. The Lynn Museum and Reading Historical Commission were also quite helpful. The interlibrary loan staff at Saint Anselm College have been invaluable.

My colleagues at Saint Anselm College have provided the warmest of Benedictine hospitality as well as intellectual challenge. I am particularly grateful to Ward Holder, Dante Scala, Br. Isaac Murphy, and Don Cox, who provided humor, support, and motivation in a summer writing group. Julie Alig read and commented on every chapter, which was beyond the call of friendship. My department colleagues have been unfailingly interested and sympathetic as I have struggled through the bookmaking process. Their support made my work far easier. Thanks go to Silvia Shannon, Philip Pajakowski, Sean Perrone, Hugh Dubrulle, Fr. James Cassidy, Fr. William Sullivan, and Andrew Moore.

Many far-flung historians have had a hand in this work. I thank Carolyn Williams and Jean Fagan Yellin for their comments on a section of chapter 4 presented at the 1999 Berkshire Conference of Women Historians. Stacey Robertson provided both good advice and research materials on western antislavery women. Deborah Van Broekhoven provided useful suggestions and early access to her research. Michael Pierson and Carolyn Lawes read versions of the entire manuscript and greatly improved the argument. They were also models of enthusiastic support. The anonymous referee from NIU Press and Anne Boylan further refined the work with careful readings.

I never knew exactly what editors did prior to this book. Now I know—they seek out works that people need to read, and they encourage, push, and bug authors until the work gets done. I thank Martin Johnson of NIU Press, who sought out this book and got it through its first reading. I am grateful to Melody Herr, who stepped into Martin's shoes, accepted the book, kept it moving through the system, and did the encouraging, pushing, and bugging I needed to get it done.

I cannot afford what my husband and parents deserve for having lived through this work. My parents have never asked for anything more than a signed copy, yet they provided so much in return. My husband wanted much more—a sane wife at the end of the process. He gave me a room of my own in which to write, followed me to my job at Saint Anselm, and said only encouraging things when I raged that there was no way I could possibly finish this book. There are not words enough with which to properly say thank you. Perhaps I will wait just a little before I mention the next book to him.

SISTER SOCIETIES

The Power of Association

"It is the order of nature, that when human beings earnestly wish the
accomplishment of any particular object, they look around them for
help—they unite their forces—they become associated."
—Boston Female Anti-Slavery Society annual report, 1842

The women were determined to finish their meeting.[1] Outside the Concord (NH) courthouse, a crowd of thirty or forty young men hurled rocks and insults against the building. Inside, more than sixty women listened to a ringing denunciation of slavery. Shouting over the mob, Englishman George Thompson described the experiences of women in Great Britain, who had formed societies, raised funds, and circulated petitions to end slavery. He stressed that slavery was a political, moral, and religious issue that demanded women's involvement. Every day slavery tore children from their mothers' arms, wives from their husbands—was it unfeminine to protest these atrocities? In the middle of his speech, a rock shattered the courthouse window, narrowly missing him and raining glass down on the women. A second rock broke another window, and shouts of "Out with the ladies—Out with the women" floated in clearly. Thompson continued amid groans and hisses from the mob, and women ducked as a rotten egg came through the broken windows.

When Thompson had finished, he asked if any woman there would step forward to form a female antislavery society. Fifty-five women walked proudly, and carefully, to the speaker's podium. In full view of the mob outside they committed themselves to the immediate abolition of slavery and the end of prejudice against black people. They signed their names to a society constitution declaring slavery a violation of the law of God and contrary to the Declaration of Independence.[2]

The Concord women found the power to challenge the mob in their association with each other. Together they could take on not only local troublemakers but the most powerful economic and political institution in the country. They were not alone in their efforts. Between 1832 and 1855 women formed over two hundred female antislavery societies across the northern United States, far more than researchers previously had suspected. Many of these societies lasted less than ten years. Some continued for decades, and a few disbanded only after the Civil War. They ranged in size from a half-dozen women to over five hundred, meeting in living rooms, parlors, churches, and town halls. Most of the women were white and middle-class, although black women, wealthy women, and working-class women could be found in many societies, and black women often formed their own societies as well. Together women paid dues, hand-stitched goods to sell, held fairs, prayed, educated themselves about slavery, and signed petitions urging their congressmen to take immediate action. They mixed private efforts among family and friends with public meetings, public fairs, and even public prayer.

The history of these "sister societies" makes clear the power of association. Female antislavery societies gave women a structure in which to meet regularly, educate themselves, stay motivated, and pool their efforts. By organizing independently from men, they were able to serve as officers, write and vote on resolutions, and run public meetings, building their skills and confidence. Meeting together strengthened women's local friendships and linked them to both regional and national networks of reformers. Knowing that they had "friends and sisters" across the country gave women a sense of belonging, and the encouragement that their small individual efforts could swell into a large cumulative contribution.

Correspondence provided the means by which local societies became connected in regional, national, and international networks. From Maine to Michigan, New England to Pennsylvania, antislavery women wrote letters, shared news and strategies, exchanged constitutions and fair goods, and provided moral support when faced by mobs or unsupportive family. Older societies mentored newer ones, providing organizational advice in exchange for new ideas. Regional networks emerged around antislavery fairs as enterprising women in larger societies solicited handmade goods and financial contributions from society members in more outlying towns. Female antislavery societies in Great Britain and Ireland provided moral and financial support, as well as an example of how effective organized women's antislavery efforts could be.

Together women accomplished organizational goals that would have been impossible for individual women. In 1837 they held the first Anti-Slavery Convention of American Women, bringing together representatives from dozens of societies across the North. They would gather again in 1838 and 1839, publishing over a dozen publications and providing a national voice for antislavery women. They organized a petition campaign that overwhelmed Congress with signatures and gave the antislavery movement new visibility and clout. At the local level, women's petitions helped to desegregate train travel in Massachusetts and blocked passage of exclusionary laws against black people in Pennsylvania. Women's antislavery fairs and other fund-raising efforts raised a large portion of the money needed to fund lecturers, newspapers, and other publications. These educational efforts, combined with women's petitioning, helped to create an antislavery constituency for new political parties. Women's national petition campaign during the Civil War helped push passage of the Thirteenth Amendment, which finally outlawed slavery.

Creating and maintaining associations at the local, national, and international level was not easy. Women had to deal with their lack of experience in organizing, debates over membership, societal disapproval, and their own disagreements on strategies and tactics. Race provided one challenge to women's unity that few societies successfully overcame. Religious divisions provided another. When the antislavery movement as a whole fractured over questions of politics, religion, and woman's role, many societies found it necessary to take sides, shattering women's unified network. In the end, the greatest challenge to women's organized efforts came from a larger societal debate over woman's appropriate role in society.

George Thompson had told the Concord women that fighting against slavery was an inherently feminine action. In calling on women's sympathy for mistreated women and children, Thompson linked the antislavery movement to a respected tradition reaching back to the Revolutionary War. For decades, women had formed societies to aid the poor, the needy, and the oppressed. Women were understood to have a particular sensitivity to the pain of others, and a responsibility to uphold the moral values of the nation.

This association between women, benevolence, and moral responsibility increased in the 1820s and 1830s, as women became more closely identified with religion while men were linked to the expanding political privilege of voting. Exclusion from direct political participation was understood to strengthen women's moral power, since they were not corrupted by the compromises necessary to messy party politics. Writers would eventually shape these assumptions into a prescriptive ideology, which suggested that men and women had different talents and skills and thus should fill different spheres in American life. Women were understood to have an important influence over the home, family, and moral decisions, while men controlled the more immoral, chaotic arenas of politics, the economy, and public life.

As Thompson pointed out in his speech, slavery complicated these supposedly neat lines. Slavery had been the subject of political discussion and compromise since the founding of the nation. Congress had exclusive jurisdiction over Washington, D.C., and the territories, and debate over the fate of slavery in these areas formed the subject of many antislavery petitions. As a major foundation of the Southern economy, slavery appeared in debates over road building and tariffs, and Southern congressmen vigorously defended the institution when challenged in any way. Thus slavery would seem to have been beyond woman's appropriate sphere, and an unsuitable topic for her attentions or efforts.

Yet an institution that gave human beings unchecked power over others had moral implications as well. At base it violated the Golden Rule that one should do unto others as one would have them do unto oneself. More broadly it enabled slaveholders to violate God's commandments against killing and adultery. Many antislavery activists saw slavery as a sin, not a political compromise, and felt immediate abolition was the only way to avoid divine retribution. On these grounds, women had every right and responsibility to fight against slavery. They were protecting the oppressed who suffered under it, and their families, communities, and nation, which were being threatened by its continuance.

How women defined slavery and how they saw woman's appropriate role deeply affected their ability to work together. Until 1837 women who joined the antislavery movement generally agreed that slavery was a moral issue on which woman's voice had to be heard. If necessary, women would send their moral message into the heart of the political system, petitioning their congressmen to act against slavery. Women challenged definitions of citizenship linked to rights, such as voting, and stressed the responsibilities of citizenship. These responsibilities fell as heavily on women as on men and required women to take public action against slavery in defense of children and country.

Women's claim to a more public and political role roused public hostility, as the Concord women's public meeting had. In 1841 "Franklin" wrote to the women of Ohio: "I am a great friend to the ladies, and it really grieves me to see so many of my fair countrywomen leaving their proper legitimate sphere of duty, the domestic circle, where they can be useful and shine as ornaments in society, and meddling in the political and civil concerns of the State." He concluded his two-page letter of advice with "Stay at home." Mr. Eli Potter, a Connecticut judge, was more direct: "It is a well known fact, that when a female takes upon herself the character of a public lecturer . . . it generally creates riot and confusion." By 1840 questions of woman's appropriate role helped to split apart the national antislavery movement. Women found it increasingly difficult to maintain their expansive definitions of woman's role, which had enabled their successful united action.[3]

By the 1850s antislavery women had vastly expanded the definition of woman's appropriate role. Female antislavery societies continued to hold large antislavery fairs, antislavery lectures by women, and in 1863 a national convention—all activities that would have caused "riot and confusion" in the 1830s. At the same time, they redefined political action by bringing the issue of slavery into their homes in sewing societies and social gatherings. Excluded from partisan politics, they continued to claim a role in shaping the nation's political agenda. They saw themselves as forcing the government to address the needs of the poor and oppressed, bringing moral arguments to bear on political contests. They also continued to debate the meaning of citizenship in a society that denied white women and most black people the right to vote. While antislavery women came to few united conclusions, their efforts would leave an important legacy for other organizations. Their debates, justifications, arguments, and successes would help to shape the suffrage movement and would play out in temperance and other reform organizations well into the twentieth century.

Organization

This book begins by tracing the associations, influences, and publications that helped inspire women to organize against slavery. Black women's literary societies, free-produce societies, British women's antislavery societies, and benevolent organizations serving black people all had antislavery aspects and provided important examples and motivation for female antislavery organizing. Two early antislavery newspapers shared a talented Ladies' Department editor, Elizabeth Heyrick, who strongly encouraged women to form societies and defended antislavery as a properly female arena for action.

Once women decided to form a society, they faced the complex questions of who could join, what activities would work best, and how to explain women's efforts to others. Correspondence networks were crucial to the success of female antislavery organizing. Through their letters women gave each other advice, shared strategies, and fostered a sense of purpose and belonging. Widespread male and female encouragement enabled women to face down mobs during these early years, including the one that threatened the Concord women.

Female antislavery organizing reached a new height in 1836–1837 when women organized, attended, and ran one of the first national conventions ever run by women. The delegates organized a massive antislavery petition campaign. Carried out by hundreds of women in almost a dozen states, the campaign made clear to legislators and women themselves the power of women's cooperative effort. At the same moment, ministers and others began to publicly question the prominent role of women in the movement. For two more years women managed to find common ground at women's antislavery conventions. In 1838 they survived personal threats of violence and the burning of their meeting hall. Yet, unlike the events of 1835, this violence prompted criticism of the women from antislavery men who openly wondered whether women had taken their organizing too far. When the male antislavery organizations began to disintegrate, in 1839 and 1840, over politics, religion, and the role of women, there were women on both sides of the debate.

In the 1840s and 1850s antislavery women adapted to the divisions that prevented united efforts. They created a diversity of new organizations and refocused their efforts. A number of female antislavery societies took on more public roles, sponsoring lecture series and ever-larger antislavery fairs. Other women turned to practical work for the slaves, forming antislavery sewing societies and providing goods for fugitive slaves. Black women in the East formed their own female antislavery societies and increased their role in vigilance associations that assisted fugitives in their escapes. Western white women, further from the divisions in the East, formed dozens of new female antislavery societies before similar questions regarding woman's role caught up with them. Although women were less united in the 1840s and 1850s, they were no less active. Antislavery energies seem to have spread into organizations previously focused on other oppressed groups.

At the outbreak of the Civil War, the majority of female antislavery societies had disbanded, but at least four groups continued to play important leadership roles in the movement. After years of quiet efforts antislavery women came full circle in 1863, uniting together in the largest female antislavery convention since 1837 and forming the Women's National Loyal League. Drawing on the correspondence networks created in the 1830s and 1840s, this organization coordinated the largest female antislavery petition campaign ever. Women's demand for the end of legal slavery culminated in the passage of the Thirteenth Amendment in 1865. A few societies continued to coordinate efforts to provide basic needs and political rights to African Americans until the late 1860s, but with the passage of the Fifteenth Amendment giving black men the right to vote, the final female antislavery society declared victory and disbanded.

Conclusion

The members of the Rochester Ladies' Anti-Slavery Society understood the heart of association when they wrote in 1864: "While as individuals we have done little . . . as a Society we may feel that our influence has been felt for the good." The Rochester women were talking about both the success of pooling their efforts and their success in bettering the world around them. Women who joined antislavery societies wanted to have a powerful positive effect on their world—to "do good" and "be righteous." That they could not, in the process, completely overcome divisions of race, religion, and ideology should not surprise anyone. However, their failures and their successes provide important lessons on the power and limits of association. Together antislavery women were fundamental to the spread of the antislavery movement, improved the lives of individual slaves, challenged and redefined the limits of woman's proper role, publicly debated the meaning of citizenship, and tackled the most difficult social and political problem of the day. They succeeded in their united goal of abolishing slavery. The nation is still debating the issues that divided antislavery women—questions of racial equality, equal rights for women, and the most appropriate means through which to accomplish moral goals. Antislavery women could leave no better legacy than the inspiration of their successes, and the motivation of their efforts toward moral and political change.[4]

CHAPTER ONE

Antecedents, 1760–1831

Influences and Organizations

"To plead for the miserable... can never be unfeminine."

—Elizabeth Margaret Chandler, 1829

Female antislavery societies grew out of women's rich tradition of helping their neighbors, working for the oppressed, and pleading for the miserable. Antislavery activist and writer Elizabeth Chandler counted on that tradition when she encouraged women to join the antislavery cause.[1] In her early newspaper columns, Chandler claimed that aid to the slave was an extension of women's benevolent activities. In this way, she tried to avoid controversy about whether women should play a role in a political and thus unfeminine cause.

Women worked against slavery in a variety of ways. Societies to educate former slaves, Colonization Society auxiliaries, literary societies, and free-cotton associations all provided women with early arenas for fighting slavery. For some, membership in these early organizations prompted further engagement in the antislavery cause. For others, the earlier societies were an alternative, often less controversial, forum for antislavery activism than female antislavery societies. By the end of 1831 women were engaged in most of the activities that would come to define their participation in the antislavery movement. This included fund-raising, information distribution, petitioning, and networking with English women. They were also engaged in quiet debate over whether antislavery agitation was an appropriate activity for women. Despite Chandler's attempts to portray antislavery as an extension of women's benevolent activities, the question of whether women had a role in political issues would have repercussions beyond the Civil War.

Early Antislavery Efforts Exclude Women

Antislavery agitation in America probably began with the first slave to resist after being led onto shore. It took longer for white Americans to take up the cause. In the late seventeenth century, members of the Society of Friends, or Quakers, began to organize against slavery. Following the lead of their brethren in England, Quakers in Pennsylvania concluded that holding slaves was inconsistent with Christian principles. With encouragement from Benjamin Lay, Quakers Anthony Benezet and John Woolman urged each other to give up the sin of slaveholding. Some Quaker meetings passed resolutions requiring manumission of slaves owned by members of the meeting.

More widespread interest in antislavery principles remained limited until the 1760s and 1770s. Prompted by religious evangelism growing out of the First Great Awakening and logical argument drawn from Enlightenment principles, antislavery activism grew amid the republican rhetoric leading up to the American Revolution. African Americans used Enlightenment definitions of liberty as they petitioned the Continental Congress for their freedom, rights, and an end to slavery. While patriots fought the British at Lexington and Concord, a few Philadelphia men formed the Pennsylvania Abolition Society, the first antislavery society in America.

Using petitions and lawsuits to force state and federal governments to address the slavery issue, these early societies did have some important successes. The U.S. Constitution, ratified in 1789, incorporated language that would result in the end of the slave trade in 1808. Additionally, by 1784 every northern state except New York and New Jersey had provided for gradual emancipation, and by 1804 those two states had passed such laws as well. The enactment of these laws, however, turned out to be the high-water mark for the early antislavery movement. The dissipation of revolutionary and evangelical fervor, increasing concerns over property rights, and racism aggravated by changing economic conditions all slowed antislavery progress in the North. Activists found themselves battling to maintain basic civil rights for free African Americans and fighting to free the slaves that remained after gradual emancipation.[2] The development of the cotton gin and new, more restrictive slave codes mitigated against continued progress in eliminating slavery in the South. Although the American Convention of Delegates from Abolition Societies met twenty-four times between 1794 and 1829, antislavery activists made little specific progress in promoting the elimination of slavery.[3]

Neither African American men nor women of any color were invited to join these early antislavery societies and conventions. During the Revolution, some patriots had called on white women to play a role in achieving America's freedom from Britain. However, there was little sense that women would be of much use in the legal and political maneuverings through which abolitionists hoped to achieve freedom for slaves. There are occasional references to white women who manumitted their slaves or African American women who "manumitted themselves" by running away, but generally women played little role in the early antislavery movement.[4]

Quaker women form the one exception to this general rule. Each Quaker congregation had separate business meetings for men and women, and both sexes were able to speak out during worship services if they felt so moved by the Holy Spirit. Thus Quaker women were able to express opin-

ions regarding slavery, and their names appear on printed petitions and letters from meetings. Two northern women were among the Quaker ministers who traveled south in the 1790s, hoping to convince Southern Quakers to mend their ways. However, Quaker tendencies to shun association
with non-Quakers kept these women from having a strong influence on
others until the 1820s.[5]

Women Take Up Reform

Women's antislavery activism came into its own, beginning in the mid-
1820s, as the result of religious ferment, economic change, and cultural de-
velopments. The revivals of the Second Great Awakening, the emergence of a
middle class in a developing capitalist economy, and the spread of a prescriptive ideology of separate spheres were deeply intertwined and synergistic in
their effects. These forces provided women with the impetus and rationale
for an explosion of women's benevolent organizations and, ultimately, propelled some women into specifically antislavery organizations.

The Second Great Awakening, usually understood as a series of revivals
from the late 1790s to the early 1830s, transformed the American religious
landscape. It refocused Protestantism away from Calvinistic determinism
and toward the doctrine that each Christian had the power to effect their
own salvation. As individuals could be saved, so perhaps could society, if
each individual worked to bring the "perfection" of God's heaven on earth.
Downplaying the importance of ministerial learning and centering on
emotional appeals to personal conscience, the Awakening resulted in newly
energized Baptist and Methodist denominations and a much larger per-
centage of "churched" Americans than before or after. Congregations split,
ordinary people debated the talents of their ministers, and Christians were
encouraged to take personal responsibility for expanding God's dominion
on Earth. One major result of the explosion of new religious congregations
was the completion of the long process of disestablishment in New England. First Connecticut, then New Hampshire, and finally Massachusetts
stopped requiring taxpayer support of the established Congregational
church, releasing religion from direct political influence. Religion increasingly became a personal decision, through which converts could express
their hopes and their goals for themselves and the nation.

Economic changes played an important role in the spread and direction
of the Second Great Awakening. The rapid growth of cities and the increased involvement of ordinary people in the cash economy created a
sense of upheaval that led many men and women to seek religious expla-
nations for so much change. The previous belief that poverty was caused
by the status of one's soul was challenged as people began to feel the negative impacts of capitalism's boom-and-bust cycle. Freed (or torn) from hier-
archical economic relations between master and apprentice, and often far
distant from family members due to the search for work or the relocation

of marriage, young people were particularly likely to be converted to the more egalitarian religious denominations. For the most part, the Awakening was experienced according to one's class status: there were few converts from the wealthy, staunchly Congregational, politically connected upper class and many converts among the expanding ranks of the middle and lower classes.[6]

Middle-class women made up the clear majority of those experiencing religious conversion and were instrumental in converting their families and friends. As economic production moved out of the New England household into newly built factories, many middle-class women experienced both economic dislocation and a sense of personal uselessness. Religion provided them with a sense of identity and self-worth, a supportive and encouraging community, and a moral impulse to make change in their communities. The increased association of women with church and religion led to a conflation of femininity and piousness. At the same time, the expansion of the vote to most white males in this period resulted in the linking of political activity with maleness. Writers and publishers developed these gender associations into the ideology of separate spheres. According to this set of ideas, proper "true women" would dedicate themselves to the domestic, religious, and moral sphere while men handled the less virtuous arenas of politics and business.

In reality the lines between men's and women's "spheres" were not nearly so clear. Women's religious convictions and perceived moral duty encouraged them to look beyond the home to eradicate sin in the world. They rapidly formed hundreds of benevolent organizations dedicating to clothing, feeding, teaching, improving, and converting others. Women took on problems ranging from temperance to prostitution to slavery, all of which sometimes involved female intervention in the economy and politics. As long as women could define their reform activities as moral rather than political, few questioned their activities outside the home.[7]

Women's Early Antislavery Activities

Given the vast proliferation of reform causes in the 1820s and 1830s, why did some women choose antislavery? A woman's class status, race, religion, or geographic location, the support of her family, her reading material and acquaintances, or the presence of an antislavery lecturer might have turned her toward antislavery. Yet even women of very similar backgrounds sometimes chose very different types of or approaches to reform, making it difficult to determine just what caused a particular woman's choices. In addition, a woman's desire to combat slavery could propel her into a variety of different organizations. Black women organized mutual aid associations and literary societies, both of which had antislavery aspects. Some white women joined benevolent organizations focused on uplifting free African Americans while others supported the Colonization

Movement, which hoped to free slaves and then return them to Africa. Women of both races participated in the free-produce movement, which worked against slavery through abstention from slave products. An examination of the variety of pathways to antislavery activism sheds further light on the diversity of women who joined the movement. Since many of these pathways continued to be viable alternatives to female antislavery societies throughout the 1830s, they help make clear the distinctiveness of women who chose to join a female antislavery society. Yet they also make clear the continuities between female benevolent and female antislavery societies, since female antislavery societies often contained elements of many of these earlier movements.

Black women were usually excluded as members of white women's benevolent organizations and as recipients of their charity. In order to respond to the needs of their community, black women formed their own women's associations to support churches, bury the dead, and aid orphaned children. Although class divisions did exist within the black community, even economically well-off families faced racism, the danger of riot, and the oppressive awareness of slavery. Therefore, black women's benevolence often focused on mutual aid and self-help more than charity for a lower class.[8]

One of the earliest black female self-help societies was the Clarkson Society, founded in Salem (MA) in 1818 to promote religion and knowledge amongst the "colored people." Like many other similar organizations, the Clarkson Society did not address slavery directly. However, these associations felt they could help to eliminate slavery by eliminating poverty and the low education levels in the African American community. Through uplift and benevolence they would undermine the prejudices that justified black slavery. The Salem women went a step further than most by naming their organization after one of England's most well-known antislavery politicians, Thomas Clarkson. Thus, they made clear the connection they felt between their work and antislavery agitation.[9]

By the early 1830s African American women had founded dozens of similar societies in Boston, New York, Philadelphia, and other cities throughout the North. Many of them strengthened the connection between mutual aid and antislavery work by donating part of their society's funds to support antislavery newspapers and lecturers. It is not clear how many women active in the black benevolent community went on to join either black or interracial female antislavery societies. One prominent woman who did was Clarissa Lawrence, president of the Colored Female Religious and Moral Society of Salem in 1818, and a founding member and officer in the biracial Salem Female Anti-Slavery Society founded in 1834. She would ensure that the black antislavery movement in Salem retained strong ties to other mutual aid societies, and that it integrated a clear concern regarding the economic and educational status of free blacks into antislavery work. Mutual aid and antislavery work would remain far more intertwined for black women than for their white counterparts. Members of the Colored Ladies' Literary Society and the Rising Daughters of Abyssinia of New York City would provide funds to print the *Proceedings of the Anti-Slavery Convention of American Women, 1837.*[10]

This connection between benevolent work for northern black people and the eradication of slavery was rare among white women prior to 1830. However, it may have enabled some white women to express their antislavery sentiment within the accepted parameters of female care for the poor. The best example is the Cincinnati Female Society, founded in 1821 and later named the Female Association for the Benefit of Africans in Cincinnati, Ohio. The members ran a Sabbath school for freed African Americans and made a clear connection between their work and their antislavery convictions. They recognized that if they were going to demand of Southern slaveholders the financial sacrifice involved in freeing slaves, they had to do their part as well. They could not "withhold the scanty pittance necessary to teach [slaves] to read the holy scriptures which are able to make them 'free indeed.'"[11]

Organizations such as these integrated benevolent work to ameliorate the condition of African Americans with a reformist outlook that placed their work in a broader social context. While radical in its crossing of racial boundaries, women's work among the African American poor was understood as an acceptable outgrowth of women's domestic responsibilities. It did not challenge the ideology of separate spheres in the ways later female antislavery activism would. For white women, like black women, benevolent societies would continue to provide an alternative route for antislavery activism even after the foundation of female antislavery societies. In 1836 the Female Benevolent Society of Hanover would donate funds to an antislavery newspaper, although its members never joined a specifically antislavery organization. This would become increasingly common after 1840.[12]

After 1817 white men and women who wanted a more activist role in the antislavery crusade could support the American Colonization Society (ACS). Founded in that year, the ACS focused on the exportation of black people to Africa where they could supposedly live without racism and without causing any racial disruptions in America. This idea salved the consciences of those concerned with the inequalities of slavery and race without demanding a major social and sectional disruption that might threaten the new and fragile Union. The idea appealed to many white Americans as a way to encourage Southern slaveholders to free their slaves, since it would help eliminate the free black population that Southerners feared could encourage slave revolts. ACS auxiliaries spread rapidly, with over eighty in Pennsylvania alone by 1831. The ACS is often seen as having provided an intellectual training ground for radical male antislavery activists such as Gerrit Smith, Arthur Tappan, and William Lloyd Garrison. Originally supporters of its gradual emancipation policies, these men were eventually convinced by the African American community to renounce the ACS's racist philosophies, facilitating their conversion to a philosophy of immediate emancipation.[13]

White women were quite active in the colonization movement. The ACS's tendency to organize through churches meant more opportunities for women to become involved in its activities, since women dominated church membership throughout the 1820s and 1830s. Women made substantial donations to the society's coffers by buying life memberships for their ministers and holding fund-raising fairs, many of which were organized by female auxiliary societies. It is currently unclear whether the ACS provided a training ground for antislavery women as it did for some male leaders. We also do not know whether significant numbers of women moved from the gradual emancipation philosophy of the ACS to the more radical demand for immediate emancipation. Sketchy evidence suggests that some did. In North Carolina, women founded four or five auxiliaries to the North Carolina Manumission Society between 1824 and 1828. While each originally supported voluntary colonization, by 1825 they had moved toward a decidedly anti-expatriation stance. By 1829 a newspaper article referred to them as "Societies for the Abolition of Slavery."[14] In Connecticut, the Ladies' Anti-Slavery Society of Norwich decided to declare themselves auxiliary to the Colonization Society, *despite* their rejection of colonization and dedication to immediate emancipation. This may reflect confusion on the women's part regarding the platform of the ACS. However, it may also highlight the contribution the Colonization Society made in providing an early space for women to agitate against slavery. The ACS, like benevolent work, may have provided some white women with a route from inactivity to full engagement in the antislavery cause.[15]

Black Americans never saw the ACS as an antislavery organization and denounced it regularly. Although black women's names do not appear on the petitions and publications put out by black male organizations, it is clear that they agreed with the sentiments expressed therein. Maria Stewart, a well-known African American lecturer in Boston, castigated the Colonization Society in an 1833 speech. Like many African Americans she saw the ACS as a thinly disguised attempt to further entrench slavery by ridding America of the positive example of free, educated, and economically productive black Americans. She called on colonizationists to erect a college for African Americans instead of shipping them overseas; "for it would be most thankfully received on our part," she noted, "and convince us of the truth of their professions and save time, expense and anxiety."[16]

By 1833 African American denunciations of the ACS and calls for immediate emancipation without colonization forced anyone interested in the end of slavery to choose between the two methods. Until the 1840s most white Americans saw the Colonization Society as a more respectable way to challenge slavery, whereas antislavery societies were radical, potentially dangerous, and, for many, far beyond woman's appropriate sphere. At the formation of the Dorchester Female Anti-Slavery Society in 1836, a woman with strong leanings toward the Colonization Society tried to dissuade the ladies present from forming an antislavery society. She felt that women "cannot submit to the shame and contempt which will be heaped upon us if we act and pray in behalf of the cause of anti-slavery." This incident makes clear that for some white women colonization societies provided a means to aid freed black people and slaves without entering into the controversial arena of immediate emancipation or female antislavery societies. It also enabled white women to challenge slavery without questioning their prejudices against free African Americans. In general, through the 1830s, wealthier white women supported the ACS while a few white middle-class women advocated more widespread antislavery reforms.[17]

This pattern supports previous research that wealthier women tended to focus on causes that ameliorated the conditions created by poverty or inequality but did not challenge the roots of those conditions. Some middle-class women, with less family wealth to risk and fewer family connections to political power, preferred to challenge the system rather than support it. Coming from or marrying into families whose stability rested on the new market economy, they were dramatically affected by the Second Great Awakening and the belief that one could and should perfect one's moral and economic community. Antislavery did attract some socially prominent and economically well-off women, particularly Maria Weston Chapman and her sisters, who helped to turn Boston's antislavery fairs into fashionable social events. There were also a number of seamstresses and school-teachers, often single women whose antislavery activities were limited by their need to earn a living. However, the majority of abolitionist women in the 1830s saw themselves as members of an emerging class balanced between the wealthy and the economically precarious.[18]

Among African Americans as well, the most active abolitionists tended to come from the middle class. These women had the time, the desire, and the financial resources to engage in reform activities. African American culture in this period stressed each black person's responsibility to uplift the race by acting in a manner that would counteract racial stereotypes of black Americans. Black women in particular were expected to adhere to a high moral standard, thus providing living refutation of the white prejudice that they were lustful and debased. In an 1831 speech, Maria Stewart "strongly recommended" that black women improve "their talents" and prove to the world, "Though black your skins as shades of night,/ Your hearts are pure, your souls are white." The education of children fell squarely within black women's responsibilities, thus providing support for black women's own educational desires. "O, ye mothers," wrote Stewart, "what a responsibility rests on you!" Therefore, in addition to mutual aid and benevolent societies, some African American women organized female literary associations, particularly in Philadelphia, Boston, and New York City. Pursuing a strategy of respectability, these women hoped that improving their mental accomplishments and those of their children would undermine arguments for slavery that relied upon an assumption of African American inferiority.[19]

African American female literary societies were not overtly antislavery organizations. The first two, founded in 1831 and 1832, did not mention slavery in their constitutions or bylaws. However, many literary society members published antislavery poems and conversations in the *Liberator* and donated money to the antislavery cause.[20] Societies founded in the next few years spoke out against the colonization movement, racial discrimination, and the erosion of civil rights for black people, as well as the horrors of slavery. The Garrison Society, named after prominent abolitionist William Lloyd Garrison, included in its constitution a requirement to pay attention to plans to ameliorate the condition of female slaves. The society also donated the money needed to make Garrison a life member of the New England Anti-Slavery Society as thanks for his work against the American Colonization Society.[21] Sometimes women's literary societies shared officers with female antislavery societies, particularly in Philadelphia. The formation of female antislavery societies may actually have weakened the strength of literary societies by calling on their membership to attend antislavery events and make antislavery speeches, taking time and energy away from literary pursuits. Yet literary associations persisted alongside their antislavery counterparts through at least 1860.[22]

For many black women, literary societies served as a recruiting and training ground for female antislavery societies, a place where they could read about, write about, and discuss the problem of slavery prior to organizing or joining a more activist antislavery organization. Literary societies also provided a space for some black women to work against slavery without stepping into the more controversial arena of female antislavery societies. Self-improvement and the education of one's children were seen as laudable female activities in ways that participation in antislavery societies was not. Literary societies seem to have served a role similar to that of benevolent societies—a route for some into more direct antislavery organization, and a route for others to continue working against slavery in traditionally accepted ways. Literary societies also enabled black women to focus their energies more directly on the black community than they could often do in mixed-race antislavery societies. The Colored Ladies' Literary Society of New York held fairs to raise money for the *Colored American,* a black newspaper, as well as for the New York Vigilance Committee, which aided fugitive slaves. Neither of these activities was broadly supported by white women's antislavery organizations until the 1840s.[23]

Free-produce organizations provided women with another avenue through which to attack slavery. Originating among the Quakers in the eighteenth century, free-produce ideology suggested that anyone benefiting from the labor of slaves contributed their support to slavery and thus participated in its sinfulness. Only by avoiding slave-made goods—such as sugar, cotton, and dyes—could one remain untainted. Although Quakers originally promoted the ideology within the framework of personal abstinence, soon they were advocating a more widespread boycott of slave-made goods. One of the earliest advocates was Alice Jackson Lewis of Chester County, Pennsylvania, who in 1806 drew upon women's expanding commercial role as the main purchasers of household goods to suggest that women had the power to help topple slavery.[24] The first two free-produce societies in the United States, formed in Wilmington, Delaware, in 1826 and Philadelphia in early 1827, had all male officers and members, but women were active participants at least in Philadelphia. In 1829 a group of white women in Philadelphia, mostly Quakers, formed the Female Association for Promoting the Manufacture and Use of Free Cotton. This organization took their monthly dues and purchased free-labor cotton (that is, cotton that had been produced without slave labor) and had it made into items most needed by women, including aprons, bed ticking, shawls, and dresses. In 1831 the black women of the Bethel African Methodist Episcopal Church in Philadelphia joined these efforts by forming the Colored Female Free Produce Society of Pennsylvania. The Philadelphia organizations also corresponded and cooperated with a sister organization in Green Plain, Clark County, Ohio, begun by Quaker women in 1829 and formalized in 1832. Numerous other societies followed among both men and women.[25]

By emphasizing the essentially moral nature of the battle against slavery, free-produce organizations helped to justify the formation of later female antislavery societies, particularly in Philadelphia and Rhode Island. Many female antislavery societies inserted free-produce resolutions into their constitutions. Women were also long-term supporters of the movement, passing free-produce resolutions at all three of the women's antislavery conventions in the 1830s and including discussions of free produce in their antislavery materials through the 1850s. Free-produce societies themselves took on antislavery activities beyond abstention, including printing antislavery tracts and creating workbags and other goods that were sold or given away as reminders of the antislavery cause.[26] Women were the main producers of these workbags, their main distributors, and the main recipients. Women also appear to have been the intended audience of free-labor tracts, with frequent dialogues and conversations printed in the Ladies' section of the *Genius of Universal Emancipation* and other antislavery newspapers. Middle-class women's increasing association with purchasing decisions and the domestic sphere, and their status as the primary consumers of luxury goods such as fine cotton and refined sugar, made them the most appropriate targets for free-produce ideology.[27]

The free-produce movement has generally been dismissed as a utopian idea that had little direct impact on the demise of slavery.[28] Free-produce goods were difficult to find and of a higher cost and a lower quality than similar slave-produced goods. Although a core of believers kept the cause alive through the late 1850s, free-produce enthusiasm dropped dramatically after the 1830s. Nevertheless, free-produce ideology had a crucial long-term effect on the antislavery movement. By focusing on private decisions about household goods, the free-produce movement enabled women to undermine the economics of slavery without ever leaving the domestic sphere or their household roles. At the same time the abstention from slave products politicized women's purchasing decisions, turning private choices into public statements. Sugar bowls with chained slaves crying "Use free sugar" engraved on the front encouraged the discussion of public, political issues at private family dinners and ladies' tea parties. Some of these women recognized the connections between their moral boycotts and the efforts of Revolutionary women to boycott English tea. Quaker demands to avoid "unnecessary vanities" in order to attend to more important issues echoed early Revolutionary calls to eschew British luxury goods in the name of republican virtue. Lists of free-produce supporters, like earlier lists of those who would not import or use British goods, gave political voice to many who otherwise would not have entered the political process. Boycotts politicized everyday actions and tied antislavery to a beloved history of Revolutionary action.[29]

Those willing to avoid all slave-made products were always on the fringe of the antislavery movement, insisting on personal, daily sacrifices for the slave rather than the potentially more fleeting commitment of a signature on a petition. Yet regular conversation about free produce drew politics into the domestic sphere and politicized the most basic domestic chores. Free-produce organizations stressed the economic nature of slavery and the economic role women could play in undermining the institution. It also made women central to the cause by focusing on boycotts of luxury goods used primarily by women. By helping to erase the distinctions between the economic, moral, and political aspects of the fight against slavery, the free-produce movement provided important justifications for women's antislavery activism.

The free-produce movement also highlights the role British female antislavery activists played in encouraging American female antislavery sentiment during this early period. English and American Quakers had maintained an active correspondence related to slavery since the late eighteenth century, sharing pamphlets, organizational guidelines, and tactics. In 1825 a prominent British Quaker, Mary Lloyd, used that network to send a letter to "an unknown but fellow member of the same Christian society." Her letter described British women's success in raising money and awareness for the Bible and missionary societies. Lloyd had drawn on that example to help found the Birmingham Ladies Society for the Relief of Negro Slaves, which served as a model for most early British female antislavery societies. She called for American women to form societies on a similar basis, "to diffuse information and excite attention" regarding the state of slavery in the South.[30] Her letter was delivered to Lucretia Mott, a Philadelphian well known by her Quaker meeting to have antislavery sympathies. Mott would take eight years to act on Mary Lloyd's suggestion but then would be central in the formation of both the Female Association for Promoting the Manufacture and Use of Free Cotton (1831), and the Philadelphia Female Anti-Slavery Society (1833). Lloyd's correspondence to Mott marked the very smallest beginning of a transatlantic collaboration between English and American antislavery women that would span forty years. In this early period, British women's activities provided a crucial example and ideological encouragement to American women beginning to enter the antislavery arena.[31]

Many of the American benevolent movements—whether organized by men, women, or both—looked to Britain for models and encouragement. This pattern was particularly true for antislavery in the 1820s and early 1830s. During this period the British were deeply engaged in debates over slavery, which provided the economic foundation of their West Indian sugar plantations. From legislative halls to pub tables to women's sewing meetings, men and women discussed all aspects of English slaveholding. British women formed dozens of female antislavery societies during this decade, which boycotted slave-grown produce, circulated pamphlets and tracts, raised funds, and collected signatures on petitions. English abolitionists generally, and women particularly, were rallied to the cause by a British Quaker and antislavery agitator named Elizabeth Heyrick. Her pamphlet *Immediate Not Gradual Emancipation* took a hard look at previous antislavery activities and determined that the gradualist approach, which sought to phase out slavery over time, had failed miserably since it required the English to accommodate a terrible sin in their midst. She made one of the first calls for immediate emancipation and, further, called upon women to lend their moral and pious hands to the work. This focus on immediate emancipation would develop independently in America's black communities and would be adopted by leading abolitionists in the United States. It revitalized the antislavery cause and drew thousands of new adherents ready to scour the sin of slavery from the earth. Every female antislavery society founded in the United States would demand immediate, not gradual, emancipation.[32]

According to Heyrick, women could most effectively eliminate slavery by organization, influence, and abstinence. She encouraged women to form female antislavery societies to unite their efforts. While societies would give women a more public voice, Heyrick also stressed women's private power to influence their families and to refuse to purchase slave-made products. She followed up her immensely popular pamphlet with two other works in 1828, an *Apology for Ladies' Anti-Slavery Associations* and an *Appeal to the Hearts and Consciences of British Women*. In these works Heyrick expanded her arguments for women's antislavery activism, drawing upon the examples of powerful women from the Bible. She drew on the common conceptions of women as more religious and less tainted by politics than men to argue for women's fitness and responsibility to work against slavery.[33]

Given the limited circulation of Heyrick's pamphlets in America prior to 1838, her arguments might have had little direct impact on American women without the intervention of Benjamin Lundy.[34] Editor of the anti-slavery newspaper *Genius of Universal Emancipation,* Lundy reprinted Heyrick's arguments as part of his decades-long emphasis on free produce and female antislavery agitation. In the first issue of his paper, Lundy included a section for ladies titled "Temple of the Muses." "Believing . . . that the virtuous matrons of our country will have an important part to perform in the great work of emancipation," Lundy published as much as he could about women's work for the slave. In addition to reprinting Heyrick's work, Lundy printed numerous excerpts from British female antislavery society reports, addresses, and publications, many of which strongly encouraged the formation of similar societies in America. In order to guide American women, one issue of the *Genius* reprinted a British formula for the formation of ladies' antislavery societies, which included information on the numbers and kinds of officers to select, how to run a meeting, what tasks to take on, and how to present society news to the public. Lundy was also interested in other forms of female antislavery activism and at times almost a quarter of his newspaper was filled with models of organized female effort, including not only the British societies but the Philadelphia female free-produce societies, North Carolina ladies' manumission societies, and Cincinnati women's benevolent societies.[35]

From the beginning Lundy provided a public arena for women to express antislavery views. In November 1822, "H.C." in Baltimore expressed her embarrassment about celebrating the Fourth of July when many Americans still did not have their freedom. She wondered how other women, "to whom has been peculiarly ascribed all the fine feelings which adorn human nature," could set their hearts against the needs of the slave. "Oh! Woman, woman . . . where is thy blush?" she demanded. A letter "From a Female Pen" encouraged women to work against slavery and not to be afraid "to stand alone in a good cause." Lundy's columns tended to stress the inherently moral and virtuous nature of women and their important role as mothers. He also assumed his female readers would need a "blending [of] the useful and the sweet" in order to keep their interest. Yet Lundy's regular references to "patriotic" women made clear his understanding that women had a role to play in upholding the honor and dignity of America. Neither "delicacy nor diffidence" should stand in the way of female participation in the "great work of moral and political reformation."[36]

In September 1829 Lundy hired Elizabeth Margaret Chandler to anonymously edit what was then known as the Ladies' Department of the *Genius.* Chandler was a young Philadelphia Quaker who had been contributing antislavery poetry to the *Genius* for three years. As editor she continued to fill the Ladies' Department with free-produce articles and British abolitionist news, while also writing regular calls for women to form female antislavery societies. In 1832 she also took on the Ladies' Department of William

Lloyd Garrison's year-old weekly, the *Liberator,* ensuring that between the two papers, almost everyone interested in antislavery read her views.[37]

From her first column in the *Genius,* Chandler was obliged to address concerns that antislavery involvement would draw women out of their appropriate sphere into the male realm of politics. Elizabeth Heyrick had addressed this issue by claiming antislavery was a moral crusade rather than a political campaign. Chandler expanded Heyrick's arguments that women were crucial to the fight against slavery because of their sympathy for the poor and oppressed, their capacity for moral outrage, and their influence over men and children. She accepted as true the ideology that women were more naturally inclined toward benevolence and the eradication of sin than men. Thus, according the Chandler, women were only being true to their highest impulses when they joined the antislavery movement. While she recognized that antislavery was "a question of government and politics," she stressed that it encompassed crucial questions of justice and humanity that demanded women's attention. She argued that any woman could engage in antislavery without its "leading her one step beyond her own proper sphere."[38]

Chandler's arguments did not silence her critics. Questions regarding woman's appropriate sphere and engagement in politics would hang heavily over women's antislavery activities for decades to come. However, Chandler did provide other women with a convincing rationale for more extensive antislavery involvement. In November 1831, the "females of Philadelphia" sent a small sum to support the *Liberator.* Writing about themselves in the third person, they noted "although it is not in their power, as females to do much, yet they are willing to aid, according to their ability, in giving a more extensive circulation to the *Liberator.*" In this early letter the women of Chandler's adopted city identified what would become two of antislavery women's major contributions to the movement—raising funds and circulating antislavery publications.[39] Later that same year a group of Quaker women circulated an address to the women attending the Philadelphia Quaker yearly meeting. It discussed the propriety of a female petition to Congress requesting the abolition of slavery in the District of Columbia. Over the course of the next few months, the petition garnered over two thousand female signatures, with one woman gathering three hundred signatures alone.[40] At the same time black women circulated a petition asking the Pennsylvania legislature to drop a bill prohibiting the migration of free colored people from the South into Pennsylvania.[41]

Since the American Revolution women had adopted petitioning as a legitimate form of supplication to the government, a right that women claimed as subjects of the republic. Building on the concept of republican motherhood, which recognized women's role in maintaining the moral foundations of the new country, women used petitioning as a means to express moral concerns that might otherwise get lost in the give and take of immoral party politics.[42] Women had previously petitioned regarding widows' pensions, the need for orphanages, and other issues. In 1830 prominent female educator Catherine Beecher had organized a widespread petition campaign to protest Andrew Jackson's Indian Removal Act, which would have evicted thousands of Cherokee Indians from their native lands in Georgia.[43] The *Genius of Universal Emancipation* published numerous examples of British women's antislavery petitions to Parliament, most of which claimed both a moral and political base for their interventions in this important issue. The early Philadelphia petitions placed antislavery into a predominantly moral context, claiming petitioning as a benevolent, religious work and thus justifiably within women's responsibilities. This may have worked particularly well in this period as the nation's two political parties tried to avoid any discussion of slavery, preferring to fight their battles over the tariff, internal improvements, nullification, and the national bank. As both Whigs and Democrats placed their hopes in the legacy of the Missouri Compromise and silenced most political debates over slavery, they facilitated women's efforts to place slavery on the nation's moral agenda.

Conclusion

Thus by the end of 1831 women were already combating slavery through a variety of organizations. In benevolent and mutual aid societies, many black and a few white women expressed an early antislavery sentiment, and some women learned the organizational and ideological skills they would later need in the antislavery movement. Literary societies provided a space for black women to improve their own abilities while undermining the assumptions of black inferiority often used to justify slavery. Both black and white women joined free-produce societies advocating abstention from slave-produced goods, in the hope that moral and economic pressure together might ruin the profitability of slavery. Women in Philadelphia raised funds for the cause in order to support the *Liberator* and petitioned their political representatives on issues of slavery and African American rights.

These various streams of female antislavery activity would come together in 1832 with the formation of female antislavery societies. While specifically dedicated to the immediate emancipation of slaves, many of these societies would incorporate aspects of women's previous antislavery work, especially the uplift of the free black population and the avoidance of slave products such as cotton and sugar. Inspired by religious enthusiasm, enabled by economic changes, and drawing on new and unstable understandings of woman's moral duties, these women united in small bands from Maine to Michigan. They would continue to debate whether they were engaged in a moral cause or a political movement, and they would draw on the arguments of Elizabeth Heyrick, Benjamin Lundy, Elizabeth Chandler, and others to justify their efforts. In the process they would help to redefine the meaning of political action in the early republic.

CHAPTER TWO

Organizational Beginnings, 1832–1837

Networks and Spheres

"But why form societies, separate organizations, you may ask?

Union is strength."

—"Address to the Women of New Hampshire," 1837

On February 22, 1832, a group of black women organized the Female Anti-Slavery Society (FASS) of Salem (MA).[1] The women resolved to help the *Liberator* in its efforts to eliminate prejudice against free people of color and in its campaign against the Colonization Society. They also planned to use their funds to buy antislavery books and to provide aid to the needy. With a resolution defining good society behavior, including not interrupting when other members were speaking, the society chose officers and put their signatures on the constitution.[2]

The Salem society was not remarkably different from the women's societies of the 1820s, including the Clarkson Society (one of the black women's benevolent organizations that preceded the antislavery society in Salem). With a focus on assisting the needy and on associating "for mutual improvement," the society looked very similar to a black female literary or benevolent society. The emphasis on behavioral rules was typical for black women's organizations, which felt pressure to live up to the social norms of respectability. Two factors make this society different enough from its predecessors to stand out as the first female antislavery society. First, the women chose to call their society a female antislavery society, putting their commitment to the elimination of slavery in the forefront of their other goals. Second, this society was rapidly followed by another, and another, and another, reaching far beyond Salem. By the end of 1833 there were seven female antislavery societies—one black, four white, and two interracial. Women formed at least seventeen more in 1834, twenty-nine in 1835, forty-one in 1836, and a record forty-five in the peak year of 1837. Thus five years after the black women met in Salem, there were at least one hundred thirty-nine female antislavery societies in the northern United States, and probably many more.[3]

Many of these societies were similar to the one founded in Lynn (MA) in 1836. Antislavery women there agreed to meet once a month, with absent members making a donation to the treasury for every meeting they missed.

This ensured that every month members contributed either their time or their money. Each meeting was opened with an appropriate passage from scripture, and the minutes of the previous meeting were read. The women would then transact "whatever other business" they had planned for the month, which could be reading and answering letters from other societies, organizing a fair, signing petitions, or even teaching African American girls how to sew. The Lynn women were particularly concerned that all their members be well educated about the cause, and thus they spent much of their meeting reading from antislavery works "with remarks or conversation relating to the object of the society." The monthly minutes also announced the "proceeds of work done at this meeting," indicating that women usually did needlework while they read and conversed, creating a pile of goods that could eventually be sold to raise money for the cause.[4]

The importance of women's decision to organize themselves often went unrecognized by others. As one observer wrote in 1837 when women formed an antislavery society in Haverhill (MA): "Nothing of moment transpired." Yet he goes on to explain that women traveled as far as six miles for the meeting, wrote a preamble and a constitution, elected officers, and discussed the most appropriate ways for women to effect the abolition of slavery. As the Lynn records show, creating a society meant creating a structure through which women could make regular donations and coordinate their efforts. It required that a group excluded from national politics write constitutions and hold elections for officers. Organization required decisions about who could belong to the group and in what types of activities the association should engage. By offering structured activities and political education, societies were powerful organizational bases. They enabled women to share information, combine their financial contributions, and hone their political impact in ways individual efforts simply could not match.[5]

Once women had formed a society, they usually took a second step, linking their organizations with others across the Northeast through frequent letters, mentoring relationships, and joint activities. From Maine across to Michigan and south to Pennsylvania, antislavery women created a correspondence network through which women coordinated their efforts and multiplied their effectiveness, particularly through antislavery fairs. Increasing criticism of abolition itself and women's engagement in the cause required women to defend their activities on religious, patriotic, and gender-based grounds. At times they had to face physical violence and verbal assault as they attempted to meet or organize. However, antislavery women found bravery by banding together and strength in a community of correspondence. "We believe with you," wrote Harriet Guzzam, president of the Pittsburgh (PA) FASS, "that societies engaged in this unpopular, tho blessed cause, may be mutually assisted and strengthened by maintaining a regular correspondence." By working together antislavery women could more effectively produce the "mighty moral revolution" of emancipation.[6]

The Process of Forming Female Societies—
Encouragement and Barriers

The first few female antislavery associations grew out of women's previous antislavery concerns. The Female Anti-Slavery Society of Salem referred back to black female literary and benevolent societies, while also challenging the ideas of the Colonization Society. The FASS of Hudson (NY) formed in direct opposition to the Colonization Society. Drawing on Maria Stewart's arguments, they published an address suggesting that colonization money could be more profitably spent in benevolent education for African Americans to prepare them for free life in America.[7] The FASS of Providence (RI) was strongly influenced by free-produce ideology. In their constitution they pledged to renounce "the productions of slavery," while also extending the circulation of antislavery and free-labor publications.[8] Women did not wait for men to ask them to organize. Their organizational efforts paralleled—and in a few cases preceded—those of William Lloyd Garrison, who is often credited with initiating the immediate emancipation movement in the United States. By December 1833, when a few hundred men gathered together in Philadelphia to form a national antislavery society, there were already at least six female antislavery societies in existence.

The formation of the American Anti-Slavery Society (AAS) did have a powerful impact on women's organizing, in part because women were originally excluded from its membership. No female delegates were invited to the convention from the existing female antislavery societies, or from the female literary or free-produce organizations in Philadelphia where the convention was held. Both the female literary and free-produce organizations had published in the *Liberator*, so they were well known for their support of the antislavery movement.[9] Inviting women probably did not occur to the men since previous antislavery conventions had always been all-male affairs. However, on the second day of the convention, four Philadelphia women with long ties to antislavery work were invited to come if they wished to listen to the deliberations. It is unclear what prompted this belated invitation, but the women were delighted to be present at this historic meeting.

After listening quietly for a while, one of the invited women, well-known Quaker minister Lucretia Mott, felt the urge to speak. Recognizing her place, she did so only after asking and receiving permission from the assembled men. After all, even articles in the *Liberator* strongly encouraging women's participation in the movement still suggested that "the voice of woman should not be heard in public debates." Yet Mott urged the men forward when their resolve was fading and also helped them word a particularly troublesome passage in their Declaration of Sentiments. In keeping with the belief that only men were official delegates to antislavery conventions, the women's names were not listed in the official proceedings, nor were they invited to sign the Declaration of Sentiments, despite Mott's contributions to its wording. Instead the men thanked them for their "deep interest" in the convention. The bylaws indicated that all "persons" might participate in the society, thus opening the potential for female membership. However, the women present recognized that the AAS was clearly formed by men for men, and they did not request membership. They would instead help found the Philadelphia Female Anti-Slavery Society.[10]

The exclusion of women as delegates or members reflected widely shared—yet rapidly changing—understandings of gender roles in this period. Participation in public conventions connoted maleness in a gender system that divided the world into public and private domains, dominated respectively by men and women. In most benevolent organizations with both male and female members, men filled all the formal offices, ran the meetings, and served as delegates to national conventions. Women tended to raise funds, to distribute information, and to perform other crucial support roles that, while they may have had public aspects, could be more clearly associated with women's domestic roles. While a few mixed-sex antislavery societies did exist prior to 1839, only one seems to have had a female officer, which may reflect the egalitarian beliefs of its Quaker members. Rather than hold leadership positions, women in many mixed-sex organizations appear to have enjoyed taking on projects as their own particular responsibility, on which they could work separated from men. In Limington (ME) the women of the mixed-sex society created and ran an antislavery lending library for use by the community.[11]

However, the long tradition of female benevolent organizations provided women with an alternative model. All-female associations gave women the opportunity to serve as officers, to write constitutions, and to dictate policy in ways unavailable to them in mixed-sex organizations. Female societies also conformed more closely to the prevailing gender ideology that suggested that men and women had different backgrounds, habits, and roles in life and thus women would find a greater communion of interests with members of their own gender.[12] Women often preferred all-female societies since they presumed these would provide a less competitive atmosphere and more genteel interaction, while relieving them of the embarrassment of debating public issues with men. At least five Massachusetts antislavery associations began as mixed-sex organizations. The women rapidly seceded to form their own single-sex societies.[13] As the men of Dorchester wrote to the *Liberator* after forming a mixed-sex society with all male officers, "The Ladies are about forming a Society by themselves, which no doubt, will far more conduce to the good of the cause here." In Dunbarton (NH) one woman felt that her sisters got little done when they organized with men. "But why form societies, separate organizations, you may ask? Union is strength—and while connected with male societies our strength be weakness—we do not as societies act at all." Many women felt that if they wanted to get something done, they had to do it themselves.[14]

There were some women who found all-female organizations to be less useful than mixed-sex organizations. Well-known writer Lydia Maria Child alluded to her dislike of all-female societies in a letter to Boston FASS president Charlotte Phelps: "My opinions concerning the formation of a distinct female society have remained unchanged since my first conversation [regarding the formation of the Boston FASS]. . . . The plain truth is, my sympathies do not, and never have, moved freely in this project."[15] Child did join the Boston FASS and remained a member for over a decade, but she regularly argued that women could get more done by working with men. She and other like-minded women would eventually advocate for equal membership in male antislavery societies, fueling a major division in the antislavery movement. In the early 1830s, however, these women were a tiny minority, as few women questioned their exclusion from the all-male American Antislavery Society. As Lucretia Mott would reminisce thirty years later: "I do not think it occurred to any one of us at that time that there would be a propriety in [women] signing the [Declaration of Principles]." Thus female antislavery societies developed both from male exclusion of women and women's own desire for all-female organizations.[16]

The American Anti-Slavery Society strongly encouraged the formation of female antislavery societies, recognizing that women could be powerful allies in the antislavery cause. The AAS had dedicated itself to eliminating slavery through "moral suasion" or persuading the nation of the sin of slavery and the need for immediate repentance. Both men and women believed that women had a more inherently moral nature and a sensitivity to the sufferings of others. They were also seen as having the domestic power and influence to shape the opinions of their husbands and children. Thus many male AAS members felt the antislavery movement's success depended on the involvement of women. Men may also have recognized that women's long tradition of fund-raising for moral causes and churches could be very useful, since they needed funds for newspapers, pamphlets, and traveling lecturers. The AAS Convention hailed the already extant female antislavery societies as "the harbinger of a brighter day" and called for further societies along the same lines. Convention delegates justified women's involvement in the cause by citing the "one million of their colored sisters . . . pining in abject servitude," as well as the example of the women of Great Britain who had been "signally instrumental" in obtaining British abolition in 1833. The men also claimed that women's "example and influence operate measurably as laws to Society," drawing on the cultural belief that, while women did not have direct political power, their moral influence on husbands, children, and society in general gave them significant social power. Within the next two years, many of the male auxiliaries to the AAS would pass similar resolutions calling for and justifying female antislavery societies. This ideology crossed racial lines as the predominantly black Convention for the Improvement of the Free

People of Color believed women's "untiring exertions and irresistible influence to be a most powerful auxiliary in the great cause of emancipation." By 1835 many men saw women's organized participation in the cause as "essential."[17]

While the enthusiasm of the AAS delegates could only have encouraged female antislavery organizing, it might have had a smaller effect had it not been backed up by institutional and financial support. The AAS immediately began to send out antislavery lecturers and agents with a specific commission to form both male and female antislavery societies. Even the smallest societies were seen as "centres of light" through which antislavery pamphlets and petitions could be spread to a wider community.[18] Often agents would convert only one or two women in an area, but these converts would then serve as catalysts, organizing other women in the community. In a series of lectures in Ohio, James A. Thome converted two women who had been decidedly proslavery, and they swiftly began to "visit amongst their acquaintances and to labor with the first Ladies of the place to *convert them.*" Their agitation resulted in the formation of the Canton (OH) FASS in 1836. Making clear the centrality of those two conversions, Thome wrote that he was not able to form an antislavery society among the men. "They chose to defer that step awhile. They were rather timorous," he noted. Charles Burleigh, an agent in New England, made a similar observation about women in Marlborough (MA) when they voted to form a society despite the protests of the men. Other agents drew up generic constitutions, which they would read at the end of a lecture to a large group of women. At times, audience members would immediately vote to adopt the constitution and would come forward to affix their names.[19]

Between August 1834 and November 1835, one particular agent had a crucial impact on the formation of female antislavery societies. Englishman George Thompson had been involved in the antislavery movement in Britain for many years and had met William Lloyd Garrison when the latter visited England in 1834. Garrison invited Thompson to lecture in the United States and Thompson accepted. He received support and encouragement from the Glasgow and Edinburgh Emancipation Societies, as well as the Glasgow Ladies' Auxiliary Emancipation Society, which formed particularly to finance Thompson's trip. Due in large part to the Glasgow women's financial support, Thompson considered the formation of female antislavery societies in America as central to his work.[20] In Lowell (MA) he addressed over one thousand women, urging them to become involved in the antislavery movement. In his view, antislavery was "not a political, but a moral and religious question. All were called upon to labor in the cause— all were able to do so." The Lowell women were convinced they had a responsibility to act, and they formed a female antislavery society shortly after his visit. After another Thompson lecture in Providence to approximately eight hundred women, one hundred came forward to form a FASS and adopt a constitution. Thompson also helped to form female societies in Dover and Concord (NH) and New York City and facilitated significant membership additions to the FASS in Boston, Portland (ME), Philadelphia, and Lynn.[21]

Building on a tradition begun a decade earlier when Mary Lloyd's letter reached Lucretia Mott, Thompson helped to expand the transatlantic communications network that encouraged and enriched women's antislavery activism on both sides of the Atlantic. British women had been forming female antislavery societies since the early 1820s, often after an address by Thompson, and had printed numerous addresses to American women over the years. Both the *Genius of Universal Emancipation* and the *Liberator* frequently printed news of the British women and urged American women to emulate their example. When Parliament abolished West Indian slavery in 1833, based in part on women's significant petitioning activity, British women turned their attention to their "transatlantic sisters" in order to help eliminate slavery in the world. Quaker women on both sides of the Atlantic were particularly likely to share direct correspondence, as Elizabeth Dudley did with friends in the Reading (MA) FASS. A Quaker preacher and member of the London FASS, Dudley provided the Reading women with encouragement and a reminder that pleading for the oppressed was a holy duty for both men and women. She also provided tracts, newspapers, and suggestions for how the American women might begin their fight against slavery.[22]

Thompson's lectures made American women much more aware of the power and example of their allies overseas. The women of Concord credited Thompson with pointing them toward "the bright example of our sisters across the Atlantic" and exhorting them to "go and do likewise." The women of Lynn asked Thompson to "assure the ladies of Great Britain, that their voice, which has been addressed to us through you, has not been listened to in vain." The Ladies' New-York City Anti-Slavery Society, formed with Thompson's assistance, rapidly took advantage of the British women's prior experience in the cause. They wrote directly to England, inquiring which types of sewn goods the British women had found most salable and most effective in promoting the cause. They also wanted to know whether any antislavery blocks or engravings remained in England that the New York women might purchase and use to print silks for sale.[23]

The New York City women's questions highlight an advantage they had over many other antislavery women's organizations. A few of the New York City members had been active in other reform causes and thus could bring organizing experience to the antislavery society.[24] In other towns many women lacked the skills they needed to run an effective antislavery organization. Even though women had been forming charitable and benevolent organizations since at least the American Revolution, many women who joined the antislavery movement had not participated in the large charitable organizations of the 1810s and 1820s. They therefore could not apply any direct experience to the new antislavery societies.[25] The Boston FASS, which would become one of the largest and most powerful societies and an able advocate of women's rights, began with twelve women who relied heavily on a male Congregational minister to instruct them in the basic forms of association and assist them in writing a constitution.[26] The Philadelphia Female Antislavery Society, the longest-lasting FASS in America, had similar start-up problems. As Lucretia Mott explained regarding the early 1830s:

> At that time I had no idea of the meaning of preambles, and resolutions, and votings. Women had never been in any assemblies of the kind. I had attended only one convention—a convention of colored people—before that; and that was the first time in my life I had ever heard a vote taken, being accustomed to our Quaker way of getting the prevailing sentiment of the meeting. When, a short time after, we came together to form the Female Anti-Slavery Society, there was not a woman capable of taking the chair and organizing that meeting in due order; and we had to call on James McCrummel, a colored man, to give us aid in the work.[27]

This is a strange comment since Mott had already helped to organize a successful free-produce organization. Mott may have wanted to stress the competence and assistance of a respected African American man. She may simply have been dramatizing women's exclusion from previous antislavery organizations. Yet the comment rang true for many women as they faced the task of organizing a society.[28]

Some female antislavery societies chose to follow the model of early benevolent societies in which women filled the internal officer positions, while men handled the public aspects of the work. This meant having men chair the annual meeting and read all public addresses. The Ladies' New-York City Anti-Slavery Society chose this arrangement, an early indication of their desire to maintain a low profile and not challenge traditionally accepted female roles. The majority of female antislavery societies adopted the other main model for female reform organizations, in which women filled the internal positions and served in the public capacities as well. Both models required women to engage in activities for which many had little prior training, and women had to develop that expertise over time.

Membership, Race, and Rural Residence

Once women decided to form a female antislavery society, they immediately faced the question of who would be permitted to join. In their desire to bring everyone to the cause they possibly could, most societies threw wide open their doors and made clear that every female who wished to join could. This immediately raised the problem of race, particularly within those societies founded solely by white women. Few white women saw their commitment to the end of slavery as a positive commitment to racial equality. This would be a sharp tension within the antislavery movement for decades. The different approaches societies took toward the question of interracial membership illustrate the diversity of opinions and the range of racial acceptance within the movement.

The Philadelphia FASS was an interracial enterprise from its beginning with the active participation of a half-dozen black women. Grace Douglass and Margaretta Forten helped found the organization, and other members of their two families served as officers or board members over the years. The relatively well-off black women who joined the Philadelphia FASS may have shared certain cultural assumptions with the white Philadelphia Quakers who dominated that organization. Both African American and Quaker culture encouraged women to engage in religious and benevolent activities outside the home. This position contrasted with the more common pronouncements that limited women's engagement in the public sphere. The Society of Friends also had a long history of antislavery activism and an emphasis on the equality of souls, which may have provided a more welcoming, less racist atmosphere for interracial cooperation than was often possible in other organizations. This history did have limits, as Grace Douglass recognized during her years of faithful attendance at the Arch Street Quaker meeting. She was relegated to a "colored bench" and was never invited to join the meeting.[29] Yet fellow Arch Street meeting member Lucretia Mott traveled to African American churches to discuss antislavery and held interracial gatherings at her home. Other founding members of the Philadelphia FASS had similar interactions across racial boundaries. These personal connections may have encouraged interracial organizing. In its first two years, eighteen black women and ninety-eight white women joined the Philadelphia FASS.[30]

Boston women had much more controversy over the admission of black women to the Boston FASS. Just a few months after the founding of the association in October 1833, William Lloyd Garrison heard from an "unquestionable authority" that the white women in the society were unwilling to admit black women. Garrison took them to task for their inconsistent principles, since one of the stated objects of the organization was the elimination of race prejudice. "Remember," he reminded them,

> that you are not called upon to decide, that you will make bosom friends of colored females, or invite them into your parlors, or eat and drink with them, or walk with them in the streets, (although, if they are truly virtuous and intelligent, you ought not to shrink from the juxtaposition)—But the question is, simply and only, whether females who are anxious to combine their influence, and to throw in their mites, for the destruction of prejudice and slavery, shall be denied this privelege [*sic*] on account of their complexion.[31]

Garrison's truth clearly stung a few of the women. There was a fundamental conflict in professing to fight racial prejudice while excluding black women. Yet Garrison's reassurance that an interracial society need not mean inviting black women to dinner must have soothed and comforted others. No records remain of the discussion held by the women, but it was quick and decisive. Within two days the corresponding secretary assured Garrison that the society would now welcome black women and that Susan Paul, the light-skinned daughter of a prominent local minister, had been given a seat on the board of managers. The Boston society would never be as integrated as the Philadelphia society, but it did eventually enroll twenty-five African American women among its over six hundred members.[32]

In Fall River (MA) the question of admitting black women as members almost split the society. As Elizabeth Buffum Chase recalled years later, she and her sister had invited a couple of African American women to join the society rather than simply attend meetings. The leading members of the society responded angrily, saying they "had no objection to these women attending the meetings, and they were willing to help and encourage them in every way, but they did not think it was at all proper to invite them to join the Society, thus putting them on an equality with ourselves." Chase and her sister held their ground, and the black women were eventually admitted as equal members. It does not seem to have been a comfortable integration.[33]

The Ladies' New-York City Anti-Slavery Society did not specifically exclude black female members. However, they did not particularly welcome them either, failing to appoint or elect a black officer during the entire life of the organization. This exclusion and other disagreements would encourage New York City black women to form their own antislavery organization in 1840, the Manhattan Abolition Society. In Rochester (NY) black and white female antislavery societies existed simultaneously without apparently ever working together. Interracial cooperation would have to wait until 1851 there. In the end, many mixed-race antislavery societies limited black women's opportunities to join, lead, and shape policy just as mixed-sex antislavery societies did for women of both races. While black women had leadership roles and power in interracial societies in Philadelphia (PA), Salem (MA), and a few other places, in most cases black women preferred to form their own organizations.[34]

Race does not seem to have been a question in many of the smaller, less urban societies, in large part because of the scarcity of African American women in those areas. However, rural geography provided its own barriers to organization. Marshfield (MA) was not very thickly settled, had no village center, and was divided in half by a deep woods. Therefore women in that town debated the utility of forming two distinct female antislavery societies (north and south). Each would be small in numbers, but they might be better able to meet than a larger, geographically separated society. The members of the New Lyme (OH) FASS found it difficult to meet in winter, since "those members who feel most interested in the Society live very remote" and the poor roads made travel quite difficult. Women in Connecticut faced a similar problem, as veteran antislavery organizer Abby Kelley reported after a lecturing tour through the area. "The women, I think, will form a society as soon as the weather and traveling will permit," she wrote. "They would have done so while I was there, had it not been so muddy." The opening of the Erie Canal in 1825 meant that people, mail, and trade goods were traveling ever faster across New York State and into the Midwest. Travel by road improved much less quickly. As long as road surfaces were made of dirt, mud and road ruts were major factors in the ease of travel and in the organization of reform societies.[35]

However, small town residence did not necessarily inhibit antislavery activities or organizing. In 1830 the town of Boylston (MA) had a population of 820, in contrast to the 4,173 people at the nearby county seat of Worcester.[36] But Boylston had a minister sympathetic to antislavery, Rev. William H. Sanford. Sanford opened his church to antislavery lecturers, giving Boylston a much wider diversity of lecturers than many larger towns with less accessible facilities. Boylston was close enough to Worcester that many lecturers would drop in after their talks in the larger town. Many antislavery luminaries presented lectures in the church in 1836, while over the next few years others would speak in the town hall. All of this activity helped to form and was encouraged by the formation of the Boylston FASS on June 10, 1837. One member of that society, Mary White, kept a daily diary, a rare, rich source on more rural women's antislavery activities. Mary sewed for the antislavery fair during sewing circle meetings. She helped found and attended meetings of the local female antislavery society every month. She attended over a dozen antislavery lectures in half that many years and recorded seven separate occasions on which she and her daughter collected antislavery petition signatures. She also regularly enjoyed the "monthly concert for the slave," which was an evening of united prayer held at Rev. Sandford's church. Clearly, rural residence did not inhibit her antislavery activities. However, many rural women were not as lucky as Mary White. With fewer resources in their local area, they turned to the larger antislavery community through correspondence networks.[37]

The Power of Correspondence and Mentoring

Women's personal interactions with nonlocal female abolitionists were limited prior to 1837. Most did not attend the national antislavery society meetings held by men, since women were not chosen as delegates to these all-male conventions. However, letters enabled women to transcend the barriers of geography and isolation in this early period. Even women who had never met felt joined together in common cause. Anne Warren Weston of Boston stressed this sense of community when she wrote to the women of New York that "though strangers in all other respects, we are yet made friends and sisters, by a common recognition of the same holy and sublime principle." Mary Clark, the recording secretary for the Concord (NH) FASS, made the point even more strongly: "We who are attached to 'the sect that is every where spoken against,' are not strangers," she argued. "[T]he intervening of a few hundred miles, and the lack of personal acquaintance form no bar to communion of feeling and sympathy." While antislavery gained advocates at a rapid rate in the 1830s, abolitionists were never more than a tiny minority in any given area, making many women feel alone and in need of support. As the women of Plymouth (NH) wrote in a letter to the Philadelphia FASS: "We have embarked in a cause which I regret to say has but few advocates in this part of New England, and we are anxious to establish a correspondence with some of the Sister Societies, which are thinly scattered over the land." Joining a female antislavery society gave women membership in a larger moral community. Letters helped to expand that community beyond the local area, to include the companionship of "friends and sisters" across the North.[38]

Lack of local organizing expertise encouraged women to seek information from others. Women wrote to each other for copies of a society constitution, information on how to raise funds, or a discussion of the best means to promote antislavery. Within a few years, larger societies emerged as mentors for smaller, more recent organizations, providing basic information on how to organize and later developing into central nodes for the organization of fairs and the circulation of petitions. The Concord FASS played this role in New Hampshire, while the Salem FASS served Essex County, Massachusetts. Providence may have played a similar role in Rhode Island. The FASS in Philadelphia, Ashtabula County (OH), and Boston had even broader reach, as the three best-known and most active societies in their areas. They played central roles in developing and strengthening female antislavery networks.

The members of the Philadelphia FASS fielded a remarkable number of requests for organizational assistance. Lucy B. Williams wrote to Lucretia Mott "on behalf of those Ladies in Brooklyn who have become much interested in this subject, and who are desirous to unite themselves together in an Anti-Slavery Society." The women looked to their "elder and more experienced sisters for advice and direction," including "the articles of your constitution, a little outline of your plans for the future, the success of your past exertions, and anything else you think will be interesting to us."[39] A woman from rural Pennsylvania felt even more in need of assistance. "I stand alone here," she wrote. "I know of no one[,] of no female in the village who entertains similar sentiments." She formed a society with a few other women who lived three miles distant, and they almost immediately adjourned, hoping to receive by their next meeting a letter from Philadelphia explaining how they should proceed. "We are all new hands in this work," they noted, "and need instruction."[40] Unfortunately, while the Philadelphia women carefully preserved all the letters they received, they failed to make copies of their own correspondence, making it difficult to find evidence of their actual assistance to outlying societies. However, their reputation as an important source of information over twenty-five years and their continued receipt of requests for guidance suggest that they responded quite readily with organizational materials and advice.

In Ohio the women of the Ashtabula County FASS served as a central organizing node for their entire county. At their first anniversary in 1835, the women passed a resolution strongly encouraging the formation of Ladies' Auxiliary antislavery societies in the various towns of the county. They further resolved to "employ an agent for the purpose of presenting the subject and assist[ing] in forming auxiliary societies among the Ladies in the several towns of the county." They chose Mrs. J. O. Beardslee as their agent, and her mission was quite effective. By February 1836 eight new auxiliary societies had been formed, with 202 members total. The County Society had grown to 446 members. Women in other towns also looked to the Ashtabula Society, and particularly to its corresponding secretary Betsy Mix Cowles, for encouragement and advice. As a woman from Tallmadge (OH) wrote, "As you started before us we wish to avail ourselves of your experience and correspondence we trust would be mutually pleasant, and profitable."[41]

The Boston FASS realized quite early that an extensive correspondence would enable them to draw on and coordinate the experience of other female antislavery societies. In their first two years, they sent out dozens of letters to "sister societies" throughout the northeastern United States, which asked for and shared advice and advocated collaboration. "The rapid multiplication of Anti-Slavery Societies in this vicinity," they wrote, "suggests the expediency of forming plans of efficient co-operation between them, that by combining they may increase their strength and influence." The Boston women asked for support of their desire to write an address to the women of the South and offered copies of the latest antislavery books. They also asked for the privilege of continued correspondence, feeling strongly that "the simple act of intercommunication will 'stir up our minds,' strengthen faith, confirm hope, and increase the ardor of love and the fervor of prayer." It would also enable them to spend less energy repeating other women's mistakes.[42]

The Boston FASS members quickly developed into mentors of women's antislavery efforts. They purchased extra subscriptions to the *Liberator* and sent them to women in neighboring towns. This helped to spread knowledge of antislavery activities and to encourage women to further action. The copy they sent to Sudbury (MA) resulted in the formation of a female antislavery society there in 1835. The society made itself auxiliary to the Boston FASS for one year and paid over all its receipts to the Boston treasury. The Boston FASS had auxiliaries in the Bangor (ME) FASS and the Randolph (VT) FASS, and they were central to the formation of a society in Roxbury (MA).[43] The copy of the *Liberator* sent to North Marshfield (MA) prompted a society there in 1837. The women in North Marshfield also became a Boston FASS auxiliary. The Boston FASS sent them sewing materials and projects to provide them with a focus for their meetings, books (on loan) to better educate themselves, and assistance in distributing their proceeds through appropriate channels.[44]

Networking and Antislavery Fairs

These mentoring relationships and communication networks paid off most directly for the antislavery cause when women coordinated their efforts at antislavery fairs. These provided an opportunity for larger societies to concentrate the donations of many smaller societies into a grand event that combined fund-raising, socializing, and education. The cooperation of multiple societies was crucial to the success of these events, since they drew upon the organizational power of a small number of women and the labor power of hundreds. These fairs would eventually provide major funding for the national antislavery organizations and link together women across the country and across the Atlantic in networks of exchange and cooperation. In these early years, they were smaller and more local events that strengthened regional networks.

Fund-raising fairs for children's hospitals, missionary activities, and even the American Colonization Society were relatively common by 1834. Women in Philadelphia held a small antislavery fair in 1833 but left few records of their efforts.[45] The first antislavery fair to draw on the efforts of multiple societies was held in Boston in 1834. Hoping to raise money for the New England Anti-Slavery Society, Lydia Maria Child and other female abolitionists in Boston asked the members of female antislavery societies, particularly those in Portland, Concord, Newburyport, Amesbury, and Reading to contribute goods for the sale.[46]

This first fair (or "exhibition" as it was advertised) was quite small, but probably similar in its outlines to later Boston fairs. Prior to the opening of the doors, energetic women would arrange tables of needlework, clothing, and household items, as well as a "cake table" or refreshments area. Banners and evergreens provided decoration, and on occasion there would be inspiring musical presentations, perhaps from Miss Susan Paul's choir of African American children. Tickets were sold at the door for a small price, thus ensuring that even those who came simply to browse contributed to the antislavery coffers. The first fair raised an impressive $360. By comparison, a fair in the first few years of the twenty-first century would have had to raise over $6,000 to be as monetarily successful.[47]

Eager to expand their efforts, the next year the Boston women asked for donations from an even wider area, and by 1836 they had clearly established the beginnings of the far-flung network of "country societies" that would provide the vast majority of the donations for the fair. They received articles that year from female antislavery societies or antislavery women across Massachusetts, including East Bradford, Lynn, Amesbury, Bedford, Hingham, Andover, Haverhill, Reading, Cambridgeport, and South Weymouth. For many of these societies, sewing for the Boston fair gave them a focus for their meetings and a concrete sense of contributing to the cause. At the same time they found a welcome outlet for their sewn goods, which they often could not sell at a profit in their local area, since most of their neighbors also did their own sewing. As the market revolution progressed in more urban areas, city women, particularly those in Boston, found it more convenient to purchase their aprons and winter gloves than to make their own, thus providing a ready market for the rural women's goods.[48] Country societies that could not provide goods for the fair often provided evergreens for decoration or sent refreshments and donations for the cake table. Both fresh greens and fresh eggs were becoming harder to find in rapidly expanding urban Boston. While the Boston fair would eventually evolve far beyond homemade goods to include an international array of high-priced items, most antislavery fairs would remain very dependent on the handiwork and contributions of rural women.

The socializing that went on as members from a dispersed set of female antislavery societies met together was just as important to some of the women as the money they raised. It enabled them to meet in person women with whom they corresponded regularly, filling out relationships previously developed only by letter. Fairs also gave women a concrete sense of involvement in the antislavery cause and strengthened ties among female antislavery societies as women talked, laughed, and worked successfully together. When country societies sent a representative along with their goods, the society hosting the fair gained crucial on-site assistance with decorating and sales. Women from outside Boston gained experience running fairs and a chance to participate in one of the "grand events" of the abolitionist year.[49] Boston women often housed out-of-town assistants at their own homes, ensuring that the cooperation and conversation of the day would continue late into the evening, over meals, and in the sitting room. In this way fairs both drew upon and reinforced the networks created by correspondence, as women exchanged goods and experiences and conversed in person rather than by pen.

Fairs were predominantly designed to raise funds for antislavery newspapers, lecturers, and national organizations. Yet they were also intended as venues for antislavery education. Pithy mottoes and political comments were sewn on, printed on, or baked into articles. In 1834 the *Liberator* noted a wide variety of creative comments placed on or near goods for sale: "iron holders were marked 'anti-slave-*holders*,'—a flag thus, 'Stripes on the banner, none on the back.' Pinned on an evergreen shrub was a slip of paper, containing the following hint, 'Persons are requested not to handle the articles, which, like slavery, are too "delicate" to be touched.'"[50]

By 1836 the women had definitely gotten the hang of handmade political commentary. The *Liberator* report for that year glows with examples of women's inventiveness:

> Bunches of quills bore the label, "Twenty-five Weapons for Abolitionists." On the wafer-boxes was written, "The doom of slavery is sealed." On one side of the pen-wiper was inscribed, "Wipe out the blot of Slavery"; on the other, "Plead the cause with thy Pen." On some needle-books was printed, "May the use of our needles prick the consciences of slaveholders"; others were made in the form of small shoes, and on the soles was written, "Trample not on the oppressed." Even the refreshment table contributed its mite to the cause. Cakes and candies made without slave sugar were prominently displayed as "free labor goods."[51]

Those who attended the fairs got a crash course in antislavery ideology, whether by engaging in conversations or simply by reading the goods for sale. Those goods continued their lessons once bought and taken home. As the New England Anti-Slavery Society noted, when praising the 1834 fair, "Many of the articles purchased on the occasion, will probably serve as perpetual mementos to the owners and their friends, of their duties to their oppressed countrymen." Thus antislavery women not only raised money for antislavery newspapers but created "publications" of their own, turning ordinary household items into antislavery tracts.[52]

Blurring the Boundaries: Public, Private, Moral, and Political

Women's incorporation of political commentary into privately made goods, which were meant to be sold in public and then used in the privacy of the home, blurred the distinctions between public and private for antislavery women. The public nature of the fairs immediately raised questions about this type of organizing. While sewing could easily fit into conventional definitions of woman's sphere, the mechanics of locating and renting a hall, putting advertisements in the local newspapers, and handling economic business transactions could not. Conversations regarding making the Boston fair an annual event under the auspices of the Boston FASS met with dissension due to "conscientious scruples on the part of some of the members."[53] For some, these scruples revolved around the focus on worldly goods and display at fairs. They felt that fairs were an insufficiently serious method by which to raise money for so serious a cause as abolition. Even William Lloyd Garrison shared this opinion, editorializing in the *Liberator*: "We entertain very decided objections to these trumpery exhibitions. Their origin, we fear, may oftener be found in a love of display, than in a philanthropic spirit; and their tendency is unquestionably pernicious."[54] But most of the Boston women who objected to fairs did so on the grounds that fairs were too public a forum for women to organize. The Boston society eventually agreed to take on the responsibility of organizing the fair, but only a particular cadre of women worked on it, and no money was used from the treasury, thus preventing offense to those who did not really want to be involved.

These concerns may have influenced women in other antislavery societies as well. Women in Concord devoted a portion of their monthly meetings to needlework and used the proceeds to aid the cause. However, they do not seem to have held a fair to sell their goods until many years later, preferring at first a quieter (and undocumented) method. The women of the Ladies' Anti-Slavery Sewing Society of New York City raised one hundred dollars through needlework in 1834, but they sold their goods through a display at the Antislavery Offices, rather than a public fair.[55]

Even antislavery women who did not hold fairs found themselves having to defend their antislavery activities on a regular basis. In part this stemmed from the common assertion that slavery was a political issue and thus unsuitable for female attention. The women who formed the FASS of Chatham St. Chapel (NY) were "grieved to see that some . . . regard the members of the Female Anti-Slavery Society as meddling with politics. They try to put us to shame, by holding us up to ridicule and scorn, for aspiring, as they say, to the place, and assuming the responsibility of statesmen." In response, they cited the example of the women who had succored Jesus at Calvary and claimed they too were succoring him when they cared for "his oppressed poor," the slave. More directly, they claimed that "[w]hatever else it may be, slaveholding must be eminently *a domestic evil*." Because slavery worked its mischief in the home, among the family circle, it was thus inherently a female concern.[56]

The AAS Declaration of Sentiments supported the women's interpretation of slavery as a moral cause. It stressed the necessity of ending slavery since it threatened the relationships among families, tearing "the tender babe from the arms of its frantic mother—the heartbroken wife from her weeping husband." It also called upon Americans to "repent" for the guilt of holding human beings in bondage. This language placed antislavery squarely in the tradition of female benevolence, in which women were to feed the hungry, clothe the naked, and eradicate sin from their family and nation. While the AAS called for the removal of slavery "by moral and political action," they heavily stressed efforts involving "moral suasion" or the effort to persuade Americans to see slavery as a moral evil needing to be scoured from the earth. This definition made antislavery not only suitable for women's attention, but requiring of their attention as the more pious and more moral sex.[57]

Women also drew upon patriotic arguments to defend their antislavery activities, placing themselves in the historical tradition of women protecting their families and country. In ringing terms, Boston women drew upon the memory of those foremothers who battled for freedom in the American Revolution. "*We,* at least, shall never forget the noble daring of those from whom we are descended. *We* shall devoutly cherish the memory of those who never shrunk from any duty because it was a new and painful one. We shall not cast carelessly by the recollection of the women of every New England hamlet who shrunk not from sacrificing their first born, when the question was of freedom or slavery." The women of the Chatham St. Chapel FASS also understood women to be defenders of the nation. "We hope," they wrote, "that female modesty does not require us to regard our country with indifference. We have fathers, brothers, husbands, sons. *Are we not something in, and something to, our country?*" Women in New Hampshire echoed the mixture of civic and religious responsibility. The women of Concord opened their first annual report with a history of powerful women in America from Puritans and pioneers to the proud women of the American Revolution. Mixing images of women defending liberty with conceptions of women as religious reformers, the Concord women made clear that they saw themselves as justified in their work by both national history and personal Christian responsibility.[58]

Whether defending their activities in moral or patriotic terms, many antislavery women attempted to fit their activities into traditional understandings of woman's role, thus undermining criticism that they had moved beyond their sphere. The Ladies' New-York City Anti-Slavery Society's first annual report contained a strong call for female antislavery societies, yet it carefully delineated the appropriateness of the activities they were asking women to undertake: "We are not calling upon them for any thing that would interfere with the sacredness of the feminine character, but rather for what is essential to prove its existence. The duties which we urge may be performed without calling them from their own firesides, or identifying them with the scenes of political strife." They argued that woman's role was to pray for the slave, teach hatred of oppression to children, and disseminate antislavery principles among family and friends. While this was a fairly conservative definition of woman's duties, reflecting the New York City women's roots in evangelical churches, even it provided room for a wide variety of antislavery activities.[59] Praying for the slave could be done privately at home, in women's antislavery societies, or at a public monthly concert of prayer for the slave, a custom that came to be quite common by the late 1830s.

Women in Boston took the idea of educating children at the fireside into the broader community. They had antislavery messages printed on handkerchiefs for children, which they distributed at fairs, schools, and churches. Lydia Maria Child produced books specifically designed to aid mothers in the antislavery education of their children. Some women helped children to form juvenile antislavery societies, for which they served as advisors. The circulation of antislavery materials among family and friends was central to women's antislavery goals. It was a silent but highly successful means of "preaching" the antislavery message, and one that could be done without moving into the public sphere.

Other common female antislavery activities could also be fit into conventional female responsibilities or roles. Drawing on the customs of religious benevolence, many female societies purchased life memberships for their ministers in the American Antislavery Society or other, more local organizations. These donations provided much-needed funds for the antislavery treasuries, while also showing women's respect for and willingness to support their local clergymen.[60] Many female societies also continued to stress the importance of the avoidance of slave-made goods and the patronage of free-produce stores. Through their ordinary household purchases, women could contribute to the economic downfall of slavery. The purchase of free-produce goods, while private in the sense of personally determined, was often actually quite public. Free-labor cotton was not of the same quality as slave-grown cotton, often requiring public explanation of why one would wear such "coarse and colorless" material. Free-labor sugar was often placed in a special sugar bowl on household tables, which made quite clear its antislavery connections. Although taking place primarily within the home, free-produce decisions thus had public aspects and public consequences, blurring the boundaries between what was an acceptable or private activity and what was not.

Mob Violence against Women

Antislavery women's public activities and advocacy of so unpopular a cause combined to make them the targets of mob violence. Attacks against antislavery women were part of a dramatic upsurge in violence and riot during the 1830s. African American institutions and individuals were particularly at risk, with mobs burning orphanages, churches, and individual businesses. Abolitionists were the other main target.[61] There were over 165 reported anti-abolition mobs and riots between 1832 and 1837. Particularly large anti-abolition confrontations occurred in New York City in 1833 and 1834, Utica (NY) and Boston (MA) in 1835, and Granville (OH) in 1836, each of which involved attacks on both male and female abolitionists. In 1837 a mob in Alton (IL) presented abolitionists with their first martyr by killing abolitionist editor Elijah Lovejoy during an attack on his press. Conflict over the mailing of abolitionist pamphlets to the South resulted in a mass burning of the mails in Charleston (SC) and the hanging of many fiery effigies of prominent abolitionist men.[62]

Violence against male abolitionists was specific to their antislavery principles and their advocacy of rights for African Americans. Violence against women resulted both from the women's abolitionist activity and their supposed violation of the separation of spheres that relegated women to the home while reserving public meetings for men. This is clear in 1834 when a Concord mob refrained from attacking a men's antislavery convention but felt compelled to "devise methods of scaring" the women, who met the very next day. A crowd of boys and men continually disrupted the women's meeting with shouts of "Out with the ladies."[63]

Benevolent women, involved in less controversial causes, had been permitted to meet in Boston and most other cities for some time prior to October 1835, when the Boston FASS published notice of their annual meeting. They indicated they would gather to pray and organize against slavery and have an address by English abolitionist George Thompson. The local newspapers immediately protested the choice of speaker, accusing abolitionist women of disgracing themselves by "running after" Thompson. This was a comment on the women's supposed sexual as well as intellectual interest in Thompson. The papers also claimed that the women were overstepping appropriate boundaries on female behavior. "Has it come to this, that the WOMEN of our country—not content with their proper sphere— the domestic fireside—must hold public meetings to encourage the efforts of a foreign Emissary?" complained one writer. In response, the owner of the hall the women had rented for their meeting backed out of their agreement. He cited the threat of violence by "the most influential and respectable men in the community."[64]

The Boston women felt obligated to defend their right to meet and their choice of lecturer. Maria Chapman complained, "It comes with an ill grace from those who boast an English ancestry, to object to our choice on this occasion; still less should the sons of the Pilgrim Fathers invoke the spirit of outrageous violence on the daughters of the noble female band who shared their conflict with public opinion." The Boston women felt they were following in a long tradition of women, stretching back to the American Revolution, who stood up for what they believed to be right and for the good of the nation. They were rather shocked at the public outrage regarding their public meeting.[65]

Although George Thompson decided not to attend, the women rescheduled their meeting for a few days later and asked Boston mayor Theodore Lyman for appropriate protection. Thirty women succeeded in meeting by arriving almost an hour early. Shortly after their arrival the building was surrounded and the staircase thronged with angry men, such that over one hundred other women were unable to enter. Despite the clearly violent crowd pressing against the small partition that kept them outside the women's meeting hall, the women opened their meeting as scheduled and knelt to pray. The crowd continued its verbal assaults and at one point "hurled missiles at the lady presiding." The mayor needed three officers to clear a path into the room where the women were meeting. Pushing aside the "twenty or thirty" men pressed against the door, the mayor urged the ladies to withdraw. They refused, claiming that the mayor could stop the violence if he wanted. "If this is the last bulwark of freedom," one woman supposedly announced, "we may as well die here, as any where."[66]

Many of the other women were less sure about becoming martyrs for the cause and agreed to follow the mayor out, if he could secure them a path. He did so, with great difficulty. The women formally adjourned their meeting and walked arm in arm, black women with white, through the crowd of men who hissed, groaned, and (perhaps worst) laughed at the women. They did not, however, attack them. Instead they took out their anger on William Lloyd Garrison who had made the mistake of being in the building. With a noose around his neck, they dragged him through the streets intending to tar and feather him until someone reminded them, "He is an American." He was placed in the city jail for his own safety, ending the excitement of the evening. The women finally completed their annual meeting a few days later at the home of Francis Jackson, a prominent Boston abolitionist. Despite the continued threat of violence, over 130 women attended this second meeting and the society actually added a number of members that day.[67]

The story of the Boston women's proud resistance to mob violence became a central part of antislavery literature and lore. This was due in large part to the Boston women's excellent and extensive publication of their actions. Facing violence helped unify that small, diverse society and propelled it into one of the most powerful organizations in the antislavery movement. By 1836 the Bostonians were elder women in the cause, "more accustomed to the heat and burden of the day" and held up as models for other women in the antislavery movement. Yet other antislavery women had also braved violence in order to organize on behalf of the slave. Antislavery women in at least three other towns faced dangerous mob violence; two of these incidents occurred at the founding meetings of female antislavery societies.[68]

The December prior to the Boston riot, women in Concord faced "violent and insulting language, stones, rotten eggs and other missiles" in order to hear George Thompson lecture. At the close of his remarks, he read a previously prepared constitution, and fifty-five ladies walked proudly forward, despite the mob, to sign their names.[69] Shortly thereafter, Thompson's three-day lecture tour in Lowell was also disrupted by riot. On Sunday, a stone was thrown during his lecture. On Monday, brickbats and other small missiles regularly disrupted the talk. By Tuesday, the threat of mob violence was so serious that the men planning to attend the lecture rescheduled it for Wednesday. The women, however, decided to meet without George Thompson present, and they formed the largest female antislavery society in the nation with over 980 members. This society drew on the large numbers of women who had moved to Lowell to work in the textile mills.[70] Only a few months after the Boston incident, thirty-five Providence (RI) women faced down a mob of fifty to sixty men. Undeterred by the loud cries from outside, the women would not be turned out and they continued their antislavery meeting despite the disturbance. Clearly female antislavery defiance was not limited to Boston.[71]

Women rarely faced serious physical harm in these early antislavery riots. An occasional stone or egg did hit its target and a few women must have suffered bruises from the jostling, but there were no reports of any serious hurt. Mayor Lyman wrote in his memoirs that the Boston women were never "in any danger of their lives or of personal injury—at the worst, exposed only to insult and to be the spectators of a disgraceful riot." However, while women did not have to fight for their lives, they did have to fight for their reputations. These were particularly vulnerable to the "insults" Mayor Lyman so casually shrugged off.[72]

The Boston women accurately understood that the violence against them had to do with both the cause they espoused and a broader effort to enforce appropriate gender roles. They therefore attempted to link their antislavery efforts to the benevolent work for which women were usually lauded. "When before, in this city," the Boston society asked, "have gentlemen of standing and influence, been incensed against a benevolent association of ladies, for holding their annual meeting?" They directly contrasted the treatment of their society with the treatment given to the members of a Fatherless and Widow's Relief Society, "*Those* ladies are designated as 'woman, stepping gracefully to the relief of infancy and suffering age'; . . . no one talks of 'binding over' [their leader] 'to keep the peace,' as has been proposed with regard to the secretary of our society. . . . No one said *then* 'women had better stay at home.'" Yet the distinction between benevolent and antislavery societies did not protect the Ladies' Moral Reform Society meeting, or a group of women holding a church fair, both of whom were disrupted by a mob that saw women in public and concluded they were abolitionists. The Boston women therefore felt compelled to defend their right to meet not in terms of free speech but on the grounds of women's understood responsibilities as wives and mothers. They published the following fiery defense in local newspapers, antislavery newspapers, and their own annual report:

> We must meet together, to strengthen ourselves to discharge our duty as the mothers of the next generation—as the wives and sisters of this. We cannot descend to bandy words with those who have no just sense of their own duty or ours, who dread lest the delicacies of the table should be neglected, who glory in the darning-needle and whose talk is of the distaff. This is a crisis which demands of us not only mint, and annise [sic], and cummin, but also judgment, mercy and faith; and God being our helper, none of these shall be required in vain at our hands. Our sons shall not blush for those who bore them.[73]

Boston women claimed antislavery activism as a fitting part of woman's moral and familial responsibilities. Boston's antislavery women were strongly influenced not only by the example of the city's Puritan founders but also by the actions of Revolutionary women who stepped outside women's previous responsibilities in order to protect their families from the danger of British oppression. Believing that women of the American Revolution "never shrunk from any duty because it was a new and painful one" and were willing to make incredible sacrifices "when the question was of freedom or slavery," the Boston women saw no reason to back down from their own battle against slavery. The power of their argument lies in their reinterpretation of women's traditional duties to include antislavery organizing.[74]

Developing Commitment through Adversity

While mob violence in this period did cause fear among antislavery women, it also inspired in most a fiery dedication to the antislavery cause. Many saw their persecutions as similar to those suffered by both early Christian martyrs and early American patriots. In Boston the women claimed proudly that, in the moment of worst mob violence, "Our souls were strengthened and borne above the violence and insult with which we were surrounded. Our hopes, our faith, our fortitude, were increased. We felt grateful that we were accounted worthy thus to express our devotion to TRUTH."[75] At their annual meeting one year after the mob disruption, the Concord women expressed gratefulness that the mob had taught them "how persecution for righteousness' sake strengthens the hearts of the persecuted—viz. by driving them for protection and succor to the Almighty, whose name is a strong tower. . . . Never saw we more clearly on which side we were arrayed."[76]

Women who faced mobs reiterated in ringing terms their fundamental right and responsibility to work for the slave, and they refused to be intimidated back into their homes. In Providence women dealt with the threat of a mob by meeting in larger numbers than anyone had expected. As an observer reported: "the ladies mustered strong—so as to fill all the seats—and made a very respecta[ble] appearance as to numbers—probably twic[e] as many as there would have been—had all been quiet."[77] A Providence woman subsequently wrote a letter to the *Providence Journal* expressing her pity and contempt for the rioters. She declared, "We are not to be *deterred*—we are not to be *frightened*—we are not to be *flattered* from our purpose."[78]

Even those women who did not face violence directly often risked social reproach and rejection when they took up the antislavery cause. Formerly a popular writer of books for children and housewives, Lydia Maria Child lost her reading public and many of her friends when she published her first antislavery work. While this undermined her ability to earn money and care for her family, she found a new supportive community among abolitionists.[79] The women of South Reading reported that they regularly endured the "frowns of the indifferent" while women in Uxbridge felt threatened by "prejudice, persecution and danger." The women of Groton had "obloquy and reproach heaped upon them." Maria Weston Chapman herself was vilified by a local congregation after asking that an antislavery meeting announcement be read in their church. As a friend reported to Chapman's sister, churchgoers muttered, "It must be Mrs. Chapman [who had the announcement read,] for no one but she would have the impudence to do it," and "If Mrs. Chapman will insult this congregation in this way, she must expect to be insulted herself." Chapman seemed actually to relish both insults and mob violence. When a few men arrived at her home fresh from the Boston mob and looking for trouble, Chapman invited them in for tea. She then spent an hour "giving it" to the proslavery men, who seemed unable to escape the polite confines of her living room. Her sister later reported that Chapman "said that she had never had such a delightful time in her life. She had said everything she wanted to."[80]

Whether women faced down mobs, strangers, or friends and relatives who disapproved of their activities, they drew crucial support from the antislavery community. Antislavery newspapers lauded women facing mobs for their "great heroism and exemplary devotion." William Lloyd Garrison christened the Boston women "Christian heroines," combining images of Christian martyrs and American patriots into a powerful justification for further female antislavery organizing. After hearing of the attack upon the Boston women, the Ladies' New-York City Anti-Slavery Society resolved that "they too could bear such indignities," particularly when one compared them to the much greater indignities endured by women in slavery. The awareness of opposition seems to have stirred the New York women to greater exertions, and they lauded the Boston women in their correspondence. Rhode Island women recognized the connection between their own mob experiences and their willingness to move beyond limited understandings of woman's proper role. "Think not delicacy or weakness of the sex may be an apology for idleness or ignorance!" wrote Frances Harriet Whipple from Providence. "Have not some of our number already suffered public indignities?"[81]

The strength of the community created by correspondence helped antislavery women to see violence as an organizational stimulant rather than a barrier. Their ability to stand up for their beliefs in the face of violence and receive encouragement from people they respected increased their sense of belonging to a tight-knit, supportive, moral community. Unified by their sense of dedication and purpose, few women seem to have left the movement due to external criticism in this period. After 1837 when the antislavery community itself divided over the appropriate role for women in the movement, the women would have a decidedly less united response to mob violence and the network would begin to fracture.[82]

Conclusion

Between 1832 and 1837 women interested in bringing about the end of slavery organized themselves into over 140 separate female antislavery societies. Excluded from but encouraged by the national male societies, women created their own national network through correspondence. Hundreds of letters provided important advice on how to form a society, how to interest members, and what kinds of activities were most effective. The women created regional networks, usually centered around a well-organized central society, and exchanged goods and personnel as well as advice and encouragement. Encouragement was necessary as women drew upon each other for moral support, particularly in the face of anti-abolition violence. Mobs and fairs both required women to justify their antislavery activities, although both provided spurs to increased participation. Fairs served as recruiting tools, fund-raisers, education venues, and a chance to socialize. Mobs inspired heroines, group cohesion, and a strong sense of dedication to the cause.

The discussion of woman's appropriate sphere was more muted in this period than it would be later, in part because antislavery men were united in their support for female involvement in this moral cause. Women's roles also remained less contentious because women themselves remained less public during this period. The vast majority of early female antislavery meetings were held in women's homes or local churches and involved sewing for the fairs, reading antislavery periodicals, distributing literature to friends and family, or other fairly private activities. The experiences of Boston women make clear that the question of whether antislavery was a moral or political issue percolated just under the surface, and women who met in public found themselves negotiating increasingly gerrymandered boundaries of public and private, moral and political. These questions would become more widespread and would affect the majority of antislavery women once they entered the more clearly public spheres of conventions and petitions.

CHAPTER THREE

United amid
Differences, 1836–1837

Conventions and Petitions

"To meet—to talk ... —to interchange plans of action ...

—these are the soul of the enterprise."

—Maria Weston Chapman, writing about the 1837

Anti-Slavery Convention of American Women.

Between 1836 and 1837, antislavery women moved beyond the realm of letters and encouragement into the realm of petitions and conventions.[1] In 1836, with the Boston, New York, and Philadelphia societies taking the lead, antislavery women petitioned Congress in record numbers. In the fall of that year these three organizations discussed creating a national executive committee to coordinate antislavery women's activities across the North. Maria Weston Chapman suggested that "great good" would result from a meeting of a small executive committee.[2] However, the three organizations ultimately decided to convene the grand Anti-Slavery Convention of American Women in 1837. The convention brought together hundreds of female antislavery leaders, enabled extensive sharing of ideas, tactics, and strategies, and cemented female networks that had previously been dependent on long-distance correspondence. The face-to-face meetings and centralized organization allowed women to coordinate a massive petition campaign in 1837, which doubled the previous number of female signatures sent to Congress. The petitioning effort itself increased correspondence among societies and contributed to a powerful sense that women across the northern half of the country were united in their antislavery efforts. In these years the networking, organizing, and mentoring of previous years bore productive and public fruits.

While the extensive networking required to coordinate petitions and organize a convention drew antislavery women into closer cooperation, it also made clearer the issues on which they disagreed. Questions of interracial cooperation and church membership emerged as problematic issues. Women also continued to debate how to organize most effectively against slavery. Throughout 1836 societies discussed whether to push for more equal cooperation with men in the all-male American Anti-Slavery Society, or whether to build an all-female national society parallel to the men's organization. These divergent plans reflected two different understandings of how women might best serve the antislavery cause: by working jointly with men or by maintaining independent, separate organizations. These choices were constrained by male antislavery activists' unwillingness to permit women into their organizations and by the rising volume of criticism against women's public antislavery activities. The women's convention and their petition campaigns made women's antislavery activities more effective and more visible, adding weight to existing complaints about women meddling in the highly divisive, political issue of slavery. Women hotly debated how best to organize in an atmosphere full of new opportunities and old criticisms. Yet women continued to unite their efforts despite and amid these differences.

The Question of Female Delegates

By 1836 women had founded at least fifty-three female antislavery societies, and the number grew rapidly in the course of that year. Many of these affiliated themselves with the American Anti-Slavery Society (AAS) as auxiliaries. Both male and female societies could become auxiliaries of the AAS. Doing so meant that a society agreed that slavery could best be eliminated by persuading Americans it was a terrible sin, and that members of that society committed themselves to raising money to help the AAS spread its message. Some societies affiliated themselves with a county or state society instead, and some female societies became auxiliary to other female societies. Auxiliary status simply meant "affiliated with a larger society" and did not imply a subservient position or limit the organization to fund-raising for the national society.

Auxiliary status gave women the right to send delegates to the national AAS meetings. In April 1836 members of the Philadelphia FASS began to wonder whether the right to send delegates meant they could send female delegates to this all-male society. Wishing to obtain a wider opinion on the subject, they sent letters to many of the female societies with whom they had corresponded over the past three years. Replies from three female societies remain: Brooklyn (CT), Concord (NH), and Boston. Little is known of the Brooklyn society, but New York area societies in general tended to adhere more closely than many other female antislavery societies to conservative definitions of woman's sphere. The Concord society generally supported a broader understanding of woman's role. The Boston society regularly experienced tension on this issue between its more radical and more conservative members. Thus these three societies provide a particularly useful sample of female opinion on the question of woman's appropriate role.

The fifty-two society members in Brooklyn unanimously agreed that they could send delegates to the annual meeting, but they felt these delegates should be male. They had sent two male delegates to represent them at the 1835 annual meeting. This may have been common among female societies, but one cannot tell from AAS meeting records. Representatives from female societies were rarely listed as delegates. Most likely, the men were also delegates from a male society and were thus listed under that affiliation, or attended as at-large delegates listed by their hometown. Only one delegate from a female society—the Female Juvenile Anti-Slavery Society of Providence (RI)—is listed in the minutes for 1835. If there were delegates from other women's organizations, they did not speak or sign their names specifically as representatives of women.[3]

The Brooklyn women recognized that they might have a right to send female delegates, but they did not feel comfortable contravening custom: "Had we a right to send [delegates] at all, we think we should have a *right* to send females," they wrote, "but in so doing we should be acting without a precedent, we should expose ourselves to additional, and needless odium, and custom has hitherto been such, that we think few females among us would be willing to attend as delegates, and that no advantage would be gained thereby—therefore, that it is best to send gentlemen." Their reference to "additional odium" underscores that these women were already participating in a cause that provoked riots and they felt no need to take any "unnecessary" actions which would cause further complaint.[4]

Women in Concord agreed unanimously with their sisters in Brooklyn. They had been represented at previous meetings by men and wondered "whether our more experienced *brethren,* who are accustomed to sit and to speak in such assemblies, could not more *justly* represent us than we could represent ourselves." Here again the women were influenced by public opinion regarding women's appropriate roles. The Concord women assumed that appointing female delegates would invite reproach for "stepping out of our appointed sphere."[5]

Boston women found themselves terribly split on the issue. Twenty-three women were in favor of sending female delegates, and twenty-five were opposed. The division was sharp enough that "many of the women were unwilling to express their opinion." These same women had been willing to face violence and insult to hold an all-female antislavery society meeting. That they could not agree to send female delegates to a traditionally male convention makes clear how serious an issue this was and how much of a line they were thinking of crossing.[6]

The Philadelphia women did not limit their inquiries to female-only societies. After asking the opinion of women in a mixed-sex society in Lancaster County (PA), the Philadelphia FASS received a reply that neatly captured both sides of the debate. Lindley Coates, the male secretary for the society, suggested that women simply form their own national society, rather than joining with men. He made clear that he did not think this was the result of female inferiority, believing that women's talents "are in no ways inferior to ours." He argued that "such is the force of Custom and habit," that if women joined men in convention, they would generally remain quietly in the background rather than truly exercise their abilities. Coates did hope that at some point "an effort was made to join the men and Women in a national Society, believing that it might be the means of breaking down this Lordly distinction" between the two sexes. But he was not sure now was the time.[7]

A letter from the AAS secretary in regard to this request failed completely to clear up the issue. In a masterly example of avoiding the question, Elizur Wright, Jr., wrote that the constitutional article regarding the sending of delegates applied to female as well as male auxiliaries. They were *allowed* to send whomever they wanted. "In regard to the propriety of such auxiliaries sending delegates, please to excuse me from saying more than that such delegates would doubtless be received with the courtesy and high respect which it is the glory of the *Christian religion* to pay to the *better half* of human nature." Female delegates would most likely be treated like female congregants at a church: with great respect, but not with equality.[8]

The Philadelphia women chose not to send a female delegate to the AAS convention that year. However, their letter clearly stimulated further thought among the women of Boston. The Boston FASS had been actively involved in circulating petitions regarding slavery in the District of Columbia and recognized that more cooperation among female antislavery societies would greatly facilitate this process. In mid-1836 they proposed a general executive committee to coordinate the efforts of antislavery women across the country, very similar to the suggestion from Lindley Coates in Lancaster County. The committee would be composed of "the officers and most deeply interested members of female Anti-Slavery Societies in the U.S." and would "advise and consider plans for the advancement of this cause." It would serve as a parallel female organization to the American Anti-Slavery Society.[9]

The General Executive Committee for Women

The debate over this general executive committee tells us a great deal about antislavery women's rapidly evolving understandings of their appropriate roles and their organizational niches. In just nine months the Boston women changed their opinion completely, from general support for to a complete rejection of the separate female organization. By tracing out the arguments women used for and against the committee, we can see two competing visions of female antislavery organization: one that saw power in women working side by side with men, and a second that saw power in women's separate organizations. The search for compromise indicates both the potential divisiveness of the issue and the women's determined ability to work through the disagreements over this issue.[10]

The women of New York strongly supported the idea of a general executive committee since "the available talent and energy now scattered throughout the country, will be brought to a common centre, and rendered tenfold more available." The New York women, like those in Boston, had been heavily involved in circulating petitions and were thus aware of how useful a centralized organization might be. Their location in New York City, the annual meeting place of dozens of national reform associations, would also have emphasized the usefulness of national organization. An executive committee would give a "national character to all important documents." Like their male counterparts, female abolitionists considered it crucial that the antislavery movement be (and be perceived to be) national in scope, including both Northerners and Southerners, New Englanders as well as midwesterners. This justified their pronouncements that antislavery was not a sectional or political issue but rather a moral issue that transcended region. A single, national, female antislavery society would provide anti-slavery women with an official, unified voice that was lacking when they spoke as individual societies.[11]

The New York women also supported the idea specifically because it united women, as opposed to women and men. They felt there was "much to be un-dertaken for the cause, for which woman and she alone, is fitted." In their view, women had gender-specific responsibilities for the raising of children, the raising of female consciences, and the raising of prayers to Congress on the issue of slavery. They felt that women's "situation in society" placed them in a "sphere of action" shielded and protected from the dangers and mocking that faced antislavery men. Therefore, joining men in their societies would be particularly inappropriate. By contrast, forming an all-female organization need not raise the issue of women "stepping out their sphere," since women would thereby be filling their religious and civic responsibilities.[12]

The idea of creating an executive organization separate from men re-ceived mixed support in Philadelphia. The Philadelphia FASS found the plan "expedient and desirable in the present state of society," though clearly some of the women "would much prefer a recognition of female members and delegates, in the American [Antislavery] Society." Unlike the women in New York, they did not see women as having a separate role to play from men. The Philadelphia FASS agreed to support the plan since the recognition of female members at the AAS "seems to be at present unat-tainable." They suggested a meeting of the executive committee in New York City in mid-May, at the same place and time as the American Anti-Slavery Society annual meeting. In this way, the Philadelphians could both attend the all-male society meeting (as gallery observers if not delegates), while also committing to working with other antislavery women.[13]

When the Boston society next wrote to Philadelphia, they had appar-ently begun to have mixed feelings about the committee they had pro-posed. They had decided that it "would be presumptuous in us to present *any* [plan for the committee], when a better might certainly be devised by the united wisdoms of *all* the societies." They had been in correspondence with their extensive network of female antislavery associations and had re-ceived the names of dozens of women who were "by zeal and experience qual-ified to carry into execution" a plan for closer cooperation. Thus they decided to invite all of these women to "A Meeting of Ladies from all parts of the free States at N. York, at the time of the National Anti Slavery Convention" at which the entire female antislavery community could decide the issue of a national female executive committee.[14]

The Boston women had clearly received a wide range of opinions on the issue in their correspondence. As they wrote to the Philadelphia women: "Some Societies would doubtless prefer the organization of a National Ladies' Anti Slavery Society; while others would prefer that no change should take place, fearing it might paralyze the *State* societies." By pulling away the energies of the most devoted female activists, integration could help the cause of women's rights, but not necessarily the cause of the slave. The Boston letter also reflected debate within their own society, which had sent such a divided response to the Philadelphia women's original query regarding female delegates. Some Boston women wanted to join the all-male national society, "which an article of their constitution *authorises* us to do, and which I have no doubt we shall be *requested* to do." Others felt strongly that a "Conference of Ladies," rather than a national society, would "perhaps avoid the charge of deserting our sphere (if it were worthwhile to do so)." The Boston women were divided on what constituted woman's appropriate sphere of action, and also on whether women should worry about the boundaries of that sphere.[15]

In this way, antislavery women planned the 1837 Antislavery Convention of American Women, a tentative compromise between the radical step of integrating the male antislavery societies, and the only slightly less radical step of creating a national female antislavery organization to parallel the men's. Women disagreed over how best to organize and what types of activities would take them beyond their sphere. However, they fully agreed that meeting together and discussing the issues would be a powerful asset to women's antislavery organizing. As the Boston women wrote: "To meet—to talk—to pray together;—to compare feelings and opinions; to interchange plans of action, to devise new means of usefulness; to see on earth the *faces* of those beloved fellow-labourers whose *names* and whose *hearts* we know so well—these are the soul of the enterprise." The convention enabled women to transcend the limits imposed by long-distance correspondence, and it greatly strengthened the personal relationships between far-flung women. It also required them to face and discuss some of the opinions that divided them, and to devise strategies to remain united amid their differences.[16]

The Anti-Slavery Convention of American Women
—Membership and Race

The 1837 convention brought together 175 women committed to antislavery, representing 10 states, at least 20 female antislavery societies, and almost 48 towns. Society delegates attended from New Hampshire (2), Massachusetts (22), Rhode Island (3), New York (19), New Jersey (1), Pennsylvania (22), and Ohio (2). Corresponding members—unaffiliated individuals who were given full voting privileges—arrived from Maine (1), Massachusetts (4), Rhode Island (2), Connecticut (2), New York (90), Pennsylvania (3), and South Carolina (2). Their goal was to interest their fellow women in the antislavery cause and to "establish a system of operations throughout every town and village in the free States, that would exert a powerful influence in the abolition of American slavery."[17] Never before had women from such a broad geographic area met together in public, and rarely had white and black women met in such relative equality. The convention organizers recognized the need for as broad a representation of female antislavery societies as possible so that "the counsels of the wisest women" could be heard on various issues. As Angelina Grimké noted: "Responsibilities will rest on us as an American Convention which have never belonged to any individual Society." Therefore, all female antislavery societies were requested to send official delegates, while "individuals of kindred feelings and principles, who may reside in places where no such societies exist," were also invited to attend.[18]

Many factors worked against gathering a broad diversity of women. First, being chosen as a delegate to the convention was an honor bestowed by female societies on their most reliable, powerful, or prominent members. Unfortunately, many of these were the least likely to attend. They were often older, and thus more likely to be married, have children, or be ill or frail, all factors that could inhibit their attendance. Older, single women could also find it difficult to attend as they cared for parents or other family members.[19]

The depression of 1837, the most severe depression since the Panic of 1819, also took its toll on the number and type of delegates who were able to attend. As banks sharply contracted available credit, unemployment rates rose rapidly, land values collapsed, and many people went bankrupt. "[T]he times—the hard times" prevented Concord delegate Mary Clark and many others from attending the convention. The society in Uxbridge (MA) chose four delegates, none of whom were able to attend, and Pittsburgh could only afford to send one delegate.[20] Working-class women would have been particularly affected by the depression, which sharply depressed their already low wages. Few would have been able to pay for travel costs and give up their small wage for the four-day-long convention. The depression caused Lydia Maria Child to have strong second thoughts, despite the willingness of her society to pay her expenses: "I had rather put money into their pockets, than take it from them," she wrote. She did eventually attend the convention but bewailed the high cost of gathering so many women.[21]

To be chosen to attend the convention was an honor, but traveling there was a tribulation. One delegate from New Hampshire did not mind the "pleasant ride of seventeen hours" from Boston, nor the long boat ride that had preceded it, but she was definitely an exception. Others had even more difficult itineraries. Sarah Southwick did not attend the 1837 convention, but her travels to the 1838 convention make clear how problematic travel could be. She "went to Providence, took a steamer at night round Point Judith to New York, took another steamboat by day from New York to Amboy, then by rail to Bordentown, then by steamer to Philadelphia." On her return trip, she was "anchored in a steamboat off Point Judith for two days and two nights in a fog. Everybody was sick, from the swinging of the boat and the creaking of the cables." Women's willingness to negotiate the difficulties and cost of travel highlights how seriously they took their antislavery responsibilities. Yet the frustrations and cost also prevented some women from attending.[22]

Some of the convention organizers, particularly the Grimké sisters, wanted to ensure that black women attended the convention. They felt that black women's presence would be crucial to the convention's success in eliminating Northern prejudice and attacking Southern slavery. Sarah Grimké wrote to the Boston FASS encouraging them to send black delegates, a request she repeated to the women of Philadelphia. She noted: "It is all important that we begin right and I know of no way as likely to destroy the cruel prejudices that exist as to bring our sisters in contact with those who shrink from such intercourse[. T]he modest worth and unassuming yet dignified deportment of many of our colored friends must I think put the supercilious arrogance of their fairer countrywomen to the blush and compel them to acknowledge that of a truth God is no respecter of persons."[23] Grimké was unconsciously repeating William Lloyd Garrison's early rebuke of the Boston women. How could a convention hope to speak against prejudice if it did not specifically invite black women to attend? Boston appointed Susan Paul and Julia Williams as delegates, and Philadelphia encouraged many of its black members to attend. However, only three black delegates and two corresponding (or at-large) members officially attended the convention. Other black women may have attended but not have been listed as official or corresponding members.[24]

Many factors help explain this limited black female presence. First, the total number of black women enrolled in female antislavery societies always remained fairly small. In the most integrated societies, black women made up no more than 10 percent of the members and rarely reached more than 5 percent. The Colored Ladies' Literary Society of New York City and the Rising Daughters of Abyssinia each sent at least one delegate to the convention, underscoring the convention's appeal to middle-class black women, but not adding significantly to the numbers attending.[25] The economic demands that forced black women to earn an income and the racial prejudices that limited most of them to domestic service, all placed severe constraints on the time and resources they could devote to reform causes.[26] Most black women who joined antislavery organizations either were economically secure or had middle-class occupations such as schoolteaching, millinery, or shopkeeping, which gave them some margin, however slim, of economic security and leisure time. Even the poorest black women appear to have taken seriously their responsibility to do "race work" and engage in reform activities. However, few black women could afford the funds or time to attend antislavery conventions, and fewer still were willing to face the difficulties, embarrassments, even harassment faced by black female travelers.[27]

Discrimination against black people was common on most forms of transportation. Julia Williams, a black delegate from Boston, was forced to take her meals separately from the many other delegates traveling to the 1837 convention, because of her color. Williams was also not accommodated with the white delegates. Upon her arrival in New York she was referred to a "colored boarding house."[28] Two years later Clarissa Lawrence and two other black women were refused accommodations on a steamer on their way home from the 1839 convention. They had valid cabin tickets, prepurchased by a white abolitionist, but they were not permitted to go below unless they were ladies' maids. This treatment of black women would result in the death of Boston FASS member Susan Paul in 1840. Refused admittance to the ladies' cabin on a trip that year, she spent the night on the lower decks in a rainstorm. She caught a cold, which led to consumption, and shortly thereafter she died.[29] Rather than face these difficulties, most black women preferred to work within their own communities. This also enabled them to avoid the "supercilious arrogance" Sarah Grimké had worried about and the potential for discrimination in antislavery gatherings themselves.

The Question of Woman's Appropriate Role

Despite the difficulties, both the black and white women who gathered in New York took seriously their responsibilities to represent the American female antislavery community. The convention chose the best-known and most active women as officers, including Mary Parker, Lydia Maria Child, and Anne W. Weston from Boston; Angelina and Sarah Grimké from South Carolina; Lucretia Mott, Grace Douglass, and Mary and Sarah Grew from Philadelphia; Ann Smith from Peterborough (NY); and Abby Ann Cox from New York City. In keeping with their wish to be seen as a national movement, delegates were listed by state and town, and both Sarah and Angelina Grimké had their names struck from the Pennsylvania delegation and listed as present from their native South Carolina. In this way the convention could have representatives from the South as well as from the North.[30]

The women recognized the radical nature of their public meeting and the potential disapproval it could cause. They opened their meeting with the Twenty-seventh Psalm: "The Lord [is] my light and my salvation; whom shall I fear? the Lord [is] the strength of my life; of whom shall I be afraid?" Many of the attendees had already faced riot and ridicule and were not to be deterred. They also recognized the membership of "absent friends" from whom they read letters of encouragement and support. These letters reminded the delegates of the strength of their united efforts and of the many far-flung abolitionists who were united in spirit with the convention. Only after these necessary and important markers of community were completed—listing the delegates, appointing officers, reading letters, and offering a prayer for strength—did the convention get down to the business at hand, under the direction of Mary Parker, president of the Boston FASS.[31]

No speeches remain from the convention itself. One delegate reported, "Much do I regret that the excellent remarks which followed each resolution must be lost to you. . . . They melted on my heart and left an impression there which time will not erase, but I cannot repeat them."[32] It seems that very few letters describing the convention have survived, leaving a surprisingly paltry record of this important event. However, since all convention business was conducted in the form of resolutions recorded in the official proceedings, we do have a basic outline of what occurred, and one delegate wrote a more thorough description, which she published at the request of her society.

The women submitted and passed resolutions on a wide variety of issues. They claimed antislavery activity as the duty of every Christian, thus claiming religious ground for women's involvement in the cause. They took Northerners to task for attempting to suppress free speech and discussion, for surrendering fugitive slaves in violation of God's commandments, and for intermarrying with Southern slaveholders. They recommended the use of free-labor goods, praised the work of interracial educational institutions, and urged attendance at a monthly concert for prayer. Given the diversity of the resolutions passed, it is somewhat surprising that only three caused any controversy. These all focused on woman's appropriate role in the antislavery movement.

Many of the resolutions at the convention drew upon conventional understandings of woman's role in a reform movement. Women were asked as the wives, mothers, sisters, and daughters of male abolitionists to vindicate the men's characters against aspersions and stand side by side with them in the antislavery cause. Female relatives of clergymen were asked to strengthen their husbands and fathers on the issue of slavery. However, one resolution challenged women to move beyond these relationship-based activities, beyond the "circumscribed limits with which corrupt custom and a perverted application of Scripture have encircled her." Angelina Grimké asked women to accept that "certain rights and duties are common to all moral beings." Woman's duty and province included using "her voice, and her pen, and her purse, and the influence of her example" to overthrow slavery. Whereas all the other resolutions regarding woman's duties passed without dissent, Grimké's sparked extensive discussion and two amendments were offered. The wording of these amendments is unfortunately not listed in the proceedings. However, they probably addressed the claim that women and men had the same rights and duties, and that to think otherwise required a "perverted application of Scripture."[33]

"An animated and interesting debate respecting the rights and duties of women" ensued. It reflected the division between women who felt current interpretations of woman's appropriate role limited their engagement in the antislavery cause and those women who drew authority for their moral reform work from women's identification with religion and the domestic sphere. The resolution eventually passed without amendments although *"not unanimously,"* and twelve women who voted against the resolution had their names recorded in the minutes as "disapproving of some parts of it." In the interests of harmony, some women who had approved the resolution attempted to have it reconsidered later in the convention "in consideration of the wishes of some members, who were opposed to the adoption of the resolution." The attempt failed, leaving one of the dissenters to offer her own resolution regarding woman's role, which emphasized the claims of the antislavery cause on mothers. This passed without debate.[34]

Two other points of contention make clear that the divisions among women were quite complex. Three of the twelve women who had voted against Angelina Grimké's resolution also dissented from a resolution that chastised evangelical and missionary associations for accepting money from slaveholders. Although the resolution's sponsor, Lydia Maria Child, couched her complaint in the most respectful of terms, these women felt it was too harsh an attack on worthy organizations. Yet these women did not dissent from a resolution by Martha Storrs, which called upon Northern churches to rebuke slaveholding members and declare slavery a sin. The dissenting women may have objected to the slights inherent in the Grimké and Child resolutions, which implied that churches had erred in their understanding of woman's role and the ways in which churches carried out their benevolent work. The Storrs resolution recognized the power of the church to effectively aid the antislavery cause, a position that the more conservative women could strongly support.[35]

The next day the women found themselves similarly divided over "whether the names of the members should be published with the appellation of Mrs. and Miss." After discussion the convention resolved that "the members be designated according to their individual wishes." Titles tended to suggest identification through marriage and family connections and were more common among members of the New York City delegation. Eleven of the twelve women who had objected to Grimké's resolution on the role of women chose to use a title, including nine of the New York City members. Yet overall only slightly less than half of all the New York City delegates chose to use a title, along with only fifteen of eighty corresponding members from that city, which indicates that New York women were not uniformly conservative in their views. The New York women had been strongly supportive of the idea of a women's convention, despite worries by other societies that meeting in such a way might move women beyond their appropriate sphere. On the other side, many of the Philadelphia women may have protested the use of titles on religious rather than "feminist" grounds, since

Quakers did not believe in the use of titles. However, it is striking that not a single Philadelphia woman and only six of twenty-six Massachusetts women chose to list a title, suggesting geographic battle lines for future conflicts.[36]

Despite these small disagreements, the convention was marked by a remarkable degree of unanimity. Women had not yet taken strongly opposing positions on the issues of woman's role or the role of the church, and they focused on the cause that had drawn them together. The closing resolution came down firmly on the side of unity and stressed the cooperative efforts of the convention. The women resolved that "laying aside sectarian views, and private opinions, respecting certain parts of the preceding resolutions, we stand pledged to each other and the world, to *unite* our efforts." They complimented the chair on her impartiality, and with a prayer for strength, they left to implement their plans.[37]

While the convention did enable women to unite their efforts, it did not result in the overarching general executive committee it had originally convened to discuss. When a resolution was presented to form a female executive committee, the Boston delegates made clear that they had been instructed by the majority of the society to vote against the idea. As they stated in their annual report: "We think that the best hope of the sexes are in each other; and that the plan of separate sources of knowledge, and separate means of mental and moral improvement is likely to produce a characteristic difference, fatal to the happiness and the usefulness of both." These women objected to a female executive committee because such a permanent structure would continue to segregate men and women and limit women's ability to integrate the male American Anti-Slavery Society. On similar grounds, the committee killed the idea of a women's antislavery newspaper. As the Grimké sisters wrote: "[W]e do not want to separate the sexes any more into different organizations if it can be avoided." More conservative women objected that a national executive committee would require women to step too far from their appropriate spheres.[38]

While this division over the appropriate format for female activism would probably have been enough to kill the planned committee by itself, issues of prejudice also played a role. In a letter written in late March 1837, Angelina Grimké reported that the Ladies' New-York City Anti-Slavery Society, which would have been a major player in the united committee, was "utterly inefficient" because of their sinful prejudice against race. Grimké noted that no black woman had ever sat on the board, none was welcome in the sewing society, and few were welcome to any meetings at all. Grimké preferred to have no national society until one could be formed "of the *right stamp*," which would include black women equally with white. It was unclear that this would ever occur if the New York City women were involved, and the committee could not serve as a national organization without them.[39]

Without support from radical or conservative women or the Grimké sisters, the national executive committee idea was roundly defeated. However, the women's convention had proven a powerful tool and a useful compromise among the various factions. Thus the 1837 delegates decided to continue this successful compromise course by holding another convention to convene in Philadelphia in May 1838. As reported by the *Genius of Universal Emancipation,* the convention "unanimously agreed that an Annual Convention would effect all the great objects of a society without any of its cumbrous machinery."[40] It would also not require perfect unanimity of its members on questions of race or woman's appropriate role.

Convention Results—Increased Cooperation

Although the convention did not result in a national executive committee, it did have a powerful effect on antislavery women's organizing. First, it provided women with an opportunity to meet in person and thus reinforce and strengthen relationships previously carried on primarily by correspondence. As the *Genius* noted, "Hitherto many . . . [delegates] had only heard of each other by the hearing of the ear, but now, they enjoyed the satisfaction of seeing each other, face to face, and hearing from each other's lips 'thoughts that breathe and words that burn.'"[41] The desire to keep down convention costs, as well as the tradition of hospitality within the antislavery community, had encouraged some women in New York to open their homes to friends and to strangers recommended by friends. This may have reassured many women that the convention was respectable since it did not involve staying in a public hotel. Sharing accommodations also strengthened the sense of community among delegates and provided additional opportunities for conversations and planning, which carried over into women's postconvention correspondence.[42]

By bringing them together to the same place, the convention enabled geographically separated women to work together more easily. While in New York, women from the Boston, Philadelphia, and New York societies discussed sharing the use of engraving plates that had been sent to New York by an English female antislavery society. The plates could be used to print images onto silks, cottons, or paper for use at antislavery fairs. Information tended to spread more quickly through personal interactions than the laborious process of writing letters. The Boston FASS noted shortly after the convention that they had learned "from various members the number, strength and efficiency of the respective Societies with which each [delegate] was connected," information they had previously obtained by an extensive, time-consuming, and costly correspondence. Other networking activities doubtless occurred, though they were not recorded in the official minutes or in extant correspondence. Sarah Grimké had suggested prior to the convention that such a gathering could serve as a catalyst for the creation of sewing societies if the larger societies brought pieces of silk, mottoes, and other materials to give away. It is unclear if this ever happened, but the rapid expansion of antislavery women's fund-raising after the convention suggests that ideas, if not materials, were definitely circulated.[43]

The convention seems to have encouraged more interactions between black and white women than had occurred previously, on both the individual and the societal levels. One delegate felt the convention challenged her racial prejudices simply by exposing her to African American women (as Sarah Grimké had hoped when she encouraged black women to attend). "I was happy," she wrote, "to have our feelings tested with regard to that bitter prejudice against color which we have so criminally indulged, and to find it giving place to better feelings. In the cabin of the boat, our colored companion slept near my side—she rode with us in the carriage—sat with us at the table of a public boarding house—walked in company with us." The convention built upon experiences like these by passing numerous resolutions against race prejudice and encouraging women to "act out the principles of Christian equality by associating with [African Americans] as though the color of the skin was of no more consequence than that of the hair, or the eyes," sentiments that may well have affected women's attitudes when they returned home.[44]

An Address to Free Colored Americans, one of seven publications written by the convention, made clear the connections between black women's uplift projects and both races' abolitionist aims: "Nothing will contribute more to break the bondsman's fetters, than an example of high moral worth, intellectual culture and religious attainments among the free people of color." While this letter was a very middle-class document, insufficiently sensitive to the economic realities of many African Americans, it did represent an alliance between black and white female abolitionists in their efforts to eradicate slavery. Black women were specifically appointed to the committee that wrote the document, and their concerns for the free black population appear to have been taken more seriously by female antislavery societies for a few years after the convention.[45]

In *An Appeal to the Women of the Nominally Free States,* the convention delegates suggested that women could best fight slavery by joining female antislavery societies. They saw membership in an antislavery society as both a personal and a public commitment of support: "By joining an Anti-Slavery Society we assume a responsibility—we pledge ourselves to the cause—we openly avow that we are on the side of the down-trodden and the dumb . . . —and we swell the tide of that public opinion which in a few years is to sweep from our land this vast system of [slavery]." Women were encouraged to move beyond the signing of a society constitution, "a very little thing," and actively engage in the work of the association, be it reading antislavery materials, circulating and signing petitions, or boycotting slave-grown products. The *Appeal* also encouraged both white and black women to interact with each other, particularly in all-female organizations. In association, white women would overcome their prejudice, black women would educate white women, and all women would find the means to fight slavery. This optimistic hope was more tempered in a circular addressed to FASS across the country, though this too stressed that "those societies which reject colored members, or seek to avoid them, have never been active or efficient." The circular suggested that any women afraid of ridicule or of retarding the cause because of interracial gatherings should heed the example of Jesus who mingled with the despised.[46] While this could not have been a comforting analogy for black women, it did allay the fears of some white women.

Convention Results—A National Petition Campaign

The most powerful result of the convention was the dramatic surge in women's antislavery petitions in 1837. Women more than doubled the number of petitions they had previously sent by creating a network across the north to circulate petitions and solicit signatures. After canvassing family, friends, and antislavery acquaintances, women went door-to-door spreading the antislavery message among people unlikely to hear it any other way. This process broadened the antislavery constituency but also generated sharp criticism of women's public efforts to influence their political representatives. The petition campaign raised the question of women's rights as citizens and further blurred the boundaries between political and moral efforts against slavery. It also strengthened and extended the relationships among female antislavery societies, creating a sense among women that they were part of a powerful, united, national campaign.

The idea of a national petition campaign had been in the air earlier that year, and both the women's convention and the American Anti-Slavery Society committed themselves to an all-out effort. The women passed resolutions stressing the "natural and inalienable" right of petition and the moral duty of every woman to petition Congress. Women were also encouraged to petition their state legislatures for the repeal of Northern laws supportive of slavery and their ecclesiastical institutions for a declaration that slavery is a sin. Each of the states was "called in rotation" so that delegates from that state might rise and formally pledge their willingness to coordinate and circulate petitions.[47]

The convention delegates chose three women each from the New York, Philadelphia, and Boston societies to serve as "Central Committees." These representatives of the largest and best-known female antislavery societies were to serve as correspondence nodes "with whom persons, favorable to the cause, in all parts of the country, can correspond." They served as the main organizers of an extensive, coordinated, female petitioning network. They sent out copies of petitions, received and collated lists of signatures, and published addresses. Many other women used previous friendships and networks to supplement the work of the central committees, writing to friends and acquaintances to encourage their participation in the petition campaign.[48]

Women had been petitioning Congress for the elimination of slavery since at least 1831. In that year Virginia slave Nat Turner led a major slave rebellion that rocked the Southern states. In response, women in Fluvanna

County (VA) sent the first female antislavery petition to Congress. They were rapidly followed by the Ladies of Philadelphia in 1831, who garnered over 2,000 signatures that year, and again in 1832. By 1833 calls for female petitions appeared in the *Liberator,* along with the powerful example of British women's petitioning efforts. British women sent over 180,000 signatures on a single petition to Parliament in 1833 calling for immediate emancipation. Female signatures on all the British petitions sent that year totaled 298,785. When Parliament emancipated all slaves in the British West Indies later that year, women's petitions were hailed as a crucial factor, and American women were encouraged to emulate their efforts.[49]

Circulating a petition sometimes preceded the formation of a female antislavery society, as a few activist women went door-to-door collecting signatures and gauging interest in organizing a society. However, female antislavery societies greatly facilitated petitioning efforts, and the number of petitions rose dramatically as the number of societies increased. In 1835, immediately upon organizing as a society, the Ladies' New-York City Society petitioned both Congress and the New York General Assembly on slavery issues. They also called for petitions to members' churches in which women prayed for the church to declare slavery a sin and to bar slaveholding members from communion. That same year Philadelphia women created a committee of twelve to circulate petitions. The corresponding secretary wrote to all the female antislavery societies in the state enclosing a copy of the petition and requesting their help. Overall, Congress received twelve petitions by women in 1834 and nine more in 1835. Female signatures outnumbered male on petitions from ten Massachusetts towns.[50]

Antislavery women's petitions became more common in 1836, as various female antislavery societies petitioned Congress against the admission of Arkansas as a proslavery state. In Ohio women held a statewide meeting at which "[r]esolutions were adopted and a committee of correspondence for the state appointed." Among other tasks, this committee was to organize the circulation of a petition to Congress with the names of as many women in the state as possible. "We thought that our united voice might perhaps obtain a more favorable hearing than if a few scattering petitions were sent in," declared the women, making clear the role of organization in the petitioning process.[51] As part of their correspondence with the women of Boston, Ohio women encouraged them to join the petition campaign, a suggestion that the Boston women took up quite enthusiastically. By the end of the year the Boston FASS, the Concord FASS, the Philadelphia FASS, and the Muskingham County (OH) FASS had all published addresses expounding women's duty to sign and circulate petitions.[52]

Congress received eighty-four antislavery petitions from women in 1836, a sevenfold increase from 1834, and almost exactly half the total number received. In April 1837 the *Liberator* reported that Congress had received 43,441 male signatures and 63,178 female signatures in 1836. Female signatures outnumbered male in Maine by 900, New Hampshire by 2,200, Massachusetts by 12,000, Rhode Island by 3,200, Pennsylvania by 1,100, and Ohio by 9,000. These were all states with extremely active female antislavery societies.[53]

The huge number and controversial topic of the antislavery petitions forced Congress to react, although not in the way the petitioners had hoped. Overwhelmed by the volume of petitions, and by the acrimonious debate that occurred as each was presented, the House of Representatives explored measures to stop the presentation of petitions. In 1836 they enacted the first of a series of "Gag Rules," which required that petitions related to slavery be tabled unread and which banned their referral to any committees for action. Congressman John Quincy Adams, a former president and staunch antislavery advocate, defended the right of his male and female petitioners to a hearing in Congress. He and others would creatively evade the Gag Rules at times, by reading the first line of antislavery petitions. However, the rules generally prevented antislavery petitions from being heard until 1844 when the ban was lifted.[54]

While limiting abolitionists' ability to be heard in Congress, the Gag Rules presented abolitionists with a golden opportunity. Congress had just denied its citizens what many saw as a basic constitutional right to be heard. Abolitionists could now couple their unpopular demand for freedom from slavery with the patriotic and highly resonant demand for freedom to petition. This helped move Northern public opinion regarding antislavery from unremitting hostility to a chilly willingness to listen. Women's petitioning efforts were central to the enactment of the Gag Rules, since almost half of all the signatures received by Congress belonged to women. The congressional committee charged with handling petitions reported a heavy preponderance of female names on the petitions they examined. Since female signatures on petitions had been rare prior to 1834, the politicians were particularly agitated by the number of female signatures. The *Liberator* claimed that the debates leading up to the Gag Rules had been "excited by the petitions of the ladies for the abolition of slavery in the District of Columbia. . . . Honor to the Ladies!"[55]

Thus by 1837 female antislavery activists had a short but dramatic petitioning history from which to build a national campaign. Meeting in convention enabled them to share strategies and justifications for petitioning and to vent their anger about the Gag Rules. Drawing on their experiences and the expertise of the AAS, the women created a network-based organizational strategy, which they published as one of the major documents from the 1837 Anti-Slavery Convention of American Women. A circular to the FASS throughout the United States directed female societies in the principal towns of each state to send a copy of the circular and a roll of printed petitions to a sympathetic woman in each town of that state. These townswomen would then form a central committee with interested women from each county, with each woman taking responsibility for arousing interest in her particular area. While women were circulating petitions for Congress, they were also to circulate petitions relevant to their state legislature, if their state had any laws that supported slavery. Petitions were to be returned to the principal cities so the number of signatures could be recorded and then sent to Congress by county rather than by town. The central correspondence committees formed during the convention were listed as the central contact points.[56]

This strategy required women in the central cities to find and then initiate correspondence with sympathetic women across their state. It inevitably led to more extensive communication among women and a broader collaborative effort. The women of Boston wrote dozens of letters and petition forms over the summer, soliciting help and signatures. They may have combined their calls for petitions with calls for fair goods, thus accomplishing two aims at the same time.[57] They also published an address that exhorted women to circulate petitions and explained women's moral responsibility to do so. The Concord FASS published a similar address and coordinated the petition effort in New Hampshire. Mary Clark, corresponding secretary for the Concord society, made clear how important correspondence was in the petition campaign when she noted in a hastily scrawled postscript, "We Anti-Slavery Secretaries must learn to write fast!"[58]

Four female antislavery societies in New York City joined together to hear an address regarding their duty to petition and then agreed to divide the city into districts and share the labor of petitioning between them. One of the letters from the New York City society helped energize a petition campaign in Rochester (NY). The secretary of the Ladies' New-York City Society found herself writing dozens of letters a week, exhorting women to petition. She eventually felt compelled to switch over to a printed circular, to which she appended short handwritten appeals.[59]

The Philadelphia FASS worked with the Pittsburgh FASS to furnish every county in Pennsylvania with a set of memorials to Congress. Since they had also taken responsibility for half the state of New Jersey, the Philadelphia women wrote friends there for the names of women in each county who might be willing to circulate petitions. The letter from New Jersey abolitionist Abby Goodwin back to Philadelphia makes clear the network of friendships upon which women drew in their search for help with petitions. Goodwin took responsibility for circulating petitions in Salem County, since she had friends in many townships who would assist her. However, she did not have friends in the lower two counties of the state, and so she asked among her acquaintances to see who might have friends there. Not finding any, she suggested that the Philadelphia women ask one of their own members who used to have connections in the area. She also named a male Philadelphian who might be helpful, since his brother and sister had lived in one of the counties.[60] Family relationships, friendship networks, and relationships created through previous years of correspondence all facilitated women's antislavery petitioning and were strengthened by it.

Strengthened Networks

The petition campaign drew women out of the home and into the neighborhood, where they conducted a massive grassroots propaganda campaign. While women might not garner a signature at every household, simply getting access to people otherwise uninterested in antislavery was a victory. The convention circular describing the petition campaign encouraged women not to be easily discouraged, since each contact was a potential conversion: "If you find ignorance, try to enlighten it; if you find scruples, try to remove them; if you find indifference, try to arouse sympathy. . . . This answers a three fold purpose. You not only gain the person's name, but you excite inquiry in her mind, and she will excite it in others; thus the little circle imperceptibly widens, until it may embrace a whole town." Yet petitioning was hard. Anna Cook found women quite sympathetic when she talked to them alone, but later some "were severely reproved by their husbands . . . and cursed me." New York women called petitioning "this most self-denying labour." Their claim that they found "either blank ignorance, total indifference, or a decided preference of slavery" was echoed in many other states.[61]

Class issues also divided the moralistic reforming middle-class petitioners and the upper-class women they attempted to convert. Juliana Tappan's delightful description of her petitioning efforts to exclude Texas from the Union brings this division to the fore. "There is so much aristocracy here, so much walking in Broadway to exhibit the butterfly fashions, that we can seldom gain access to the consciences of the women. I have left many houses ashamed of my sex, and must say that I met with more intelligence in the families of some colored persons in my district, than in the splendidly furnished drawing rooms of wealthy citizens in Hudson Square." Tappan was particularly surprised at how little the women knew about the politics of the country. "Not only did I meet with utter ignorance about the subject of slavery," she wrote, "but about the affairs of our country. Ladies, sitting on splendid sofas, in the midst of elegance, looked at us, as if they had never before heard the word *Texas,* and I presume some of them would have been unable to say whether it was north, or west, or south of Louisiana, or whether, or no, it belonged to the U.S." Tappan's comments are particularly telling since she regularly stressed her own participation in a moral not a political cause. Petitioning required women to be deeply aware of political issues and the political process.[62]

Despite the difficulties, antislavery women persevered. They saw their face-to-face communications and door-to-door efforts as crucial in converting women to the cause and obtaining the moral support necessary to eliminate slavery. Their campaign was inordinately successful. The number of petitions submitted to the Boston women for forwarding rapidly overwhelmed them. In October they published a note in the *Liberator* asking all women in Massachusetts who still had petitions against the annexation of Texas to send them on to Washington rather than Boston. "It is found that their number is so great, that the expense of postage will be more than it is desirable should be incurred." Congress received petitions with signatures from over 200,000 women in 1837, a threefold increase from the already extensive numbers of the previous year. The increase in numbers was also dramatic for many individual societies: Dorchester (MA) sent no female signatures in 1835, then 150 in 1836, and 325 on each of two petitions in 1837.[63]

Petitions played a crucial role in raising the profile of the antislavery movement. Through door-to-door campaigns conducted primarily by women, thousands of individuals unlikely ever to attend an antislavery lecture or subscribe to an antislavery publication were confronted with the issue and asked to take a stand. The petition campaign may also have been crucial in moving the antislavery movement from a predominantly moral to a predominantly political focus beginning in 1839. Signature gathering helped to create the male constituency necessary for antislavery parties, while the continuance of the Gag Rules year after year showed abolitionists the uselessness of moral appeals to legislators.[64] Given the limited data on women who signed petitions, it is difficult to determine whether signing a petition encouraged women to join a female antislavery society, attend antislavery fairs, or make a donation to support the cause.[65] Yet from the extensive coordination among women across the North, it is clear that the petition campaign drew upon and strengthened the correspondence networks developed earlier by antislavery women. These would later prove central in the expansion and growth of antislavery fairs in the late 1830s and 1840s. In 1837 the clearest impact of the petition movement for women came in the form of a backlash against their increasingly public and political participation.

Backlash against Women in Public

Women's petitions seem to have been particularly annoying to both Northern and Southern congressmen, who felt women had no place in the halls of politics. One wrote that he was "pained to see the names of so many American females [signed] to these petitions. It appeared . . . exceedingly indelicate that sensitive females of shrinking modesty should present their names here as petitioners." A few congressmen did defend women's petitioning efforts, claiming that "in labors of love and works of benevolence [women] should overstep the limits, and disregard the rules" that would usually prevent women's participation in political matters. However, the very need for such extended defenses makes clear the general disapproval of women's actions.[66]

This general disapproval grew across the nation in 1837, as female petitioning added fuel to an already volatile discussion regarding woman's appropriate role in the antislavery movement. The question had been raised a few months earlier, when Sarah and Angelina Grimké began a public-speaking tour to encourage petitioning and the formation of new female antislavery societies. Natives of South Carolina who had moved north to escape the influence of slavery, the Grimké sisters felt called to testify against the "peculiar institution." They joined the Philadelphia FASS and began writing letters and publications regarding slavery. They were the only women invited by the AAS to attend the 1836 training sessions for antislavery agents, and they undertook their own lecture tour in early 1837. They originally intended to convert women "by conversations in the social circle, [and] at the fireside," as the women of the Ladies' New-York City Anti-Slavery Society arranged a series of parlor lectures to sewing societies. However, even before the first lecture, it was clear that a larger venue would be necessary and the lectures were moved to a local church. The venue raised some concerns among abolitionists who felt public speaking by women was inappropriate; therefore, the lectures were limited to women, maintaining in a public place the all-female atmosphere of the parlor. Yet men were drawn by the novelty and obvious talent of the women, and soon the Grimkés opened the meetings to the general public. Once the audience became mixed (or as they would have said, "promiscuous"), abolitionist response turned more decidedly mixed as well, and clerical response became downright furious.[67]

In June 1837 the General Association of Massachusetts Congregational Churches met and issued a pastoral letter. While addressing issues related to the powers and privileges of the "pastoral office," the ministers felt compelled to address "the dangers which at present seem to threaten the female character, with wide spread and permanent injury." Praising women's "mild, dependent, softening influence," the ministers took objection to women who assume "the place and tone of man as a public reformer." In those cases "our care and protection of her seem unnecessary; we put ourselves in self-defence against her; she yields the power which God has given her for protection, and her character becomes unnatural." While the letter never mentions the Grimké sisters by name, they were clearly the most prominent objects of the ministers' concerns, as some of "that sex who so far forget themselves as to itinerate in the character of public lecturers and teachers." The ministers reiterated often that they did not wish to discourage "proper influences against sin" but rather wanted to encourage women to return to more scripturally sanctioned types of behavior.[68]

Congregational churches were the denomination most threatened by the recent divisions of church and state in Massachusetts, since they had been financially privileged by the connection. The swift rise of both Methodist and Baptist congregations threatened their supremacy in the state. The changing role and declining political importance of ministers added to the sense of siege. The attack on women represented only one part of the pastoral letter, which attempted to reassert older, more traditional values, including "the respect and deference to the pastoral office which is enjoined in Scripture."[69] The pastoral letter was followed by other clerical denunciations of female "departures from propriety," indicating a broader concern with women's public antislavery activities. Ministers may have been worried that women, the financial backbone of many churches through their support for missionary activities, would abandon church work for antislavery work. This loss of income would have been particularly threatening in 1837 given the financial impact of the economic depression. The 1837 Anti-Slavery Convention of American Women resolution that chided the American Bible Society, American and Foreign Bible Society, and "kindred associations" for their willingness to accept money from slaveholders and recommended that antislavery women think twice before supporting these organizations could only have added to the ministers' concerns. The AAS soon felt compelled to issue disclaimers that the Grimkés "travel at their own charges" and "are not under the direction of any society. . . . They have no commission except what they have received from God."[70]

While the AAS wavered in its support for the Grimkés, many female antislavery societies rallied behind them. The Boston FASS published a letter of introduction and support for the sisters. The women of the Andover (MA) FASS wrote a letter of support and recommended the "noble-minded" and "self-denying southern sisters" to every "association of females." The members of the Philadelphia FASS felt particular interest in and support of the Grimkés since the sisters had been members of the Philadelphia FASS for a few years. The Philadelphians worried that "if the reproaches of any portion of the community were awarded [to Angelina Grimké], they must necessarily be shared by female abolitionists in general." However, even if the Grimkés might have departed from "woman's proper station," the Philadelphia women felt the evils of slavery required each woman to do what she felt was right, rather than what she felt would be universally approved.[71] The Buckingham (PA) FASS also worried at first that the Grimkés' advocacy of women's rights might retard the antislavery movement. However, they felt that setting boundaries to the Grimkés' work would be setting boundaries on God's work to "break every yoke." Thus they too gave the Grimkés their unconditional support, as did the Pawtucket (RI) FASS, the Haverhill (MA) FASS, and "a respectable number of Female Abolitionists, of Abington."[72] The Grimké controversy forced female antislavery societies to debate more openly the proper role of women. While the issue had been present from the moment women began to organize, after 1837 its more dramatic prominence in public and private discussion made it more difficult for women to ignore.

Given this context of controversy it is unsurprising that the 1837 Anti-Slavery Convention of American Women was harshly criticized outside the antislavery movement. The women of Dorchester noted in their annual report that to many, the convention "was a matter of complaint, of ridicule and contempt." The women of Philadelphia had assumed that such a novel measure would elicit surprise and censure. As they predicted, they were met with "editorial rebukes, sarcasm, and ridicule" as well as "coarse invective and rude jesting." The best example of this abuse comes from the *New*

York Commercial Advertiser, whose editor railed for a full column against the "Amazonian farce," which brought together a "monstrous *regiment* of women" in order to effect "petticoat philanthropy."[73] Women in New Hampshire felt obliged to write a defense of the convention, against those who would impugn the motives and censure the conduct of women who attended. "The daughters of America who composed the late female convention will *never* feel degraded by having mingled in that assembly," they declared. "God and angels . . . approved their conduct." Male abolitionists approved their conduct as well, hailing the convention as "one of the most cheering signs of the times." However, neither AAS encouragement nor divine approval spared women from continued editorial rebuke.[74]

Once women began their coordinated petitioning efforts, occasional complaint became sustained crescendo. Critics attacked petition gatherers as rude, pushy, unladylike, and failing to attend to their domestic responsibilities. The *Religious Magazine and Family Miscellany* claimed that signature seekers would go into tirades if the mistress of the household refused to sign their petitions. Even worse, it claimed that abolitionist women violated the polite rules of class, by demanding to see the domestic help in order to secure their signatures. The Delaware legislature responded to a female petition by suggesting that the women of the state "mend their husband's breeches instead of breaches in the Constitution." The *New York Sun* suggested women should return to shaking bedticks rather than politics.[75] In response to a suggestion that women petitioned only because they were not properly occupied with a husband, the ladies of Halifax County (VA) petitioned Congress to provide, at public expense, suitable husbands for all the female petitioners for the abolition of slavery.

These references to woman's domestic responsibilities were the most common critique of antislavery women's actions. While the critics may have disagreed with women's stance on slavery, they attacked women's presence outside the home and in the arena of politics. As a correspondent to the *Providence Journal* made clear, where would the women stop, once permitted a voice in national politics? "Would it not be well to employ females to memorialize Congress with regard to the tariff, the land bill and other important and intricate subjects, which so much try the wisdom of our national legislators?" As with antislavery violence, criticism of female petitions and petitioners was due in part to women's violation of their appropriate sphere and in part to the unpopular cause they espoused.[76]

Women Redefine Political Action

Women had faced the question of whether antislavery activity was political activity even before the organization of the first female antislavery societies. In 1829 Elizabeth Chandler felt obliged to refute the statements of "a lady whose talents and character" Chandler highly respected. The woman felt that antislavery work required "the energies of men," since its close connection with issues of law, government, and politics meant that female interference "would be a departure from that propriety of character which nature, as well as society, imposes on woman." Women were "privileged," the correspondent claimed, "by having their duties circumscribed to the domestic sphere . . . removing them from many temptations of the world." Chandler agreed that men were needed in the antislavery battle, that women should avoid politics, and that women were blessed by the privileges of domesticity. Yet none of these should prevent women from engaging in the benevolent work of antislavery. Chandler argued that women had the duty to help men in this cause, to act against an outrage to morality and religion, and to extend the blessings of domesticity to slave women. Chandler's argument was neither progressive nor feminist but rather a carefully crafted rationale for extending women's moral and domestic responsibilities out from the home.[77]

The first female petitioners in 1831 had faced similar critics who felt that the mode of petitioning was too overtly political to be feminine. Since the "females are not entitled to a vote," they "therefore need not trouble themselves about [petitioning]." Although William Lloyd Garrison would eventually become a strong supporter of female petitioners, in the early days even he had to be convinced. As late as December 17, 1831, he justified women's petitioning on the basis that women were held in slavery. "The peculiarity of the case authorizes [women's] appeal to Congress." The female petitioners agreed that unless women were to close their hearts to the oppressed, and thereby lose that sensitivity and moral sensibility which made them women, they had to do whatever they felt proper to end suffering, which included petitioning. They went further than Garrison, however, by making more direct claims for female involvement. They noted that petitioning was the right of all citizens, including women.[78]

After the formation of female antislavery societies, both the criticism and the refutations became more common. On his 1834 speaking tour, George Thompson frequently claimed that antislavery was not a political question but, rather, a moral and religious question that particularly needed the power of women. In 1836 Angelina Grimké's *Appeal to the Christian Women of America* argued that women could not agree to "be turned aside from our purpose by the often repeated objection that this is a political question with which we as females have nothing to do." She repeated Chandler's claims that while antislavery was indeed a political question, it was also a moral and religious cause with which women had everything to do. The large-scale petition efforts by women in 1836 and 1837 raised the question of women's engagement in politics in more pressing ways than previously. In order to defend their right to petition, antislavery women had to decide whether antislavery in general—and petitioning in particular—was a political activity or a religious response to a moral issue.[79]

Some women chose to argue that petitions from females were not political because women were inherently excluded from the political sphere by their inability to vote. Their petitions were thus not part of the partisan politics that governed events in Congress but rather, as they put it, "prayers" to the representatives to rethink their position on an issue with deep moral implications. These women saw their exclusion from politics as a bonus, since they would clearly be untainted by political partisanship and speaking from deeply held religious motivations. From this perspective petitioning could be seen as consonant with the accepted role of woman as moral arbiter of the community's moral behavior, using her influence over men to affect political outcomes.

Representative Dickson used this reasoning when he presented the 1835 petition from the ladies of New York City. In his introduction to the petition, he noted the long history in which "the influence of woman was talismanic over the heart of man, and roused to action all his noblest energies." Juliana Tappan, corresponding secretary of the Ladies' New-York City Anti-Slavery Society, also agreed with this line of reasoning. In a letter to the Philadelphia FASS describing the New York women's petitioning activities, Tappan wrote: "I have lately felt deeply the necessity of keeping our attention fixed upon the moral bearings of our principles, rather than the political, as there appear to be so many who place more confidence in the influence of the polls, and other appeals to the selfishness of men, than in the mighty power of truth upon the conscience." Tappan saw women's petitions as moral prayers, contrasting them to the male arena of voting. A New Hampshire woman made this connection between petitions and prayers even clearer. After noting that petitions enabled woman to "lift her voice in the ear of our national congress, and there, unseen, plead with simple eloquence the cause of suffering humanity," the correspondent went on to suggest that woman should also "present her petitions to the court of Heaven."[80]

The *Appeal to the Women of the Nominally Free States* published by the 1837 women's convention also stressed the moral basis for antislavery women's fight against slavery. After laying out eight reasons why women have a moral duty to fight for the slave, the *Appeal* called on women to petition their ecclesiastical authorities. Women's petitions should "beseech and entreat" their church to ban slaveholders from the communion table. More than any other action, including forming societies and petitioning, women should "pray without ceasing." "We have no confidence in effort without prayer, and no confidence in prayer without effort," the *Appeal* declared. In this understanding, petitions were simply the works through which women expressed their religious faith.[81]

However, while the *Appeal* ended with a statement of woman's right to "unite in holy copartnership with man, in the renovation of a fallen world," it also contained a strongly worded defense of women's political right to petition. Rather than taking the easier ground that antislavery was a moral *rather* than a political question, the authors "grant that it is a political, as well as a moral subject." The *Appeal* argued that women must take an interest in the "political concerns of the country" because the honor, happiness, and well-being of everyone were bound up therein. "Are we aliens because we are women?" they asked. "Are we bereft of citizenship because we are the *mothers, wives,* and *daughters* of a mighty people? Have *women* no country—no interest staked in public weal—no liabilities in common peril—no partnership in a nation's guilt and shame?"[82]

Many women took similar stances in their own society publications that year. In the "Address of the Boston Female Anti-Slavery Society to the Women of New England," the Boston women reminded their petitioning sisters "that the representation of our country is based on the numbers of the population, irrespective of sex." Thus women were official constituents of their congressman and entitled to voice their opinions despite their gender. The Philadelphia women put it most bluntly in their 1836 address: "Yes, although we are *women, we* still are citizens." Congressman John Quincy Adams entered the debate on the side of women as citizens. When presenting a petition with both male and female signatures, he noted it was from "my own constituents, male and female; for . . . the vote of the men is the vote of the women; and I consider the wives and daughters of the men who vote at my election, . . . as much my *constituents . . .* as if every individual had deposited in the ballot box a vote in my favor."[83]

The two defenses of female petitioning reflected two competing views of the petition in the culture more broadly, growing out of changes in the definition of citizens and democracy. Petitions had generally been seen as requests from a subject to a ruler, and women's early petitions particularly fit this definition. During the Revolutionary War many women petitioned local committees of safety and revolutionary governments, requesting permission to cross enemy lines, claim property left behind, or receive compensation for their war-related activities. These petitions were personal requests, usually containing only one signature. Women rarely petitioned as a constituency. Men often petitioned in larger groups, yet at first their petitions also contained the humble, loyal language appropriate when making a request on the goodwill of a superior. As the controversies with Britain deepened, male petition language moved incrementally from humble deference to more direct assertiveness.[84]

By the 1830s many male petitions had taken on the character of informational demands, a means by which citizens informed their representatives of the issues on which they wanted action. Since legislators were representatives rather than superiors, direct rather than deferential language prevailed. This change in language paralleled the expansion of the suffrage to all white men. Women as a group remained caught between the two forms of petition, just as their political status remained caught between that of subject and that of citizen. Single women continued to be taxed as citizens but were unable to vote. Despite their exclusion from politics, women were clearly affected by political issues. Women drew upon the two visions of the purpose of petitions, gravitating toward the one most consonant with their vision of woman's appropriate role. These different understandings of the purpose of petitions were reflected in the women's petition language.

The most popular petition form for women through 1840 was the "Fathers and Rulers of our Country" form. This petition asked Congress to "suffer" women to plead as "wives, mothers and daughters" and invoked a religious responsibility to petition. By adopting a supplicatory stance and equating their petition with religious prayer, the women could set petitioning within women's traditional responsibilities and evade the political aspects of their request. Beginning in 1837 some women began to adopt the AAS short-form petitions, which did not justify women's petitions but rather simply stated their request. Most of these forms were the same ones used by men.[85] At the 1837 women's convention, antislavery women drew on the best of both interpretations to fuel their petition drive. The convention's *Appeal to the Women of the Nominally Free States* stressed women's responsibilities as "*subjects* of the government, as members of the great human family." Yet after describing examples of female political activity from the Bible, Roman history, and the American Revolution, the *Appeal* stressed the principle that "women are *citizens*, and that they have important duties to perform for their county."[86]

This balance between subject and citizen was reflected also in the convention's *Letter to John Adams*, the former president turned congressman who regularly presented women's antislavery petitions. In the *Letter* the women thanked Adams for his efforts on their behalf and on behalf of the slave. While sending their gratitude, the women also felt it necessary to chastise Adams for his lack of support for the abolition of slavery in the District of Columbia. They beseeched him to rethink his position on this particular issue. The letter to Adams is a curious mix of new and old roles for women. Their method reflects the respected female tradition of using woman's moral influence to affect male policymakers. However, their willingness to publicly chastise a politician and have public opinions on political issues was a new departure for women and echoed their increasingly direct petitioning language.[87]

Women's creativity in blurring the boundaries between moral and political activities has made it difficult to claim their actions as clearly political. If politics is defined as voting and running for office, women were excluded from the central political activities of their time. Therefore women's activities were, as the women usually claimed, efforts to exert a moral influence on the nation, and on those men who did have access to political power. But in the modern era, the definition of politics has come to include public actions meant to influence the balance of local or national power, including riots, parades, economic choices, citizen education, and lobbying. With this definition it is clear that antislavery women were actually pioneering a modern understanding of politics, using petitions to lobby legislators, and raising funds to support the newspapers and lectures that would create an educated, active citizenry. In 1837 antislavery women wavered between two definitions of citizenship that had deep implications for their political rights. The older definition limited women's political role to motherhood or wifehood, drawing on cultural understandings of women as moral influences upon men. Women had influence but not rights. As the petition campaign progressed, women began to articulate a new definition of citizenship in which they had both a responsibility and a right to express their opinions and guide the decisions of legislators. No women went so far as to claim the right to vote or to run for office, but these implications hung in the air.

The implications worried many antislavery women, which helps to explain why most rejected any linking of their work to political action. The gender ideology that equated women and morality, men and politics, gave women the ability to expand their domestic sphere to include a wide array of activities with political implications, as long as those activities could be defined as originating in moral concerns. Party politics, with its increasingly acrimonious debates between Democrats and Whigs, did not seem moral and often seemed so corrupted with alcohol and dirty dealings that few women would want to be associated with it. Antislavery women were caught between two problematic options. The ideology that men and women by nature should occupy separate spheres empowered women to address moral issues but also severely limited their ability to affect the political system. The idea that men and women both had political duties gave women access to political influence but opened them to severe criticism and reproach for stepping beyond woman's traditional responsibilities. Neither strategy held a clear advantage in 1837. Women had definitely stepped further into the public sphere, but not all of them found the bright, open space very comfortable.

Raising Funds and Building Community

Amid all the debate, women went on working for the antislavery cause in the small and large ways that they had developed in the previous few years. They continued reading and subscribing to antislavery publications, assembling together in societies, attending monthly concerts of prayer, using free-labor goods, and raising funds for the national society. Women's antislavery fairs expanded in this period, and their fund-raising became crucial to the cash-strapped AAS during the depression of 1837. In that year, the Boston FASS donated $1,600 of the $2,305 pledged to the Massachusetts Antislavery Society, and the Philadelphia women made major contributions to the Pennsylvania and American antislavery societies. Women's financial influence sometimes extended beyond the fairs. In 1837 the all-male Cambridgeport (MA) antislavery society raised $100 for the cause and paid it over to the Boston women's society for them to designate as they felt best. Women in Groton (MA) and other towns met monthly to do needlework, thereby making a physical as well as a financial contribution to the cause, and keeping their dedication alive by regular meeting, talking, and group reading.[88]

Women also continued their extensive networking connections, with women in Dorchester corresponding with twelve to fourteen other female societies, and women in Boston helping to organize a society in a nearby town. Providence women sent out a recruiting letter advocating the formation of female antislavery societies in all areas that did not already have one. Correspondence continued to strengthen antislavery women in the face of public critique and complaint. As the secretary of the Boston society, Anne Weston, wrote shortly after the convention: "[W]ith so large a portion of the community arrayed against us it is wise as well as cheering to invigorate our strength by an interchange of sympathy and advice."[89]

American antislavery women also kept in close touch with the activities of their sisters in Britain. Interactions between American and British women had been increasing since George Thompson's tour of 1835–1836, and in late 1835 Boston women had sent an "Address to the Women of Great Britain," thanking them for their example and asking for their continued engagement in the cause. The proceedings from the 1837 women's convention included a letter of support from the Newcastle-on-Tyne Ladies' Emancipation Society to the Ladies of the American Anti-Slavery Societies. The letter mentioned the ladies' receipt and appreciation of the Boston women's "Address" and strongly encouraged the American women to persevere in their work, knowing that British women were watching, admiring, and being inspired. The women's convention published a "Letter to the Women of Great Britain," which stressed the common ancestry and Christianity of the two nations of women and highlighted how the example, support, and continued efforts of English women bolstered up and encouraged American women.[90]

The letter to the women of Great Britain was probably received in England at just about the same time as George Thompson's republication of Angelina Grimké's *Appeal to the Christian Women of the Slave States of America* appeared. Thompson's long introduction challenged British women to expand their support for their American sisters through the formation of new antislavery societies, their support for the annual fund-raising fairs, and an increase in correspondence between American and British female societies. "A regular correspondence between the American and British *Female Societies* would greatly strengthen and animate both," Thompson claimed, because letters and fair goods were "lasting memorials of your sympathy and co-operation." In order to encourage communication, Thompson published the names and addresses of women in New York, Boston, and Philadelphia with whom to correspond. Two of these were women listed as central correspondence nodes in the women's convention *Proceedings,* thus linking the U.S. and British correspondence networks.[91]

The example and encouragement of British women also appeared in the convention's circular addressed to female antislavery societies, which called on American women to petition Congress and their churches and laid out a central organization for petitioning activity. In order to make clear that women's petitioning could be extremely effective, the circular quoted a Member of Parliament regarding British women's 1833 petition: "We can delay no longer," the MP exclaimed. "When all the maids and matrons of England are knocking at our doors, it is time for us to legislate." In the long and often wearying petition campaign, American women frequently celebrated the British women's success. In 1837 British women involved themselves in another petition campaign, memorializing Queen Victoria to use her influence to speed the abolition of the apprentice system in the West Indies. Although slavery had been eliminated there in 1833, many black children still faced slavelike conditions in a mandatory apprenticeship system. The example of a woman on the throne of England and of hundreds of thousands of women petitioning her on a political issue helped to inspire American women when critics questioned their right to petition. One antislavery newspaper editorial suggested that the American clergy tell Queen Victoria she was out of her sphere, which must have brought a smile to the faces of some of the more embattled antislavery women.[92]

Conclusion

During this highly productive period of female antislavery organizing, women experienced simultaneous unity and division. While disagreeing over how exactly women could best organize against slavery, women resoundingly agreed on the usefulness of cooperation. The 1837 Anti-Slavery Convention of American Women and the petition campaigns brought women together across geography and race, drawing more women into the movement and more women into the public sphere. Women experimented with new understandings of female citizenship and demanded that their political representatives listen to their voices. Yet their firm strides into the public arena had powerful repercussions, not only in an onslaught of criticism of their roles but also in making clearer the divisions among the women themselves. It was not a case of cracks beginning to show in a united front—women had always held different opinions on how best to organize and on woman's appropriate role. After 1837, however, the divisions began to grow faster than the women's abilities to contain them, in large part because the male antislavery societies also split into factions, providing women with new opportunities and with demands that they choose sides. In some cases women were able to limit the divisiveness to come. Many female antislavery societies moved through 1838–1841 with little or no change in their organization. Others saw their membership drift apart or, as in the case of the Boston FASS, fly publicly and acrimoniously apart. In 1837 women could still agree to disagree, and their work together remains a testament to the power of women united. As the networks in which they worked began to fracture, women would take the lessons they had learned during this period and greatly expand their influence, although not their unity, during the next few years.

CHAPTER FOUR

Internal Divisions, 1837–1840

Debates and Choices

"Is it not very difficult to draw the boundary line? On the one hand, we

are in danger of servile submission to the opinions of the other sex, and

on the other hand, in perhaps equal danger of losing that modesty . . .

which our Creator has given as a safeguard. . . . How difficult it is to

ascertain what duty is."

—Juliana Tappan, July 21, 1837

Juliana Tappan's confusion over woman's appropriate duty was echoed by hundreds of other antislavery women in the closing years of the 1830s.[1] Clerical disapproval of the Grimkés' "promiscuous" lectures and editorial rebukes of female petitioners combined to inflame public debate over abolitionist women's roles. At the same time abolitionists themselves debated the role of women, as well as other important issues including the meaning of political action and the role of the church. Throughout 1838 and 1839 women attempted to create a middle ground in the controversy, meeting together at the Anti-Slavery Conventions of American Women. They faced intense anti-abolition violence in 1838, and increasing diversity within the movement itself. Harmony prevailed and the networks women had created continued to hold, although the strains evident in the male societies did overflow and lead to debates among the women.

This harmony came to an end in 1839 and 1840 when the national male antislavery societies divided into competing organizations, the American Anti-Slavery Society (AAS) and the American and Foreign Anti-Slavery Society (A&FAS). Since women raised the majority of the funds for the antislavery movement, both sides competed for their support. Suddenly women had new organizational options, as the AAS invited women to join as equal members. Many women had waited years for this opportunity, and they quickly abandoned all-female antislavery societies. Others enjoyed the recognition of their equality but chose to retain the independence of their all-female organizations. In either case, supporting the AAS meant accepting woman's right to agitate against slavery while generally rejecting political means for that agitation. The AAS maintained a primary commitment to moral suasion, criticizing the political system as corrupt and proslavery. AAS supporters also criticized the churches for not being sufficiently antislavery. Women on this side thus found themselves in the awkward position of having achieved equality with men, while rejecting both the moral institutions and political means through which they had done much of their antislavery work.

Women who chose to support the competing American and Foreign Anti-Slavery Society often did so because they maintained a strong loyalty to their churches and ministers. Yet the A&FAS placed less emphasis on moral suasion than the AAS and, for at least a few years, focused more attention on political antislavery efforts. This meant that, while the A&FAS stressed the fundamental differences between men and women, women were encouraged to support political action that had previously been rejected as being outside their sphere. While women were not welcome as equals in the national A&FAS organization, women increasingly welcomed male cooperation in the women's own organizations.

Never were the gerrymandered boundaries of public and private, moral and political, more confused than during this period. Divisions among men had created the organizations that women were invited to join or support, but the battle lines men drew up did not map well against women's own understandings of their role in the movement. Family alliances and friendships also affected women's choices and divided women who had worked together for years. Scholars have tended to label the women who demanded equality as either radicals or feminists and those who clung to a distinctive "feminine influence" as conservatives. The women themselves did not see things quite so clearly.

A Convention amid Conflict, 1838

Signs of disunion among abolitionists had existed from the very beginning, as activists judged each other's commitments to colonization, immediate abolition, the political rights of free black people, and other related issues. As early as 1835 a short-lived rival organization to the AAS emerged called the American Union Society. In the same year William Lloyd Garrison and New York philanthropist and abolitionist Lewis Tappan were already publicly disagreeing over whether abolitionists should use harsh language against the clergy, and over the issue of appeasing allies by not harping on their failures. By mid-1836 abolitionists had begun taking Garrison to task for introducing issues other than antislavery into the most widely read antislavery newspaper, the *Liberator*. They disliked his discussions of the peace movement and Sabbatarianism and worried that disagreements over these issues would pull people away from the antislavery cause. However, the movement maintained a remarkable sense of unity until mid-1837, when debates over the role of women and the power of the church began to converge.[2]

The Congregationalist clergy's attacks on the Grimké sisters had prompted an outpouring of support from female antislavery societies. When clergymen and antislavery activists with strong ties to established churches began to upbraid Garrison for his increasingly acrimonious attacks on the proslavery stance of various denominations, many women again responded with strongly supportive letters. For many female societies, support for both Garrison and the Grimkés became intertwined, as women recognized attacks against both as attacks on a person's ability to serve the cause as they felt best. The female antislavery societies of Concord (NH), Philadelphia, Buckingham, and Pittsburgh & Allegheny (PA), Kent County and Providence (RI), and Braintree & Weymouth and S. Weymouth (MA) all wrote letters for publication, indicating their strong continued support for Garrison, and often the Grimkés as well. The women of Lynn (MA) and Boston went a step further, sending much-needed cash for additional subscriptions to the *Liberator*.[3] However, some women felt torn between their strong ties to their churches and their support for Garrison, pulled in opposite directions by institutional commitments to churches and antislavery activism. The formation of a new "Evangelical Antislavery Society" in January 1838, which denounced Garrison's stand on women's rights, made it yet more difficult for women to balance strong religious ties and a desire for more equality in the antislavery movement.[4]

It was within this context of debate and division that antislavery women planned their second Anti-Slavery Convention of American Women in May 1838. The Call for Convention asked for an even wider representation of American women than in 1837, arguing that the "Pastoral Letter" and other challenges to women's place in the antislavery movement required united thought and action. The potential for divisiveness at the convention worried Juliana Tappan and the strongly church-based women of the Ladies' New-York City Anti-Slavery Society. "There are a few, a very few," Tappan reported to the women of Boston, "who prophesy that measures will be adopted, and views advanced in the Convention, which they cannot conscientiously approve, and they therefore refuse to have anything to do with it." Others were more positive that "great good will be done, and are very desirous to avoid any unpleasant feelings." However, even these hoped for "*strictly* an *Anti-Slavery* Convention," without any discussion of those topics "concerning which there are so many different and conflicting opinions." The New York women were concerned that women who supported Garrison would force a choice between antislavery activism and continued commitment to the churches or would advocate roles for women that would further antagonize the clergy. At the same time Abby Kelley, an abolitionist from Lynn who had begun a public-speaking career in the wake of the Grimkés' tour, staked out exactly the opposite ground. She wrote the Philadelphia women that she felt "great anxiety that our coming convention should take ground as high as the truth requires," even if that meant addressing issues of woman's rights and the church. Clearly women were going to have to walk a fine line to maintain a workable unity.[5]

Almost three times as many delegates attended the 1838 convention as had gathered the previous year. The proceedings list almost three hundred women, and observers reported almost five hundred attending some sessions of the convention. Delegates and corresponding members represented nine states and thirty-seven towns, with representatives from Maine (1), New Hampshire (1), Rhode Island (6), Massachusetts (34), New York (27), Connecticut (2), New Jersey (1), South Carolina (2), and Pennsylvania (207). Women from Philadelphia and the surrounding area numerically dominated the convention, although the leadership was more evenly spread among the most active antislavery societies. The absence of any women from Ohio is striking, given their intense organizational efforts in this period. This may indicate an increasing distance between the activism of Eastern and Western antislavery women.[6]

Black women also attended the convention in larger numbers, with as many as 11 black delegates among the 206, and 2 black corresponding members. This almost tripled the numbers from 1837. Susan Paul of Boston served as vice president of the convention, and Sarah M. Douglass of Philadelphia served as the treasurer. The increased presence of black women may reflect the highly integrated nature of the Philadelphia FASS or the large number of black middle-class women active in reform movements in Philadelphia.[7]

Drawn by a deep commitment to the antislavery cause, the women found common ground on a wide diversity of issues and maintained a remarkable unity of purpose. They agreed to publish an "Address to Anti-Slavery Societies," an "Address to Free Colored People," and "An Address to the Senators and Representatives of the Free States in Congress." They passed resolutions to increase their petitioning efforts, to adopt new fund-raising techniques, and to attempt to use fewer slave-produced goods. After three days of intense activity and discussion, the women expressed their gratitude that "sectarian feeling has been so far laid aside as to enable us to meet together as Christians." As one delegate wrote, the convention had enabled women once again to expand their antislavery acquaintances, learn about new plans, strategies, and techniques, and be "incited afresh" by the company of like-minded women.[8]

Only three issues prompted debate, and each seems to have been resolved in a way that permitted broad agreement. The first and most expected was a question regarding the appropriate role of women. In contrast to the 1837 convention, the women's printed resolutions regarding woman's role in 1838 did not stray from the generally accepted and elicited no debate. The women resolved that antislavery was "one of the most appropriate fields for the exertion of the influence of woman." By focusing on woman's "influence"—that magical, gender-specific power women were assumed to wield over men and the appropriate means by which they were to exercise their domestic power—convention members deflected criticism that they were stepping out of their sphere. The women also focused on other relatively unobjectionable roles for women, including teaching anti-slavery beliefs to their children, praying for the free people of color, and forming Cent-A-Week fund-raising societies, a model long common in benevolent societies.[9]

Even a resolution declaring women's responsibility to petition passed without a single objection. Juliana Tappan, a secretary of the convention and a delegate from New York City, presented the first resolution, which demanded that women maintain the right of petition. The convention resolved that women should not cease their efforts until "the prayers of every woman within the sphere of our influence shall be heard in the halls of Congress on this subject." Although literally referring to every woman "of our acquaintance," the resolution carefully uses the language of spheres to imply that every woman should be heard within the sphere of her influence, a sphere that here includes the halls of Congress. The women had come a long way from their early fears that signing a petition would improperly launch them into the political arena.[10]

The conflict arose when Abby Kelley, who had become an increasingly prominent advocate of an expanded role for women, proposed that the women's convention sponsor a "promiscuous" meeting of male and female speakers. After a debate the delegates voted against sponsoring the meeting, even though, as one delegate reported, "it was understood that the Convention, as a body, approved of the meeting, and that several of its members would take part in the exercises." Lucretia Mott later made clear that the convention had voted against the meeting, since "many of the members of that Convention considered it improper for women to address promiscuous assemblies," and the majority had deferred to their wishes. Some women felt strongly that there was still value in the separate spheres for men and women, even if the boundaries of those spheres had changed.[11]

Mott clearly was unhappy with this decision, and she expressed the hope that "such false notions of delicacy and propriety would not long obtain in this enlightened country." Angelina Grimké agreed, implying that those who upheld such notions had more interest in their reputations than in real reform. She expressed her satisfaction at seeing "so few *ladies,* and so many *women* present" at the promiscuous meeting, which did occur without the convention's backing. Mott, Grimké, and Kelley were openly disappointed in the less-than-radical stance of the convention. However, the majority of the delegates saw the compromise of supporting the meeting while not sanctioning it as an appropriate decision given the diversity of their membership. The decision was controversial enough that the committee publishing the convention minutes debated whether to include it. They seem to have decided not to publish the controversy, since the minutes make no mention of the resolution, debate, or outcome.[12]

Two other issues troubled the harmony of the convention. The first concerned the right of slaveholders to take communion, an issue that was beginning to prompt debates throughout antislavery circles. Many abolitionists felt that churches' willingness to permit slaveholders to participate in communion represented an inherently proslavery stand. Acceptance at the communion table implied that the slaveholder had committed no unpardonable sin and was a welcome member of the holy community, neither of which antislavery activists could accept. Ministers' frequent unwillingness to permit antislavery meeting notices to be read from the pulpit, occasional sermons denouncing antislavery activists, and refusal to pass resolutions against slavery added to the proslavery image of most churches. Some abolitionists began to call on antislavery activists to "come out" from their churches rather than suffer the moral degradation that could result from association with a proslavery institution.

In this spirit Philadelphia abolitionist Mary Grew submitted a resolution to the women's convention claiming it as an antislavery duty to "keep ourselves separate from those churches" that permitted communion with slaveholders. A majority of delegates accepted the resolution, but only after an extensive and unrecorded debate. Five women spoke against the resolution. Three of them plus two others inserted an explanation of their negative votes in the printed proceedings. They agreed that slaveholders should be excluded from the churches but did not feel it right to abandon the potentially useful tool of church membership until it was apparent that the churches were totally corrupt. The majority of the dissenting women came from the Ladies' New-York City Anti-Slavery Society, which continued to have much stronger connections to evangelical churches and moral reform societies than any of the other female antislavery societies. These were probably the women who had expressed their concern to Juliana Tappan prior to the convention that just such an issue would come up.[13]

While this disagreement made clear that there were important divisions among antislavery women, dissent does not seem to have inhibited any women from continuing to work together or from continuing to express their diverse opinions. Margaret Dye, a delegate from New York City who voted against the church membership resolution, felt accepted enough to enter two related resolutions the next day. The first stated that "the Anti-Slavery enterprise presents one of the most appropriate fields for the exertion of the influence of woman," stressing the importance of women's continued service in the cause. The second admitted that the churches were very implicated in the sin of slavery and called on women to petition their ecclesiastical bodies to exclude slaveholders from the communion table and pulpit. Both resolutions passed without a dissenting vote. In all, women who had spoken against the antichurch resolution offered three of the five resolutions passed the following morning.[14]

The final source of friction at the convention centered on how abolitionists should interact with African Americans. The antislavery women had resolved at the previous convention to "pray to be delivered" from racial prejudice and "to act out the principles of Christian equality by associating with [African-Americans] as though the color of the skin was of no more consequence than that of the hair, or the eyes." The broadness of this resolution seems to have facilitated its passage in 1837. In 1838 Sarah Grimké offered a more specific resolution elaborating the duty of abolitionists to refute racial prejudice by "sitting with [African-Americans] in places of worship, by appearing with them in our streets, by giving them our countenance in steam-boats and stages, by visiting them at their homes and encouraging them to visit us, receiving them as we do our white fellow citizens." The majority of the women strongly supported the resolution.[15]

However, an unspecified number of women cast a negative vote, stating that "a resolution couched in such phraseology, might, by being misapprehended, injure the abolition cause." After the convention, a few of these women, along with supportive male associates, went further and attempted to get the resolution expunged from the convention transcript in the interests of public safety. When the committee refused, these individuals attempted to coerce the black community to issue a disclaimer "in order . . . to avert the destruction and bloodshed that will result if they do not disavow it."[16]

Although the convention proceedings do not provide an explanation of the women's concerns, some white women may well have been motivated by racial prejudice and an unwillingness to associate with African Americans. Sarah Grimké made clear that prejudice did exist at the convention, even as women resolved to pray for its elimination. While a number of women moved over to give the prominent Grimké room to sit in the terribly overcrowded assembly, a black woman "was suffered to stand in the aisle" for the entire evening. Sarah M. Douglass wrote in early 1839 that even in antislavery meetings she met "The cruel language of the eye/ whose meaning kills.'"[17]

While prejudice was clearly a factor, the women's concerns may also have been a response to the claims made by anti-abolition editors and orators that abolitionists sought to "amalgamate" the races by encouraging social, and by implication sexual, interactions. These claims fueled the most memorable aspect of the 1838 convention, the burning of Pennsylvania Hall and a number of black institutions. This violent outbreak in the middle of the convention ensured that it would be remembered neither for the extensive harmony among the women nor for the divisions they managed to overcome.

The Burning of Pennsylvania Hall

Never before had such a large number of antislavery women been exposed to such personal violence. The opening of Pennsylvania Hall, the first building dedicated to free speech and abolition principles in the United States, and the meeting of three or four antislavery societies at the same time as the women's convention, spurred newspaper editors and agitators to new heights of abuse against abolitionists.[18] They were particularly concerned about black men and white women stepping beyond the boundaries set for them by prejudice and tradition, and artists and editors conjured up highly controversial images of interracial sexuality. The image in Figure 1, for example, exaggerates the interracial socializing that occurred when white women and free black men attended the mixed-sex gathering that some women's convention members had themselves considered inappropriate. Images like this highlighted white women's public presence and willingness to cross the color line, feeding anti-abolition sentiment in the city.

The mixed-sex convention was surrounded by a "noisy throng" from the beginning of the evening. A shower of stones and the sounds of windows breaking interrupted many of the speakers. Maria Weston Chapman, who had faced down the mob in Boston in 1835, was making her first public speech. She was virtually ignored as delegates attempted not to crush each other while also keeping the furiously surging mob from coming through the doors of the building. There was a "constant roar from the mob around the house" and most delegates were eager to leave when the meeting was adjourned.[19]

When the delegates to the women's convention gathered the next morning, a "noisy crowd of miserable looking people" still surrounded the hall, making it difficult and somewhat frightening for the women to enter. During the midafternoon recess, the business committee met to prepare material for the afternoon session and the brother of one woman sent a note "beseeching her, if she valued *her life,* not to attempt to attend the afternoon session." At the afternoon session the women "found the number, and noise of the mob much increased," and a few women had to push their way into the meeting "amid the hisses and imprecations of many." One woman wrote a moving account of the events to her father:

> During the two hours in which we were in session, the voices of the women were partially drowned in the loud shouts and curses of those who were watching for our adjournment. Every woman, however, and there were about five hundred present, sat calmly, and it was unanimously resolved to maintain the periled cause to the last. As we retired, the colored members of the convention were protected by their white sisters, and Oh! shame to say, at both were thrown a shower of stones.[20]

Fewer black women attended the afternoon session than had been present in earlier days. This suggests that black women felt a more serious threat to their lives than white women did. White women had felt deeply the martyrdom of white abolitionist Elijah Lovejoy only a year earlier, when a mob attacked his antislavery press. Juliana Tappan had even referred to Lovejoy in the first resolution of the convention, suggesting that women petition until their energies "like Lovejoy's, are paralyzed in death." However, white women's experiences with mobs had not included real injury or death, and

Figure 1: *Abolition Hall. The evening before the conflagration[. A]t the time more than 50,000 persons were glorifying in its destruction at Philadelphia, May 1838. Drawn on stone by Zip Coon.* Salt print photo of unrecorded lithograph, ca. 1850. Courtesy Library Company of Philadelphia.

therefore they may have been less deterred than black women. Black women had numerous examples of black deaths at the hands of a mob, including one in Philadelphia only four years earlier. Rioters had threatened black people, their homes, and their institutions since the convention had convened. The president of the Pennsylvania Hall Association had sent the women's convention a letter recommending that black women not attend the evening meeting of another antislavery society, since the mob was directing its energies particularly against black people. Prominent white abolitionist Lucretia Mott hoped that black women would not listen to the warning, not "be alarmed by a little *appearance* of danger." This comment suggests that white women may not have appreciated the real dangers faced by black women when participating in interracial antislavery organizations.[21]

As the delegate noted in the message to her father, white women did take steps to protect the black delegates from the dangers of the mob. Declaring that they had not come all the way to Philadelphia to go out the back door, the convention delegates linked arms so that each black woman was shielded by a white woman. The two or three thousand men who surrounded the building provided them with barely enough room to walk two abreast and kept up a constant stream of insult and abusive language. Only one white woman seems to have been injured by a stone, and everyone made it home safely. However, the white women's public demonstration of their willingness to mix the races socially may have put African Americans in the city at greater risk. Mobs spent the evening burning Pennsylvania Hall to the ground and threatening, damaging, or destroying many black institutions in the city.[22] The burning of Pennsylvania Hall by an anti-abolition mob is celebrated in Figure 2, which shows the fire company pouring water away from the blaze and upper-class men joyously waving their hats in the air. For women of any color to meet in the aftermath of this event took great courage.

When the women met the next morning they found that Temperance Hall, which they had rented for the day, would not open to them due to the fear of yet more violence. Unwilling to give up after all they had been through, the women chose to walk across town to the schoolroom of a delegate. African American Sarah Douglass took a great chance in offering the use of her schoolroom, given the actions of the mob the previous evening. The Philadelphia FASS would later thank her and a coworker "who so nobly risked their property on this occasion."[23]

Although the women walked in small groups so as to escape notice, one group attracted very unwelcome attention. According to one delegate: "As we passed through some lanes, several low-looking women, who I should think fit companions for the leaders of the mob, actually came out of their huts to jeer at us; pointing the finger of scorn, distorting their faces to express contempt, and saying among other things which I could not understand, 'you had better stay at home, and mind your own business, than to come here making such a fuss.'" Although abolitionist women had been willing to stretch the boundaries of the appropriate female sphere in order to hold a women's convention, many had a strong investment in the ideology of middle-class womanhood. For this reason many rejected the idea of a promiscuous meeting under the auspices of the convention and stressed women's moral responsibility to fight slavery. To be jeered at in the streets, far from their homes, by women they considered their social, if not moral, inferiors made a strong negative impression on some of the women, particularly after the traumatic events of the previous night.[24]

It was not surprising that once the women gathered together "the appearance of this meeting was very solemn. Many were in tears." When a messenger informed them that the mob was still looking for them, convention president Mary Parker of Boston asked each woman present to decide whether she would stay in the building or not. While stating her own desire that the convention continue, she recommended "withdrawal to any, who, though strong in heart, yet felt themselves not *physically* nerved to meet a repetition of the scenes of the past night." No one left and "each one, doubtless, felt it to be a rare occasion for self-scrutiny—and many felt

Figure 2: Lithograph by J. C. Wild (Philadelphia: J. T. Bower, 1838). Courtesy Library Company of Philadelphia.

more forcibly than ever before, what it was to 'remember them that are in bonds as bound with them.'" Far more than signing a petition or joining a society, choosing to stay at the convention required women to make a commitment to the movement. Many were also making a commitment to the community of women with whom they were risking their lives.[25]

The women went on to have one of the fullest sessions of the convention. They passed fifteen resolutions, including Sarah Grimké's controversial suggestion that abolitionists associate with black people in public. They also referred to the powerful example of British women, who had successfully petitioned for the end of the apprenticeship system in the West Indies earlier that year. Sarah and Angelina Grimké offered resolutions related to the burning of Pennsylvania Hall, stressing that insult, scorn, and mob activity were all part of the "spirit of slavery" and hoping that the flames that had burned the hall would light "fires of freedom" in the future. Amid the closing resolutions, the women resolved, "That when this Convention adjourn, it adjourn to meet in this city in May, 1839." The women seemed determined to affirm that neither ridicule nor mob violence would deter them from meeting again, and they defiantly chose to meet in the same city that had served up such large portions of both.[26]

The Impact of Mob Violence

As with earlier antislavery violence, events in Philadelphia had a powerful positive effect on female antislavery organizing. In 1835 the women of Boston, Concord, and Providence had drawn inspiration and organizational strength from their ability to face down mobs and from the supportive encouragement they received from the antislavery community. Many women left Philadelphia with a similarly heightened sense of commitment. Their personal ability to face the mob empowered them to continue in their activism. Sarah Baker, corresponding secretary of the Dorchester FASS, recommended the fear of violence as a moment of truth against which all abolitionists should test their faith. Although the Philadelphia women were at first despondent, sick at the events that had happened in their fair city, Lucretia Mott reminded them that they had withstood the violence, had finished their meeting, and had sent a message of commitment and dedication. The women ended up finding a new strength in their reaction to the violence, claiming that they had "passed through an ordeal whose influences are such as mould the character for after years." At their next meeting the Philadelphia women met "the denunciation and obloquy so liberally heaped upon us" with new energy and firmness, and they resolved to work even harder for the slave in the coming year.[27]

Facing violence may also have enabled otherwise privileged women to identify more closely with the slave who faced violence regularly. As Angelina Grimké noted while the mob surrounded Pennsylvania Hall: "What if the mob should now burst in upon us, break up our meeting and commit violence upon our persons—would this be any thing compared with what the slaves endure?" Although dangerous, the Philadelphia mob violence was not anything like the daily dangers of physical, sexual, and emotional violence endured by many slave women. However, whether in Boston, Concord, or Philadelphia, the violence of the mob brought the violence of slavery home to many of these Northern white women, strengthening their commitment and connection to "those in bonds."[28]

For some women, however, the severe negative comments in the press regarding women's public antislavery activism and the personal violence that met antislavery women who broke societal norms all began to take their toll. Many women could only have gasped at the news that Maria Weston Chapman, corresponding secretary of the Boston FASS and major power behind the successful Boston fair, had collapsed and experienced a nervous breakdown after the Philadelphia mobbing. Chapman's friends blamed her condition on the recent death of her son. This explanation stressed the power of mother-child bonds in proper middle-class families. The anti-abolition press, however, suggested more cruelly that she had collapsed because she was too weak to carry her point in the face of a mob and suggested that temporary insanity was the fate of all women who overstepped their bounds.[29]

The *New York Commercial Advertiser* combined news of Weston's collapse with language from the 1837 "Pastoral Letter" into a scathing critique of those who attended the convention. "The females who so far forget the province of their sex, as to perambulate the country, and assemble for such purposes," announced the *Advertiser,* "should be gently restrained from their convocations, and sent to the best insane hospitals to be found." The article then attacked antislavery women for abandoning their domestic and familial responsibilities: "the husbands and parents of these modern Amazons should be arrayed in caps and aprons and installed in their respective kitchens."[30]

The *Boston Centinel and Gazette* published a more extended attack on antislavery women's virtue. It suggested that preaching abolition, socializing with black people, and appearing without male escort were equally problematic signs of antislavery women's degraded condition:

> There is no sort of propriety in women wandering about, from State to State, preaching up abolition. Their duties are circumscribed by the domestic circle, and they appear to the best advantage at home, or under the protection of their husbands, fathers or guardians, when abroad. There is still less of decency and modesty in white women perambulating public streets, cheek by jowl, with blacks, or in addressing popular meetings anywhere. . . . The misguided and rash people who go about the country on missions of this kind, are not the most suitable characters to lead the public opinion to any beneficial conclusion.[31]

Commentary like this had occurred in connection with the 1835 mobbing of women in Boston. However, at that time, the antislavery community had fully supported the Boston women's desire to meet publicly and had acclaimed their willingness to suffer for the slave. By 1838 that community had become divided, particularly over the question of woman's appropriate role, and thus provided less support after the Philadelphia incident. Women more comfortable with conventional gender roles found it difficult to defend their public antislavery activity. The mob's violent actions and the press's violent comments reinforced their nascent discomfort with the role of women in the antislavery movement, rather than encouraging them to continued engagement.

Antislavery women could only have been more discouraged by events occurring outside Philadelphia. In Massachusetts hundreds of women had been petitioning the state legislature to repeal the state ban on interracial marriage. Almost immediately these women were portrayed in both print and pictures as sour old maids unable to find white husbands and thus petitioning for access to black men. Aroline Chase and the antislavery ladies of Lynn submitted the largest petition and were soon caricatured in a New York lithograph. The cartoonist "respectfully inscribed" the work to "Miss Caroline [*sic*] Augusta Chase, & the 500 ladies of Lynn who wish to marry

Black Husbands." His misspelling of her name was only a tiny insult compared to the cartoon itself. It portrayed a group of aging and unattractive white women gathered in a drawing room with a group of African Americans, all anxious to meet the Haitian ambassador, whose wide-lipped face and black dialect were the broadest of racial caricature (see Figure 3). Shortly after the publication of the cartoon, 193 men of Lynn petitioned the legislature to permit the women of Lynn "to marry, intermarry, or associate with any Negro, Indian, Hottentot, or any other being in human shape at their will and pleasure." While the lithograph struck at women's vanity, the petition from Lynn men insulted their virtue. Other comments regarding their assumed sexual needs appeared regularly in the press and in the comments of the legislators receiving their petition.[32]

Women who signed a petition from Dorchester on the same subject had their ethics as well as their virtue called into public question when they were called to testify in front of a legislative committee. The committee was attempting to uncover irregularities in the signing or circulating of petitions in order to discredit them. Sarah Baker, the corresponding secretary of the Dorchester FASS, had organized the petition campaign from that town and had to undergo extensive cross-examination. Forcing her to testify in a public hearing not only suggested question of her signature-gathering technique but also implied that she had given up the modesty and virtue appropriate to women. The legislators implied that a proper woman would never have had to appear in such a public political setting. The widespread public notice given the hearing and the Lynn cartoon made these episodes almost as far-reaching as the 1838 violence. While this type of harassment differed dramatically from the mob violence of the women's convention, it served the same effect by strengthening the resolve of some women deeply committed to abolition, and causing doubt and discouragement among others.[33]

The Question of Female Membership in
the National Antislavery Societies

Thus while women had succeeded in maintaining a shaky unity during their convention, mob violence, insult, and criticism all challenged women's active participation in the movement. Still other events were unfolding that would offer women new roles and shatter their efforts at compromise and harmony. Meeting in Boston while the Anti-Slavery Convention of American Women met in Philadelphia, the all-male New-England Anti-Slavery Convention passed a resolution of central importance to women's antislavery organizing. The delegates voted that "all persons present . . . whether men or women, who agree with us in sentiment on the subject of slavery, be invited to become members, and participate in the proceedings of the Convention." A few women had been members of small, mixed-sex antislavery societies since the early 1830s. However, the

Figure 3: *Johnny Q.* [John Q. Adams] *Introducing the Haytien Ambassadore to the Ladies of Lynn, Mass. Respectfully inscribed to Miss Caroline Augusta Chase & the 500 ladies of Lynn who wish to marry Black Husbands.* Lithograph by Edward W. Clay (New York: J. Childs, 1839). Courtesy Library Company of Philadelphia.

New-England Anti-Slavery Convention was the first large antislavery convention to accept women as delegates with voting rights.

It did so based on a broad definition of the term "persons." The New-England Anti-Slavery Society constitution contained an article inviting "any person" to join as a member, and article 3 stipulated that members, meaning those who signed the constitution and paid dues, were "entitled to a voice and vote in all its meetings." In 1836 the meaning of "person" had varied enough to permit numerous interpretations. While only "gentlemen" were accepted as delegates, "friends of the cause of both sexes" were invited to attend the meetings and were encouraged to speak. On one vote in that year, "all present, including the ladies, whether members of the Convention or not, were invited to vote." While this makes clear that women were not permitted to vote under ordinary circumstances, it did occasionally happen without creating any dissension in the organization.[34]

The 1838 decision to allow women to vote did create major dissension. After the vote, a "long and animated discussion" ensued as some men tried to have the decision reversed. When that move was unsuccessful, eight conservative clergymen removed their names from the membership rolls. Another seven filed an official protest. The protest complained that allowing women "to vote, debate, and aid generally as members of this body" would injure the antislavery cause by connecting it with "a subject foreign to it." This might create a precedent for linking other "irrelevant" issues to the antislavery movement and was an "innovation" on "previous usage." In other words, the clergymen felt this vote would inevitably link antislavery with the demand for women's rights, while also undermining years of tradition.[35]

The division over the role of women was part of a larger set of divisions within the antislavery movement and antebellum society in general. The economic depression of 1837 had dramatically diminished the movement's ability to field lecturers and fund publications, which undermined its effort to sway the hearts and minds of the American people. The repeated passing of congressional Gag Rules had made clear that petitions would not be effective weapons to influence politicians. Abolitionists were struggling to figure out how best to use their limited time and resources in the fight against slavery. Seeing a link between the evil of slavery and other forms of inequality and injustice in the world, some abolitionists thought that a dramatic reform of society was the only way to purge it of sin. This included attacking churches and ministers that seemed insufficiently active against slavery. It also meant uniting men and women in the same societies, thus strengthening the antislavery organizations and undermining prejudices based on sex.

Both these steps threatened many ministers, particularly those in the Congregational and Presbyterian churches. These ministers were used to social prestige and respect and did not take kindly to suggestions that they were permitting sin to run rampant in society. They also recognized the threat to their financial status if they were to take a stand unpopular with their congregants. Massachusetts had broken the formal connection between church and state in 1820, ending state support of Congregational ministers' salaries. Therefore ministers had to please their congregants in order to continue receiving the donations and church membership fees that paid their salary. Yet antebellum congregants felt free to wander from church to church, searching for the best orator, or a congenial congregation, or even more social status. Ministers had little to gain by raising controversial issues, and a lot to lose.

Few issues were more controversial than the question of woman's role in society. While there were prominent exceptions, many ministers agreed with the sentiments in the "Pastoral Letter" against the Grimkés published by the Congregational Consociation in 1837. Women clearly had spiritual responsibilities to engage in reform, particularly by providing a moral influence over their families. However, that moral influence was compromised when they acted out of their sphere and claimed the roles of men. Many ministers held a vision of woman's appropriate role based on scriptural injunctions that women should not preach and were created for different purposes than men. Women who crossed the lines sanctioned in the Bible were considered arrogant, combative, indelicate, and morally wrong. These women were seen as incapable of that humility and deference proper to true female morality. Ministers rapidly joined newspaper editors in openly condemning the virtue of antislavery women.

The New-England Anti-Slavery Convention promptly provided a perfect target for critics. For the first time ever, a large antislavery convention appointed a woman to a mixed-sex committee. Abby Kelley, an active member of the Millbury (MA) FASS and Lynn FASS and a well-known antislavery lecturer, agreed to serve. She had long argued that women had duties and abilities equal to those of men, and she was eager to push the boundaries of woman's appropriate sphere. The committee was to draw up a memorial to ecclesiastical associations to urge their action against slavery, an activity Kelley had previously supported at the Anti-Slavery Convention of American Women. Immediately upon her election most members of the committee resigned. The remainder wrote the requested memorial, but when some churches found out that a woman had been on the committee "[t]he memorial was treated with all possible indignity." The Rhode Island Congregational Consociation voted "to turn the illegitimate product from the house, and obliterate from the records all traces of its entrance." A reporter with the *Christian Mirror* attended the Rhode Island meeting and wrote a report of how the ministers felt:

> It was humiliating enough to come under [the rule of women], imperceptibly, or blindfolded; but to bow the neck with the eyes open, would be an aggravation of the disgrace and humiliation. . . . What man, who loves and honors his wife, would himself feel honored by having her closeted in close consultation with two men, in the preparation of a public document? . . . Would it not be "all one as if she were shaven?"—shorn of her honor, her loveliness, her glory?

According to these ministers, meeting in equality with men could only result in immoral promiscuity (in the modern sense) and undermine the moral character that women brought to a reform effort. It left women without loveliness, honor, or virtue, and any man who was willing to accept equality with such a woman was disgraced, degraded, and despised.[36]

Antislavery women found themselves increasingly divided by the New-England Society's decision and the resulting barrage of insult against Abby Kelley. Most agreed they would have preferred that the debate had not occurred, since it distracted everyone from the original fight against slavery. As the women of Amesbury and Salisbury wrote to the *Liberator*: "whatever may be our views in regard to the rights and appropriate sphere of women, we cannot but regret that a discussion on this point should ever in the slightest degree take the place of those eloquent appeals and appalling facts, which first awakened among us a sympathy for the southern slave." The women of East Haverhill also regretted "the discussion of the question of woman's rights in anti-slavery meetings or newspapers" and felt sorry for any woman who would "make the redress of her own real or imaginary grievances paramount to the claims of her enslaved sisters of the south." Other women attempted to avoid the radical question of meeting with men by focusing on defending women's right to meet among themselves. In a letter to her colleagues in Lynn, Sarah Baker of Dorchester wrote:

> The Conventions of Women at New York and Philadelphia have been a matter of *much* complaint, ridicule and contempt to many of our opposers. . . . We are willing to admit the meetings were of a singular and unpopular character, but they were not more so, than the cause which demanded them. The crisis *has* come when it would be sin for woman to stay at home and remain silent. It is necessary and important that *woman should consult with woman* and that they should bear their united public testimony against the brutalising system of slavery.[37]

Yet while some women hoped to avoid controversy, the debates over mixed-sex organizations provided a few women with an opening they had long been anticipating. A brave few plunged directly into the controversy and advocated abandoning all-female conventions in favor of continued efforts at integrating all-male societies. Lydia Maria Child had joined the all-female Boston FASS only reluctantly, and she refused to attend the second Anti-Slavery Convention of American Women. In perhaps one of the best-known rejections of female separatism, she wrote, "I have never entered very earnestly into the plan of female conventions and societies. They always seemed to me like half a pair of scissors." Abby Kelley, the subject of the New-England Convention controversy, expressed a similar opinion that "combined effort" of men and women was "the only correct mode of operation." These two women firmly agreed with Angelina Grimké that women "*must establish this right* [of equality with men] for if we do not, it will be impossible for *us* to go *on with the work of Emancipation*." If women gave in to demands that they engage only in certain types of reform within the bounds of decorum, might they eventually be asked to give up the controversial call for black freedom altogether?[38]

Child's and Kelley's opinions could not have pleased the Philadelphia women to whom they were sent, given that the Philadelphia FASS was actively planning the third Anti-Slavery Convention of American Women. Corresponding secretary Lucretia Mott responded to Kelley on behalf of the society, agreeing that mixed-sex societies were preferable. But, she reminded Kelley, many people were not yet ready for such innovations, as was quite clear from the objections lodged at the New-England Anti-Slavery Convention. Mott felt that those women who felt called to do so should "avail themselves of every opportunity offered them to mingle in discussions and take part with their brethren." At the same time and "without compromise of the principle of equality or sanction of any error," women could still meet by themselves "for special purposes . . . and thus prepare themselves for more public and general exercise of their rights." Meetings of women, "imperfect as they are," prepared women for eventual cooperation with men, while enabling women who wanted equal rights to "enlighten" their "less educated sisters." Mott had long hoped that men and women would be able to work equally together. She had not been supportive of the idea of a female executive committee in 1836 because she preferred to be asked to join the men as equals in the AAS. Yet in 1838, as in 1836, Mott felt too many valuable women would be lost to the cause if integration-minded women chose to "hastily withdraw and leave their sisters to serve alone." Female conventions were the best option available, where those who wanted female equality could still work with those who saw value in gender differences, and all could focus on the cause of the slave.[39]

The Women's Convention, 1839

The contentious debates regarding woman's role, the new opportunities for antislavery women in New England, and memories of the 1838 mob all had a severely negative effect on the 1839 Anti-Slavery Convention of American Women. When it convened in Philadelphia on May 1, 1839, only 102 delegates and 68 corresponding members attended, a drop of almost 40 percent from the previous year. Women attended from six states, including Massachusetts (13), Rhode Island (1), New York (10), New Jersey (5), Delaware (1), and Pennsylvania (140). While women attended from thirty-five towns, Philadelphia women dominated the membership, comprising 80 percent of the delegates and 87 percent of the corresponding members.[40]

The most active women from New York City and Massachusetts did not attend the convention. Of the twenty-seven women from New York City who had attended the 1838 convention, only two returned. While those who stayed behind gave no explanation for their absence, the fear that controversial topics would be introduced could only have been stronger this year than when Juliana Tappan worried about it in 1838. These women may also have chosen to stay close to home to watch the controversial proceedings of the American Anti-Slavery Society conference, which was to take place in New York City just days after the women's convention. Everyone was expecting extensive debate on women's participation in that organization.

The AAS meeting also drew away from the women's convention many of the most prominent and outspoken women from Massachusetts. Many were headed to New York fully expecting to finally participate as equals in the national organization. Only three Massachusetts delegates from 1838 returned in 1839, and delegates represented seven towns rather than ten. The limited number of women from Boston was particularly striking, with a fourteen-person delegation shrinking to three.

The absence of the leaders from New York and Boston deprived the convention of many of its previous officers. Mary Parker, who had led both of the previous conventions, did not attend, nor did eleven previous vice presidents. Former secretaries who missed the convention included Angelina Grimké, Anne W. Weston, and Juliana Tappan. Of the twelve officers in 1839, four had never served previously, including two vice presidents and two secretaries. Of these, three had at least attended the 1837 women's convention and the other was very active in the Nantucket FASS. The presence of the founders of the Philadelphia FASS, including Lucretia Mott, Mary Grew, and Grace Douglass, as well as Martha Ball, a founder of the Boston society, did give a weight and respectability to the convention, but this was clearly not the national gathering of antislavery leaders originally hoped for by the convention organizers.[41]

The absence of those women who strongly rejected integration with men, as well as those who passionately desired it, meant that the delegates were those most likely to find middle ground. The desire to make everyone welcome and avoid contentious issues came through clearly in the women's resolutions. The convention required all convention business to be submitted to the business committee but resolved that "any document or resolution rejected by this Committee, may be presented to the Convention, by the author or mover, if dissatisfied with the decision of the Committee." Their first substantive resolution sustained the "original principle" of the antislavery cause, that is, that slavery was a sin and should be immediately abolished. The resolution then welcomed to the ranks all who supported this original principle "regardless of their opinions on other subjects." This is the only reference at the convention to the divisions occurring within the movement at large. The women walked a careful middle ground in the debate over whether slavery was a moral or a political cause. They resolved to continue exercising their right of petition, feeling that "petitions to Congress have effected much good" and then promptly followed up with a resolution which stressed that slavery was among "the most important of our moral duties."[42]

The women shied away from the specific resolutions of the previous year that had advocated social interaction among the races. Perhaps they were attempting to avoid the horrible violence provoked by their previous convention. The Philadelphia mayor was clearly worried that violence might occur. He called on Lucretia Mott to inquire "where the Convention would be held—if it would be confined to women—if to white women, or white and colored—if our meetings would be held only in the day time, and how long they would continue." He advised the women not to meet in the evening, to avoid "unnecessary walking with colored people," and to close the convention as soon as possible. Mott informed the mayor that they had "never made a parade, as charged upon us, of walking with colored people, and should do as we had done before—walk with them as occasion offered," making no distinction on account of color. The mayor provided officers to protect the women (and the property of the Riding School at which they met), which may have been sufficient to fend off any possible trouble. The lack of promiscuous meetings and any mixing between white women and free black men probably contributed to the peace and quiet. The women did resolve to work harder to assist the free black population and to work at eliminating racial prejudice.[43]

This was not a convention of women's rights activists. In passing their resolution on racial prejudice, the women stated: "That we will continue to act in accordance with our profession that the moral and intellectual character of persons, and not their complexion, should mark the sphere in which they are to move." It would have been linguistically simple to substitute "sex" for "complexion" and turn a radical declaration against prejudice into a strong feminist statement. Some abolitionist women were moving in that direction. Sarah Grimké had just published her *Letters on the Equality of the Sexes and the Condition of Woman* in 1838. Her sister Angelina had replied to a biting denunciation of women's public antislavery activities by writing *Letters to Catherine Beecher, in Reply to an Essay on Slavery and Abolitionism*. Denying that women could best be of service to God by remaining in the domestic circle, both women claimed a public, and equal, antislavery role for women. The 1839 women's convention attempted to avoid any discussion that might raise the issue of women's rights. This position was perhaps made easier by the Grimkés' absence from the meeting.[44]

Instead the women criticized ministers for their "inconsistency" in professing a Christian belief in loving thy neighbor but opposing abolitionists who attempted to practice it. They also passed a resolution claiming that they would never "hide the truth of God in relation to the subject of slavery" even though "bonds and imprisonment" might be the result. These were the only two resolutions that resulted in any debate. The topic of debate for the first went unrecorded. The second discussion revolved around whether the women were expressing too much pride in their declarations of support for the movement. No one wanted to make vows they could not keep. In the end, however, both resolutions passed, apparently without dissenting votes. At the close of the convention, the women thanked God that they had been able "to conduct our deliberations with so much profit and harmony," an event that must have seemed all the more remarkable given the mob violence of the previous year and the divisions within the antislavery movement itself.[45]

The women resolved to meet again in 1840 in Boston, at a time "to be left to the decision of a committee of nine persons," three each from the cities of Boston, Philadelphia, and New York. Four of those persons were not present, including two of the three women listed from Boston and two of the three listed from New York. All four of those women were preparing to attend the AAS annual meeting four days later in New York. Events at that meeting would severely disrupt women's attempts at harmonious compromise, and the 1839 Anti-Slavery Convention of American Women would be the last.[46]

The AAS Grants Membership to Women and the Movement Divides

The delegates to the May 7, 1839, AAS annual meeting knew that harmony would not prevail for them as it had for the women. The Massachusetts Anti-Slavery Society had split into two organizations the previous January. Delegates divided over the question of remaining in "proslavery" churches, over whether to participate in party politics, and over the proper role for women in the antislavery movement. Those same issues promised to disrupt this AAS meeting.

In one of the first resolutions of the convention, a minister raised the issue of female membership by attempting to limit the roll to "*men,* duly appointed." An amendment changed "men" to "persons" and passed by a large majority, as did the resolution. The next day the convention reconsidered the previous day's vote. They rejected a resolution that would have entitled women to "sit, speak, vote, hold office, and exercise the same rights of membership as persons of the other sex." No one at the convention, including most of the supporters of female membership, wanted such a bald-faced statement of women's rights at an antislavery convention. Instead they suggested a very simple resolution that would make up the roll of those men and women who were members of the society or delegates from an auxiliary. This would provide women with the same rights but under the auspices of their already existing membership, rather than an imported ideology of women's rights.[47]

The question of whether women could vote on these resolutions proved complicated. Those who felt that women had never been invited to be members of the organization felt that women, as nonmembers, had no right to vote. The other side argued that the constitutional article that invited "all persons" to become members included women. Therefore, women had always had a right to vote as members but simply had not "improved upon" or taken advantage of it in prior conventions. To this group, the measures to "give" women the vote were moot. In the end the women were permitted to vote on whether they were members of the society. Fifteen took advantage of the opportunity, with thirteen voting for women's inclusion and two voting against. Contrary to claims by the minority at the meeting, women's votes did not substantially affect the outcome. The vote count excluding women still totaled 167 for women's inclusion to 138 against.[48]

A brief look at the women who voted suggests that the divisions among them may have reflected divisions between long-term activists and newcomers, as those who supported William Lloyd Garrison's side of the battle regularly contended. Ten of the thirteen women who voted for inclusion were from Massachusetts, the state with the largest number of and most active female antislavery societies. These women included members of the Nantucket, Fall River, Salem, Lynn, and Boston female antislavery societies. All but one of the Massachusetts women, and the one New York delegate who voted with them, had attended an Anti-Slavery Convention of American Women. Six of the women had traveled directly from the 1839 meeting in Philadelphia to the AAS meeting in New York. This participation marks them as among the most active female abolitionists of the period. Given the difficulties of leaving one's family for two weeks and traveling to two different cities in less than six days, these women had clearly made a powerful commitment to antislavery activism.[49]

On the other side, two women voted against their right to membership in the convention. Both were from New York City, and neither had attended any of the women's antislavery conventions. Little is known about Lucy Deming, but Mrs. G. M. Tracy's use of her husband's name and married title signals her support of a more conservative interpretation of woman's appropriate role. George M. Tracy was a New York abolitionist and a friend of abolitionist and philanthropist Lewis Tappan, himself a supporter of a more limited sphere for women. Neither Lucy Deming nor Stella Tracy was active in antislavery societies in New York City. It is a tantalizing mystery why these women who had not attended antislavery conventions held by women risked public censure to participate in a mixed-sex convention only to vote against continued female membership![50]

Although women were admitted and allowed to vote, the issue of female membership was not settled at the 1839 meeting. Lewis Tappan's brother Arthur served as president for the meeting, helping to create compromise between the two sides, but 123 delegates, including Lewis, signed a protest against women's participation. They argued that female participation was against the constitution of the society, violated the tradition of previous conventions, and was repugnant to the wishes of many members. They also pointed out that the AAS had long encouraged the formation of separate female antislavery societies, an action hardly necessary if the organization had intended mixed-sex meetings. Perhaps most important, they argued that this split would bring unnecessary reproach on the antislavery movement, already fighting to change public sentiment on one controversial issue—slavery. They saw no need to adopt yet another cause "at variance with general usage and sentiment."[51]

By the 1840 AAS Convention, any room available for compromise had completely disappeared. Strong personalities had become as crucial to the divisions as any particular issue, with harsh language and bitter denunciations on both sides. The fiery orator and newspaper editor William Lloyd Garrison personified the "old organization" or "perfectionist wing," which advocated continued moral suasion to convince the slaveholder and the Northerner of the sin of slavery. In the eyes of Garrisonians, as they were called, the churches had forfeited their moral leadership by failing to denounce slavery and to bar slaveholders from communion. Thus they advocated that congregants withdraw from churches in order to preserve their own moral purity. In keeping with their focus on the equal rights of all God's children, the Garrisonians advocated equal rights for women, as well as for African Americans. Garrisonians also denounced partisan politics, preferring a moral revolution to a politically imposed compromise. Some of Garrison's supporters disagreed with him on one or more of these issues, or on one of the many other topics he raised, such as the duty to avoid violence, to keep all the days as holy as Sunday, and others. However, the old organization was united in the belief that each person should be permitted freedom of conscience. Anyone who agreed that slavery was a sin to be immediately eliminated was welcome in the antislavery movement, regardless of their opinions on other controversial issues.

In contrast, one group of Garrison's opponents tried time and again to write out of the movement those with unacceptable opinions on topics other than slavery. These "new organization" reformers were predominantly united by their dislike of Garrison and their sense that his perfectionist demands were damaging the antislavery cause. A New York City circle centered on reformer Lewis Tappan had long-standing ties to orthodox or conservative churches and continued to see ministers and religion as powerful allies to the antislavery movement. They also saw women as powerful allies, as long as they remained within their proper sphere of home and church. This group wanted to wrest control of the AAS from what they saw as fanatics who would ruin any chance the antislavery movement had to succeed by linking it with even more radical ideas, including black or female equality. A third group opposed Garrison on different grounds. This group felt moral suasion had had its chance and the time had come to build an antislavery political party that could utilize the political system to effect emancipation. In 1840 these reformers began to organize the Liberty Party, a third political party focused almost solely on the abolition of slavery. This group supported women's rights, while also drawing on the churches for organizational support.[52]

Thus it is not surprising that at the AAS annual meeting in 1840 the antislavery movement's unity was irretrievably shattered. When the majority of the members present elected Abby Kelley to the business committee, those members most invested in a more traditional role for women protested. Finding themselves a small minority, they walked out of the convention. They quickly formed the American and Foreign Anti-Slavery Society (A&FAS), named to honor and affiliate with the long-standing British and Foreign Anti-Slavery Society. They published a constitution that avoided further debate over women's roles by specifically excluding women from any formal role in the organization. Women were invited to form separate female auxiliaries, but these could only be represented at the annual meetings by male delegates.[53]

Since the state antislavery societies were auxiliaries of the AAS, the national debates over female membership were rapidly replayed at the state society annual meetings, with varying results. In New Hampshire and Massachusetts, states with powerful female antislavery societies, those desiring female membership prevailed. In Maine, which had only four female societies, women were excluded from the state society. In Connecticut, where the female antislavery societies were very weak, the state society voted to ban women from even speaking at the annual meeting. The atmosphere became so hostile to public female antislavery activities in Connecticut that the women's antislavery fair had to be moved out of New Haven since no church would house the fair. From the state level, the divisions percolated down to the local level, and eventually individual women had to decide whom to support.[54]

Complex Choices for Women

The process of division and the resulting split in the antislavery movement forced women to choose sides in a debate whose terms were largely set by the men who precipitated the divisions. The stark choice between two antagonistic societies, the American and the American and Foreign, left women without the middle road they had honed so carefully at the antislavery conventions of American women. The Garrisonian side offered greater encouragement for women's rights and the ability to play an equal role in the movement. Women who felt strongly that antislavery required their equal participation with men in order to succeed joined this side of the fight. Since many Garrisonian men chose not to cast a vote in political elections, they further enhanced the equality between women without the vote and men who would not use it.

That equality came at some cost, however. Garrisonians condemned most churches for not taking a stronger antislavery stand, and some rejected the Bible as a proslavery tool since it was so often cited by slavery's defenders. Many Garrisonian women felt they had to "come out" from or disown their churches and reject ministerial authority in order to engage in the moral suasion activities previously encouraged by ministers. Since Garrisonians rejected politics, arguing that a moral revolution of the heart needed to precede the compulsion of political force, women who chose this side of the split abdicated any role in the antislavery political parties. These women did not give up the right to see slavery as a political issue but refused to get involved in the partisan politics of elections and campaigns.[55]

Women who had joined the antislavery cause out of a religious motivation to create God's heaven on earth and use their moral power to convert slaveholders would have been quite comfortable with the Garrisonian emphasis on moral suasion. The rejection of politics would have fit perfectly with a belief that women had a moral influence over society due to their exclusion from politics. However, many women with strong connections to churches could not accept Garrison's abandonment of churches and denunciations of the Bible, which were central features of their life and community. For many it would have meant leaving the institution attended by all their non-abolitionist friends and family, and perhaps leaving other reform groups that met at or organized through the church. These women often chose to remain within their churches, working within church-based antislavery organizations. Thus some women found themselves estranged from the Garrisonians who so supported the moral suasion stance that had originally drawn church women to antislavery.

These women ended up making a powerful statement in favor of women's moral responsibility to engage in politics. Drawing on the previous arguments that women had a moral duty to petition their legislators, the women of the Massachusetts Female Emancipation Society (MFES) wrote: "If woman has nothing to do with politics then has she nothing to do with the rising generation; then has she no duty to her husband,—none to her neighbor,—in fine none to the world; then indeed must she needs *go out of the world* to seek her duties." The MFES women saw encouraging men to vote the antislavery ticket as a necessary complement to their petitioning efforts. As they wrote in their annual report, MFES women agreed with a sister who was tired "of procuring signatures *for the brethren* to petitions for the Abolition of Slavery in the District of Columbia, while these same brethren go to the polls and vote for men who will throw these petitions under the table the moment they are presented to Congress." MFES women showed their support of the Liberty Party and men who voted by creating and publicly presenting a celebratory banner to the town with the largest Liberty Party vote in the Massachusetts tenth congressional district.

Ultimately women in the MFES would find their closeness to the Liberty Party too much of an ideological stretch. By 1843 they would withdraw their support from partisan politics and turn their attention to moral reform movements that were less contentious than antislavery. At the same time Garrisonian women who had flatly rejected party politics generally and the Liberty Party specifically, gradually moved in the direction of calling for a woman's right to vote. Few women found it easy to choose amid the competing and overlapping demands of antislavery activism, church affiliation, woman's rights, and partisan politics. Even more important, many women had good friends and beloved leaders on both sides of the division, which further complicated their alliances.[56]

Factors Affecting Women's Choices

Women's affiliation decisions depended on personal relationships, race, religion, and economic status, among other factors. The most important may have been personal relationships, and this is currently the least well documented. One study has suggested that at least 70 percent of women in the Boston FASS joined the cause as part of a family unit. These alliances tended to hold when women had to choose between competing antislavery factions. Even women without direct relatives in the movement used family ties as an explanation for their choice of alliance. Mary Clark found a "household of faith" in the Garrisonian abolitionists who dominated her female antislavery society in Concord (NH) and the Boston society that she had visited on occasion. Her close relationships with members of both societies resulted in her unwavering support of the Garrisonian faction. Yet family ties were not always the most important factor, as indicated by Mary Grew's staunch support for Garrison while her father, Henry Grew, was decidedly less enthusiastic. Family alliances seem in general to have reinforced the other factors that helped shape women's decisions.[57]

Race seems to have been the predominant factor in black women's affiliation decisions, although personal relationships and religion also played a role. Black women sincerely regretted the divisions within the antislavery movement since these took attention away from the crucial issue of black equality. Although restricted by many of the same ideological and legal barriers faced by white women, black women recognized race as the most serious of their social and legal disabilities. They wanted to remain focused on the desperate daily needs of black people, free and slave, rather than endless debates about woman's appropriate role. The AAS made clear the distinction between white and black women when, after admitting women, they failed to appoint a single black woman to a leadership position. They did elect a black man to the vice presidency, and one black woman, Hester Lane, was nominated for a leadership slot. However, this former slave had voted for political action as an abolitionist duty in 1840 and had connections to Lewis Tappan in New York, so it is unsurprising that she was not elected. No other black women were nominated.[58]

It is not currently clear how many black women seceded from Garrisonian organizations when the movement split. At least two or three did so in Boston, primarily due to their personal relationships with ministers who both denounced Garrison's anticlerical stance and hoped to find support for black suffrage in the political wing of the movement. However, most chose to remain affiliated with the AAS. These women recognized William Lloyd Garrison as a tried and true, if temperamental, friend of black freedom and rights. His support of black women's literary, benevolent, and church-related organizations had made clear that he shared their broad view of community uplift as part of antislavery activism.

In many ways, black women did not enter into the battle for equal participation in antislavery societies until 1848, eight years after the AAS divisions. In that year a black woman requested permission to participate equally in the National Convention of Colored Freedmen. With clear echoes from the AAS debates, the convention agreed to accept all "persons" as voting members. Black women would continue to face exclusion from black antislavery conventions through the 1850s, particularly as more and more black men shifted away from moral suasion tactics and toward political engagement.[59]

White women divided primarily along religious and class lines. Women with strong connections to Congregational, Baptist, and Presbyterian churches tended to secede from the AAS, either affiliating themselves with the evangelical A&FAS or leaving antislavery altogether. For example, in Boston, 85 percent of the Congregational women and all but two of the white Baptist women rejected the anticlerical stance of the Boston FASS and left in 1839. Many went on to form the MFES, an A&FAS affiliate. A similarly sized group left antislavery to form a Baptist Sewing and Social Circle. The seceders included almost all the ministers' wives. In upstate New York, most of the seceders were Presbyterians. Women who remained with the AAS tended to be Quakers, Unitarians, Universalists, Methodists, and Episcopalians.

In part, these divisions reflected denominational understandings of the role of women. Quaker, Unitarian, and Universalist doctrines saw women as more equal participants in the life of the congregation, in comparison to the more orthodox Protestant faiths where women played a more subservient role. In more conservative denominations, the religious conversion process stressed humiliation and subjugation of self to a higher power. Many male ministers played on those experiences when they called on middle-class women to stop putting the issue of their rights ahead of serving God through church-sanctioned benevolent work.[60]

To some extent religious affiliation reflected class status. Unitarian, Quaker, and Episcopalian women tended to be either the wealthy Boston elite or upstate New York farm families. In either case they tended to support the AAS side of the split. The Congregationalists and Baptists who seceded in both places tended to come from the lower middle class, with clerks, artisans, and merchants among the husbands, and teachers or shopkeepers among the women. Religious experience, economic mobility, and gender ideologies among middle-class women worked together to help explain their removal from public antislavery activism. As middle-class women attained relative economic security, they turned their attention away from activities that challenged the status quo. Instead they turned to benevolent work, which supported established political structures while ameliorating their worst effects on women and children. Clerical disapproval aided this process by encouraging these status-seeking women to leave the controversial arena of antislavery for more accepted arenas for the exercise of female power, particularly charitable, missionary, and benevolent organizations.[61]

Some women in more conservative denominations did choose the Garrisonian side of the debate, however. A few did so despite the preferences of their clergymen. In Byfield (MA) a prominent minister lectured a leading member of the newly formed female antislavery society on her "improper conduct" in joining the society. She agreed to present his concerns to the society. She did so with a series of strong, anticlerical resolutions reiterating woman's responsibility to the antislavery cause. The society responded to the minister's interference by unanimously supporting the resolutions. In this case the minister backed down.[62]

However, other clergymen made regular speeches on the topic and created an atmosphere in which activism was quite difficult. This occurred in Ashburnham (MA), where women's antislavery work withered away after 1840. The most prominent clergyman in the area lectured women to "ask their husbands at home" if they wanted to know more about the antislavery cause, strongly suggesting that women avoid any public involvement in the cause. Ultimately, a few women with such unsupportive ministers made the difficult decision to leave their congregations and "come out" from their churches, in order to work without religious fetter. Some joined more liberal congregations in the same faith, others migrated to a less orthodox doctrine, and many remained unattached to a particular denomination. For these women devotion to the cause outweighed devotion to a particular denomination, although they retained a strong sense of personal faith in God. This was an extremely difficult decision, however. It is not surprising that many other women chose to remain within the churches and support the A&FAS side of the division.[63]

Women Struggle to Maintain Community despite Divisions

It is questionable whether the Anti-Slavery Convention of American Women might have been able to provide a compromise arena for all these various women once the men formally split and began competing for women's affiliation. However, three major factors made it impossible even to try. First, the 1840 women's convention had been scheduled to occur in Boston, home of the powerful Boston FASS. Unfortunately, by late 1839, that society was coming apart at the seams in a series of angry and embarrassing confrontations. Divisions had begun to show as early as 1837, when a small group of women took objection to the anticlerical language of the society's annual report. After a series of meetings at which the disapproval was clear but no one would present an official objection, the report went to press, at which point a few women inserted an official rejection of certain portions of it. Over the next few years the split between those who condemned the churches and those who supported them continued to widen, until in early 1840 the church-supporting majority officially dissolved the organization. The minority immediately cried foul and reconstituted the society, but Boston was clearly no place to hold a unifying women's convention in 1840.[64]

The women's convention was left without some of its best organizers at the moment when they were most needed. The 1839 convention had named a committee of nine to plan the 1840 convention, and the chair, Lucretia Mott, did make some efforts in that direction in a letter to Boston soon after the third convention closed. However, the committee was split right down the middle by the larger divisions in the movement. Mary S. Parker, Martha Ball, and the three committee members from New York City eventually affiliated themselves with the A&FAS or anti-Garrisonian organization. These women, while they had been supportive of the previous conventions, may have felt that to hold another one in this period of division would have been to advocate a more prominent role for women, an argument they did not feel comfortable making. Maria Weston Chapman and the three women from Philadelphia favored the AAS side of the debate, including a more prominent role for women. Each had had reservations about female-only conventions in the past and, given prominent roles in the AAS, probably decided the women's convention was not worth the effort. By 1840 efforts to create national coordination among antislavery women were dead. Ideological divisions had proved stronger than gender solidarity, at least on the national level.[65]

Women also struggled at the local level. Many societies passed resolutions urging unity, but these often reflected their divisions as much as their hope for harmony. The Barnstable (MA) FASS resolved: "That we as a Society, will strive to lay aside all sectarian, and other prejudices, and gladly welcome to our ranks all, whatever their station, creed, or color, who esteem it a privilege to plead for those who cannot plead for themselves." The word "sectarian" as used here meant "religious prejudices" or the desire to put one's religious beliefs above the common good of the society. Its use here indicates that the women recognized the dangers of religious affiliations in dividing antislavery societies. The Groton (MA) FASS annual report stressed the "unanimity" in the society. Dissension clearly lay just below the surface, however. The women reported: "Opposite views and feelings have not been openly expressed, but if there be a solitary instance or two of shrinking from the odium hitherto poured out upon the heads of abolitionists, we will pity the weakness—we will forgive the dereliction." This type of condescension, where the majority "pity" and "forgive" the minority, may help explain why women with more traditional views of their role in the movement felt uncomfortable presenting their opinions to the society at large.[66]

This was clearly true in Boston where the Garrisonian women complained that no one would openly express complaint in a meeting, although there was much debate behind the scenes. More conservative women in the Boston FASS may have refused to express their opinions out of "sisterly regard" for other women's feelings or because they were inexperienced in public speaking. They tended to expect public consensus and the ability to express dissenting views in friendly, private meetings. Antislavery women had founded female antislavery societies in part to avoid having to compete and debate with men in mixed-sex societies. The caustic debates and antagonistic atmosphere that sometimes met more conservative women's concerns may have promoted further divisions within the women's societies.[67]

Faced with the acrimonious male splits and their own internal divisions, each female antislavery society had to figure out an organizational response. The variety of their responses reflects the diversity among the women and underscores the importance of carefully examining the women's arguments. Particular institutional forms did not always represent the same ideological choices. Garrisonian women in Nantucket chose to disband their organization, in order to re-form it as a new mixed-sex organization. The previously all-male county society had not been active for some time, "leaving all action to the Women's Society"; no one could even find the men's constitution. The women decided that merging with the men into a new county society would not limit the women's action but rather would spur the men on to new sacrifices and activity. The absence of an active group of men may have helped the women take charge of this particular merger.[68]

At least one group of church-supporting women also decided to merge with men, although it is unclear if this meant equal participation or simply a quiet, female presence at mixed-sex meetings. The women of the Wesleyan FASS (of the Methodist Episcopal Church) discussed uniting with the Ladies' New-York City Anti-Slavery Society with whom they had cooperated on various occasions. However, in early 1840, they decided to unite their quarterly meetings with the Wesleyan male society, "thus hoping to share the reproach to which our brethren are subject." For these women, uniting as women would have meant diluting their evangelical affiliation. In this case, a more church-friendly choice was to create a mixed-sex society.[69]

Most evangelical women did not have the option of mixed-sex membership, and they either retained or formed all-female societies. The A&FAS constitution barred women from membership, while strongly encouraging them to form single-sex organizations. This attitude filtered down to the local auxiliaries, most of which excluded women as well. In Nantucket a minister interested in forming a new society auxiliary to the A&FAS asked all current antislavery society members to wait after the monthly concert of prayer for the slave. He explained his opposition to Garrison to everyone present, but once he began focusing on actual organization he "dismissed the sisters," who later organized themselves into the Nantucket Female Union. Even all-female organizations did not preclude cooperation with men, however. In Boston those women angry at the course of the Boston FASS seceded to form the MFES, perhaps the most important female affiliate to the A&FAS side. Emphasizing their affiliation with evangelical men, the women asked local ministers to preside at their public meetings and they relied heavily on male cooperation to advertise their fair and help organize their other activities.[70]

Many of the women most fully committed to independent female organization were those given the option of equality with men. This makes clear that retaining an all-female antislavery society did not necessarily mean a rejection of the idea of equality for women. The women in Salem chose to retain their all-female organization, despite their strong support of the AAS. They recognized in their 1840 annual report that some people thought women's associations were weak, powerless, and inadequate. They, however, felt that their work was too great to stop and discuss such matters as "the disputed question of women's rights," or whether they had advanced beyond their sphere through antislavery work. They clearly supported Garrison and the women who joined his cause. However, they felt comfortable remaining organizationally separate from male abolitionists for another twenty-six years. In Dedham (MA) the original female society divided into two opposing organizations. The Garrisonian women debated whether to form a separate organization or simply affiliate themselves with the mixed-sex state society as individuals. Edmund Quincy, a prominent Dedham abolitionist, favored individual affiliation since "the necessity of exclusively women's Societies seems to be superseded by the admission of them on equal terms in the Men's Societies." The women apparently did not agree, finding it more useful to organize in a female society and work together than to affiliate as individuals with a mixed-sex society.[71]

Achieving the right of equal membership with men was indeed enormously important to these women. For Mary Clark in Concord, the state society's decision to permit women was not only a victory for women but a moment in which she more clearly understood the meaning of freedom: "I think I can realize somewhat of the feelings of [our] *fugitive* brethren and sisters when they arrive on the Canada shore. I feel as if we women in N. H. have fairly set foot . . . on the soil of freedom, and am inclined to prostrate myself upon it, and give God thanks." Garrisonian women also recognized, however, that they were unlikely to actually be treated as equals among the men. Two years after integrating its membership, the Massachusetts Anti-Slavery Society Convention had female delegates from at least twenty-nine antislavery societies, some of which sent only female delegates. However, only three women had any position on a committee or on the executive committee. The AAS also gave a small minority of leadership positions to women. For this reason many women stressed the continuing value of all-female organization. Powerful leaders from both the reconstituted Boston FASS and the Philadelphia FASS became officers in the AAS. They also continued to be active in their all-female organizations, which lasted until the late 1840s in Boston and 1870 in Philadelphia.[72]

Given that the form of an antislavery society did not always reflect its affiliation, women found new importance in the names of their societies. Previously, societies had been fairly loose about their official names, and antislavery newspapers and reports were even less careful. After the divisions women used nomenclature more carefully to denote affiliation with one antislavery faction or another. When the women of North Andover split over which side to support, the Garrisonian women retained the name of the Female Anti-Slavery Society. They wanted to stress the continuity between the original organization, founded in 1836, and their own. This sense of continuity was important to Garrisonian organizations, leading them to call themselves the "old organization" while descrying the A&FAS as the "new organization." The Andover women who supported the A&FAS chose to call their new organization the Female Charitable Anti-Slavery Society. The name emphasized their rejection of "new" roles for women, stressing the place of antislavery work in the long and well-accepted tradition of women's involvement in charitable organizations.

A similar debate over nomenclature occurred in Boston. When the Boston FASS was dissolved and then reconstituted in 1839, the Garrisonian women who dominated the reconstituted society reclaimed the name Boston Female Anti-Slavery Society. They stressed that their society was the true heir to the original organization, despite the defection of over half the members. Those defecting members formed the rival Massachusetts Female Emancipation Society, setting a precedent for choosing the word "Emancipation" to signify affiliation with the A&FAS side of the division. This became so standard for both American and English antislavery societies that the Weymouth and Braintree Emancipation Society, so named since their founding in 1835, felt obligated to change their name. In 1840 they became the Weymouth and Braintree Female Anti-Slavery Society so their commitment to the AAS could not be mistaken.

Another relationship between name and affiliation appears in the increased use of both "Women" and "Ladies" in the names of female antislavery societies. The use of the term "Ladies" had occurred earlier, especially in the well-known Ladies' New-York City Anti-Slavery Society. After 1839, however, the use of "Ladies" in a society title tended to mean affiliation with the A&FAS or with its general principles. It also connoted a rejection of the demand for women's rights, and an adherence to a more genteel understanding of woman's appropriate role, including deference to men in church and public gatherings.

At the same time, a few Garrisonian organizations acted on a comment made by Angelina Grimké at the 1839 Anti-Slavery Convention of American Women. She noted that she was glad to see so many *women* present and so few *ladies*. In 1840 at least two Garrisonian organizations replaced the term "Female" in their title with "Women," as in the Lynn Women's Anti-Slavery Society and the Millbury Women's Anti-Slavery Society. Abby Kelley had been an active member of both societies, which may have influenced their decision. The Boston women, had they not been bound by the need to retain "Female" for continuity purposes, would also have adopted the term "Woman." Thus in both society names and organizational forms, women attempted to negotiate the divisions that were tearing the antislavery movement apart. Few had the option of remaining neutral.[73]

Antislavery Fairs Prompt Division and Community Building

The desperate need for money by all antislavery organizations, and their reliance on women to raise it, made it almost impossible for women to avoid choosing sides. Multiple bank failures from the Panic of 1837 had resulted in widespread inflation, economic contraction, and personal belt-tightening. Cotton prices plunged, construction projects were put on hold, and many workers were made idle. The economy would not begin to improve until 1844.[74] Subscriptions to abolitionist newspapers fell, lecturers found it harder to raise money, and antislavery organizations found they had to cut back on agents. Few societies could count on donations to cover their expenses. Antislavery fairs emerged as one of the largest sources of income for antislavery societies, and thus also sites of contention, negotiation, and competition for resources. Fairs brought the divisions within the antislavery movement home to local female societies. As they debated where to send the proceeds of their labor, they inevitably had to debate the same issues that had divided the national organizations.

As the organizer of the most profitable antislavery fair in the nation, the Boston FASS had the largest proceeds to distribute. Deciding whether to support Garrison or his critics ripped the society apart. In 1838 women in twenty-nine towns had aided the Boston fair, which provided support for the Massachusetts Anti-Slavery Society.[75] In 1839 the majority of the society decided to bypass this traditional recipient, which had divided over the issues of whether the church supported slavery, whether abolitionists should engage in political action, and what the role of women should be. Instead the Bostonians would send their money to the AAS, which had remained united. One can see the competing demands within the society in the additional donations they made. To assuage the minority who strongly supported Garrison, the society designated some funds for the *Liberator,* Garrison's newspaper. For those who wanted to emphasize the links between antislavery and women's traditional benevolent work, the society continued to allocate money for the Samaritan Asylum, an orphanage supported for many years by the Boston FASS.[76]

This attempt at harmony failed. The minority who supported Garrison included almost all the women who had previously organized and controlled the fair and they were incensed at this interference by the majority of less active members. They decided to hold a separate "Fair of Individuals" in October, prior to the traditional December fair. This marked the beginning of a series of dual fairs in Boston. When the society divided in 1840, the reconstituted Boston FASS would hold its long-standing fair for the Garrisonian faction, while the rival MFES held a fair to benefit the more conservative A&FAS.[77]

The MFES members found themselves in a difficult position. Many had deeply felt scruples against fairs and had deliberately not become involved in the Boston fair in previous years. Yet their male counterparts needed money and counted on them to provide it. Limited in their commercial connections or business acumen, the evangelical women turned to what they knew—local religious and reform leaders and the model of discreet benevolent sales. The women counted on ministers to advertise the fair and asked evangelical abolitionists at the AAS to provide an official endorsement. Yet, despite this assistance from men, the women advertised their fairs as showcases of female contributions to the cause.

The MFES women wrote to female antislavery societies throughout Massachusetts and in England in order to solicit contributions. In keeping with their discomfort concerning "frivolous" or vanity fairs, they focused on simple goods, stressing the usefulness and moral purity of the contributions, and limiting the number of fancy or decorative goods unless they had a particular moral message. The women's first fair showed their inexperience and raised slightly less than two hundred dollars. In later years they would be more successful, raising over eight hundred dollars at their 1841 fair, with an additional six hundred dollars collected at affiliated fairs held around the state. Yet these women were never wholly comfortable with fairs as a form of fund-raising; they "accustomed" themselves "to the profitable method of holding fairs" at the request of their brethren. Within a few years antislavery women affiliated with the A&FAS ceased holding fairs in Boston at all.[78]

Those Boston women who supported an equal role for antislavery women had long been the main organizers of the Boston Fair. In 1839 they simply continued their highly successful efforts. In order to discredit the rival fair, Maria Weston Chapman and others wrote to all the female antislavery societies in the state asking them to support the Boston FASS October fair rather than the MFES December fair. Chapman drew on her extensive connections in England to encourage continued British contributions and to excoriate the MFES women. The Boston FASS women helped organize and run fairs in surrounding communities such as Lowell, Lynn, New Bedford, and Worcester in order to utilize donations not sold in or contributed too late to Boston. These raised additional funds for their side of the cause. The Boston FASS fairs were more sumptuous, elaborate, worldly affairs than the austere sales held by the MFES women and were major social events for the abolitionist community. While run entirely by women, the Boston FASS fairs had a commercial orientation that often had little to do with woman's traditional sphere or responsibilities.[79]

The divisions within Boston produced a ripple effect in surrounding communities as the two sides competed for donations and support. Women who had previously been united into a broad and geographically widespread network around Boston now divided into two competing groups. The Stoneham (MA) FASS and Lynn FASS sent goods to the old organization October fair, along with expressions of support for the Garrisonian side. The Cambridge (MA) FASS sided with the MFES women, possibly due to a family relationship between two of their members. Previously all three had donated to the united Boston FASS fair. Women in New Bedford decided not to support either side in 1839. They preferred to make and sell their articles locally and then spend the money locally. The women of Dorchester officially supported the Boston FASS fair but agreed to allocate funds according to the request of the donor.[80]

Most societies found themselves unable to make a unified response or a creative compromise, since the conflicted debates over fair goods substituted for similarly difficult debates on affiliation. The female society in Boylston donated its goods to the Garrison-supporting October fair, despite the contrary wishes of a minority of the organization. The next spring a member and her husband, the local minister, challenged this decision. Faced with the threat of complete division as had happened in Boston, a member of the Boylston society wrote to Maria Weston Chapman wondering if they should simply purchase antislavery publications and distribute them locally instead of contributing to future fairs. The Andover FASS sent their goods to the MFES December fair. However, a few members were so upset by this decision they left and formed a new society, which would continue to support the Boston FASS fair.[81]

Many societies were confused by the complexity of the issues involved and needed some guidance. Elizabeth Chase of Fall River felt that an agent to explain the divisions would be a great help. As she wrote: "I do think it very important that some suitable woman should visit Female A. S. Societies in Massachusetts. Judging from the state of things in our society in Fall River, I do believe that when no open division has taken place, there is much diversity of opinion among the women, on the subjects which so divide and distract in Boston. . . . The Mass. women need talking to, and it can best be done by a woman." Chase was partly responding to the agency of Martha Ball, a member of the original Boston FASS who seceded to join the MFES. The majority of the Boston FASS had hired her in late 1839 to tour Massachusetts and form female sewing societies. These groups, a form of female antislavery society that would become increasingly common in the 1840s, would meet regularly to sew for the fair. Elizabeth Chase wanted an "old organization" or Garrisonian woman to counter Ball's organizing, which openly advocated for the A&FAS side of the debate. It seems this did not happen, and most societies had to make their decisions as best they could in the absence of an agent to explain the divisions.[82]

These divisions were not limited to the Boston area, and contributors to other fairs faced similar questions of loyalty throughout this period. In early 1839 the Concord FASS decided to hold a fair for the support of a New Hampshire abolitionist newspaper, the *Herald of Freedom*. Until that point the society had managed to avoid the divisions occurring in other societies. As the president of the society wrote: "The differences which have been disturbing the brethren, have never been manifested in our female society, but we have as yet, had no test questions before us." This was not wholly true. Women in New Hampshire had been forced to choose which "Monthly Concert of Prayer" to attend since 1837, when the united gathering divided into competing prayer nights, each sponsored by a particular religious denomination. Thus each month women had to make public statements regarding where their antislavery sympathies lay. Unity within the society had held, however, and in 1840 abolitionists in Concord began to hold "Free Concerts" where antislavery sympathizers could attend and pray regardless of religious affiliation. The issue of how to appropriate the fair's profits proved a more contentious "test question," which prompted extensive debate among the Concord society members. They eventually decided to support the Boston FASS.[83]

Given the enormous financial potential in antislavery fairs, the Salem FASS embarked on an ambitious plan to create unity and closer ties among all the female antislavery societies of Essex County (MA). While county societies were common in the western states of Ohio and Illinois, the greater density of both women and towns had made this less necessary in the East. However, the Salem women saw advantages in regional affiliations of women. These could promote a broader sense of collaboration and community while developing interest in and donations for the county antislavery fair held in Salem by the Salem FASS. Therefore in June 1839 the Salem FASS commissioned Mrs. Abigail B. Ordway as their agent and sent her on a tour of all the towns of Essex County. Ordway's mission was to arouse and energize the women of the area, form female antislavery societies wherever possible, and develop interest in contributing to antislavery fairs. Salem's proximity to Boston often meant they were competing among the same societies for goods. Ordway found that most women preferred to support a local fair, to see directly the effects of their handiwork and thus were quite receptive to supporting an Essex County antislavery fair at Salem. Ordway received expressions of support and actual donations of goods from associations and individuals in at least sixteen and probably eighteen towns. The West Newbury Society also donated money to the Salem treasury to make their president a life member of the Salem FASS, an action that set up a continuing relationship between the two societies.[84]

Ordway did not find the trip an easy one, noting that "the disagreeables far exceed the agreeables on such a route." The divisions among abolitionists, which appeared with particular virulence in Massachusetts, were a problematic "disagreeable." Ordway tried to compromise between the two sides by encouraging women who donated goods to the Essex County fair to specify where they wanted the avails of their donations sent, whether to the Garrisonian AAS or the new A&FAS. This did not sit well with Ordway's fellow society members, who were strong supporters of the AAS and officially affiliated with them. Ordway defended her actions in an explanatory letter: "in my official capacity, I have advocated neither the one or the other; and I have recommended to all, to say nothing *at all,* about the difficulties existing in the men's societies." Ordway felt strongly that the divisions were a battle among the men that need not disrupt women's contributions to the cause. Some of her contributors, however, did not agree and would engage in extensive correspondence to ensure their donations were appropriated to their preferred side in the cause.[85]

While Ordway's correspondence regarding her tour is incomplete, she lectured in at least twenty-two towns, which included lectures to seven mixed-sex antislavery societies and eight female antislavery societies. At a time when some women were leaving female societies to join with men, she helped women in two mixed-sex societies leave and form their own female organization. She also assisted unaffiliated women in one other town to form a new female antislavery society. As of her last letter, she had plans to lecture in six more towns, thus completing her commission to meet with women in every town of Essex County except Lynn. Ordway's organizational assistance, mentoring, and community-building enabled women in Essex County to form united societies when many societies were dividing and to coordinate their efforts into a tight network of fair contributors.[86]

Ordway's efforts also led to the formation of the Women's Anti-Slavery Conference of Essex County in the summer of 1839. Made up of women from nine female antislavery societies in the county, the conference met quarterly to coordinate their efforts. Electing a secretary and president for each meeting, and rotating these offices among the various member societies, the group pledged itself to support the old organization. The women sent records of their proceedings to the *Liberator* to "encourage and strengthen others" by news of their formation and activities. By early 1840, the group had forty-five official members, and between thirty-five and fifty people attended each quarterly meeting. Reports from local societies indicated that "the conference had a salutary influence upon the local societies; that since its formation, their meetings had been much better attended. Greater zeal was manifested, and, in some instances, more [members] were added." These women would continue to meet through the late 1840s, providing a new level of collaboration for antislavery women in that area and a way to counteract the withering influence that division had had on women's cooperation.[87]

The Problems of Growth and the Start of Decline

The divisions among women's societies in this period can partly be seen as growing pains accompanying success. The Boston FASS had grown from its original 12 members in 1833 to a remarkable 550 women in 1838, representing a varied array of religious affiliations, economic classes, and antislavery commitments. In 1838 Abby Kelley had complained: "Abolition is becoming so popular, that we even now begin to experience the weights of *new professors* bearing us down and clogging the free circulation of the vital principle. Can there not be some test of genuine abolition?" Kelley's complaint came before the 1838 mob in Philadelphia and overestimated abolition's popularity. However, although exact numbers are difficult to come by, membership in antislavery societies did rise through at least 1839. Abolitionists had been concerned about the commitment level of their members from the very beginning. Boston women had encouraged many of their correspondents not to worry about adding lots of members but to focus on adding members with a deep commitment to the cause. Kelley's complaint reflected her concern that newer converts did not have the same level of commitment as those who had joined in the earlier days of unpopularity and violence.[88]

Yet these newer members were beginning numerically to dominate some antislavery societies. When divisions appeared within a society, the newer members were more likely to turn the society toward the "new organization," with its less contentious definitions of woman's role and strong support for religious organizations. An affiliation with the A&FAS often meant increased memberships for a female antislavery society, since it made clear that the society would be involved in benevolent work and would avoid the anticlerical and woman's rights stances of the AAS, which put off many women otherwise interested in antislavery as a religious cause. Women in the Southboro (MA) FASS wanted to make an affiliation decision quickly after the AAS split, since a large group of women had expressed interest in joining if they aligned with the A&FAS. In Dedham, "many women never seen before" joined the society in May 1840 and promptly voted to transfer the society's affiliation from the Boston FASS to the competing MFES. The Garrisonian women preferred limited membership and a broader commitment to radical change in society.[89]

Despite the large numbers of new members in already existing societies, the organization of new female (and male) antislavery societies slowed in the East after 1837. From a high of forty-five societies founded in that year, the number of new societies formed dropped to twenty-three in 1838, fifteen in 1839 (many of which resulted from Abigail Ordway's tour through Essex County), and seven in 1840 (four of which resulted from the division of extant organizations into two). Prior to 1837 the AAS had focused particularly on forming new societies in areas where they did not exist. Mob violence and the 1837 depression forced them to concentrate their efforts in areas that already had substantial antislavery sentiment. Rather than forming new societies, they focused heavily on fund-raising for their perennially empty coffers. The AAS did not keep lists of societies after 1839, and societies may have formed during the divisions and not been recorded, but their numbers were probably very few. Many likely went the way of the society Mary Grew attempted to help found in Hartford (CT) in 1839, which quickly failed. An observer claimed that most women had apparently joined "more because their husbands were abolitionists than that they themselves felt interested." The decision to join a female antislavery society had implied a willingness to face controversy since 1833. However, women now faced attack from within the antislavery movement as well as from without, making it a much less attractive arena even for those with a deep interest in the slave.[90]

Conclusion

The divisions of this period had a mixed impact on the antislavery movement. The influx of new antislavery advocates diluted abolitionists' willingness to confront society and demand radical changes in race and gender relations. Yet the splitting of the movement into different organizations that demanded different types of commitment may have enabled it to grow far faster and have a broader, more lasting influence.[91] The divisions had a similarly mixed impact on women and their antislavery organizations. They provided crucial new opportunities, as well as tremendous loss. From 1832 to 1839 antislavery women had managed to put aside differences of race, religion, ideology, and class to work together in the battle against slavery. By 1840 public censure and the divisions among men placed too many strains on women's networks and alliances. Women had to make difficult choices among complex ideological and tactical options.

For those who believed that greater equality with men was central to their ability to fight for the slaves, the divisions opened new opportunities. The ideological connections these women made between their status and that of the slave and the struggles they experienced in their efforts to achieve equality with men were central influences in their continued focus on the rights of women. Some would pioneer new paths for women at the 1848 Woman's Rights Convention in Seneca Falls, which demanded economic and legal reforms in the status of women and called for women's right to vote. But while these "feminist abolitionists" are perhaps the best-known female abolitionists, they were not the majority. A much broader group found in the divisions a different opportunity—the chance to continue their antislavery activities outside the occasionally harsh spotlight of the public sphere. Some women chose to work more closely with male ministers and female charitable organizations as A&FAS affiliates. Other female antislavery societies quietly transformed into sewing societies, where women could make goods for fugitive slaves or for the antislavery fairs run by more public female antislavery organizations.

Thus the year 1840 was a watershed year in many ways. It marked the entry of abolitionist women into many of the previously all-male county, state, and national organizations. It also meant the end of the female antislavery conventions and national petition drives, which had united abolitionist women's efforts in the previous few years. Women had managed to maintain harmony among themselves despite increasing criticism from within and outside the antislavery movement regarding women's public advocacy for the slave. Before 1839 even debates over the role of the church, while divisive, could be smoothed over. In 1839 and 1840 the virulent debates among the men finally spilled over into women's organizations, where family relationships, race, and religion helped shape the decision of which side, and which values, the women would support. Women did not disappear from the movement after 1840. The 1840s and 1850s were a crucial period of organizing for Western female antislavery societies, black vigilance organizations, and female antislavery sewing societies. However, the divisions had escalated the sharp debate over the public, political aspects of women's antislavery organizing and had changed how women would engage in the movement in the period that followed.

CHAPTER FIVE

Transition and
Transformation, 1841–1855

Morality and Politics

"While we leave to our Fathers and Brethren in the Republic, the exciting

arena of political action, we cannot but feel that woman is appropriately

employed in aiding the cause of humanity, though so gently as to be

almost imperceptible to the multitude."

—Van Buren County (MI) Ladies Anti-Slavery Society, 1846

The 1840s and early 1850s were a period of transition for antislavery women in the East, as they searched for a role in the new antislavery landscape. The divisions had sapped the energies of many in the movement, and they wondered what to do after a decade of activism and little progress to show for it. Most female antislavery societies suffered the death of one of their leaders in the early 1840s, and increasing age and apathy rather than mob violence became their worst enemies. The rise of the Liberty Party in 1840 began an era of antislavery politics that channeled much of the movement's energies into partisan arenas in which most women had little power or influence. As the movement focused on the "the exciting arena of political action," many women's activities became, as the Michigan Ladies wrote, "almost imperceptible to the multitude."[1]

After the mobs and criticism of the previous period, it may have felt like an improvement to be imperceptible. In reality, however, women's activities were neither imperceptible nor apolitical, although they were far less unified and often less public. The divisions within the movement shattered the fragile unity among the women. Some women responded to the claims that they had left their appropriate sphere by forming antislavery sewing societies. Few acts could be perceived as more private, benevolent, and uncontroversial than sewing. Yet sewing brought the increasingly politicized issue of slavery into the center of women's domestic activities. Whereas their antislavery conventions had brought women's moral goals into the public sphere, sewing societies enabled women to engage in political actions within the privacy of their homes and churches.

Other women maintained their female antislavery societies, which continued to petition, hold lecture series, and organize other events. Most important, these FASS coordinated the efforts of many of their less public sisters into large and small antislavery fairs. These tiny local or grand international events provided a focus for women's weekly sewing meetings, a social event to draw more people into the cause, and the majority of the movement's funding. Women's fairs kept antislavery newspapers, tracts, and lecturers out among the public, spreading antislavery sentiment and creating constituents for the antislavery political parties. They strengthened the regional networks, which became increasingly important in the absence of female conventions, helping women to feel part of a larger national movement. The fairs also provided a reason to strengthen existing alliances and to create new connections with English, Scottish, and Irish women. A dozen new British female antislavery societies were formed in the 1840s, dedicated to supporting the American antislavery fairs. These would provide both financial and moral support to American women and formed the basis for later international cooperation.

This period also saw a dramatic increase in antislavery organizing by black women, who found themselves excluded from some white women's societies and found it difficult to focus on their own agenda in those societies that were interracial. Thus in some areas black women formed black female antislavery societies. Other black women formed women's organizations to support the predominantly male vigilance societies. These organizations helped fugitive slaves escape to Canada and assisted them with food, clothing, education, and other needs once they were settled. These organizations became increasingly important after the Fugitive Slave Act of 1850. Black women's efforts sometimes drew white criticism, as the two groups continued to differ on the definition of what counted as "true antislavery activism." Many white women, however, adopted black women's agenda of support for the fugitive during this period. Clothing a black person provided an immediate sense of accomplishment and the chance to aid a human being rather than fight a powerful and seemingly immovable institution. Aid to fugitives also meshed well with women's accepted role of caring for the poor and needy.

Western women integrated care for fugitives into the dozens of new female antislavery societies they formed during this period. Rather than a period of retrenchment, the 1840s in Indiana, Illinois, Michigan, and Wisconsin were a period of growth, organization, and united action, much as the 1830s had been in the East. Western women petitioned, published, resolved, sewed, convened, and read, creating networks of like-minded women across the Midwest. Far from the debates in the East and less connected to the national societies, Western women temporarily escaped the Eastern debates over woman's appropriate role. When those debates caught up with Western women, they created similar divisions and disruptions and forced Western women to search for less public means of supporting the slave. Care for fugitives continued to be one important aspect.

Thus organized female antislavery activism continued through the 1840s and 1850s, although in more varied and less unified forms. After a decade of public conventions and national petition campaigns, women returned to forms of activism more like those of the late 1820s and early 1830s. Generally renouncing partisan politics, women continued to blur the boundaries between organizations dedicated to a change in the political system and organizations dedicated to the care of the poor and needy. This blurring of the moral and political aspects of antislavery, combined with many women's removal from the public sphere, muted much of the controversy over women's role.

The blurring process was greatly aided by the increasingly prominent woman's rights movement, which helped to distract critics by providing a better target for their complaints. The process was also assisted by the growth of the Liberty, Free Soil, and Republican parties, which helped to bring antislavery agitation to the center of the political process, where women's exclusion from the vote helped to mask the political nature of their other antislavery activities. Thus, while women's activities changed during this period, the context in which they occurred also changed. By the middle of the 1850s, activities that had created controversy in the late 1830s were broadly accepted as falling within woman's appropriate sphere, despite the fact that they addressed the nation's most volatile political issue.

Antislavery women were, as the Michigan ladies perceived, "effectual as the silent rill," keeping the antislavery movement funded and keeping its newspapers, lecturers, and agents in the field. Consistent antislavery agitation eventually created antislavery legislators, a national party with an antislavery platform, and a broad constituency that rejected the extension of slavery into the territories. In the early 1840s, however, most Eastern women saw the problems, not the possibilities, in their movement. Discouraged and disgusted by the constant bickering and division, they searched for ways to reenergize and refocus their societies.

Discouragements and Deaths Take Their Toll

In the late 1830s deeply committed abolitionist women had begun to complain about the lack of dedication shown by some of their antislavery sisters. As Harriet Minot wrote about her Haverhill (MA) society in 1838: "We never needed lectures more than now. We are cold and stupid, never 'remembering those in bonds as bound with them.'" Eliza Boyce in Lynn felt that women there were in even worse shape a year later: "It is indeed a dark hour with us. Were it not for a few individuals I believe the society would long before this have disbanded." The Lynn women did not have bitter arguments as were occurring in Boston, but they found themselves fighting a more insidious problem—apathy. Boyce wrote that many members "wish well to the cause and here ends the whole matter."[2]

After the harsh words and sharp divisions of 1839–1840, female societies faced even more difficulty engaging the interest of members. The Dover (NH) society dwindled from an active society of seventy-five or eighty members to a group of about four. When the women could not agree on which side of the divisions to support, many of the original members left the antislavery movement for a while. The call for the 1841 Massachusetts fair asked for donations from societies, from towns where no societies existed and from those towns "where having a name to live [the societies] are dead." This wording makes clear the inactivity of a number of female antislavery societies.[3]

The Great Falls (NH) FASS had flourished in the 1830s. It managed to hold a fair in 1841, but by 1843 only two or three members were still active in the movement. In Providence (RI) Harriet Hale wrote to the Philadelphia FASS to get advice on reenergizing her society, since it was also struggling. "Shall we go on and tell you how thinly our regular quarterly meetings have been attended, and how few have gathered at the place of prayer to pour forth supplications to God?"[4]

This decreased dedication stemmed from numerous sources. The divisions of the previous years had taken their toll on abolitionist energy, and many felt uninspired by the sniping and arguing that now made up much of the antislavery press. Lydia Maria Child had been active in the Boston FASS since 1833 and had become the editor of the largest antislavery newspaper, the *National Anti-Slavery Standard,* in 1841. By 1843 she had had it with abolitionists' inability to work together. In a letter written just prior to her resignation as editor, she wrote that she was "forever alienated from the anti-slavery organization," in large part due to the "bad spirit" showed by abolitionists in dealing with each other. She was "weary, weary of this everlasting pulling down, and no building up." In a letter to Maria Chapman, Child asked to be taken off the list of managers for the fair as "I have retired from the anti-slavery cause altogether." Child would continue to work for the cause on her own and would eventually rejoin her friends in supporting the Boston fair. For the time being, however, she was done with associated, organized efforts.[5]

This attitude was repeated by many less prominent women, much to the dismay of their colleagues who were not yet ready to give up the cause. Harriet Webster in the Danvers (MA) FASS lamented: "Our Society is small and the number of *active* members is less *this* year than since the formation of our association. Several are so situated that they cannot consistently give us much time or labor, and others, we regret to say, manifest but little interest in the cause of 'oppressed humanity.'" Many activists were still struggling with the economic effects of the 1837 depression while others, tired of controversies within the antislavery movement, turned their attention to less controversial or more rewarding arenas. Their antislavery sisters did not respond well to what they saw as defections from the true cause.[6]

In 1843 the Essex County Female Anti-Slavery Conference rebuked those members who had left active antislavery work to remain with their churches. Founded in 1839 to unite women across the county, the conference dissolved in 1844 when a large group of women simply failed to show up. A few of the holdouts wondered why their former collaborators "who once professed to feel deeply for the slave, have embraced the delusion, that there is a work greater than helping to give deliverance to the captive." This and other comments suggest that some conference members had left antislavery for benevolent work under the aegis of the churches, and their former antislavery friends were decidedly unsympathetic. Women in Boston put a letter in the *Liberator,* encouraging antislavery women to maintain their activism and not let other causes, particularly temperance, pull them away from their work.[7]

It must have been hard to continue attending antislavery meetings where debate and dissension had replaced united, productive efforts. Some women simply chose to put their limited time and effort elsewhere, where they thought it might do more good. Martha V. Ball, a founder of the Boston FASS and officer at two Anti-Slavery Conventions of American Women, left antislavery in 1840 and became an officer and member of a variety of other moral reform causes. Many other women seem to have taken their antislavery beliefs back to their churches, some of which slowly shifted in an antislavery direction over the next decade.[8]

The loss of membership was made far worse by the deaths of prominent antislavery leaders in the early 1840s. Susan Paul had been the first black member of the Boston FASS. A year after her unexpected death from consumption in 1841, Boston lost Mary Parker, former president of the Boston FASS, former president of two Anti-Slavery Conventions of American Women, and, after the divisions, the president of the MFES. Mary Clark, the corresponding secretary and central agitator of the Concord FASS passed away in 1841, and Grace Douglass, a founding black member of the Philadelphia FASS, died in 1842. Even the tiny Danvers society lost two founding members in 1840 and 1841 and the Hallowell (ME) society lost two members in 1843.[9]

These deaths left significant leadership gaps in the antislavery organizations. The majority of the most active antislavery women had joined the movement as a cohort in the 1830s, filling leadership positions for a decade. Few women came forward to fill the gaps, with occasional exceptions. In the Boston FASS, nineteen-year-old Sarah Southwick became recording secretary in 1840 and sixteen-year-old Harriet Jackson was named treasurer in 1841. However, these additions could not compensate for the loss of women who had spent nearly a decade in the cause and had felt bound together by correspondence, conventions, criticism, and mobs.[10]

Other factors also played important roles. The continued unpopularity of the antislavery message, the previous mob attacks, and the continued lack of support from ministers all discouraged new converts to the cause.

As Elizabeth Wright wrote from Newburyport (MA): "the reason we have no more young persons in our Society is . . . because the cause of the Slave is so very unpopular in this place. . . . [N]one of our ministers are interested enough to say anything on the subject." In Leominster (MA) the minister's unwillingness to support any cause associated with William Lloyd Garrison kept his wife and fifty other women from supporting the local female anti-slavery society. Leominster women also had to deal with local opinions about woman's appropriate role. Women were told they should not fight a battle that belonged "to *men* in high office."[11]

In Ashburnham (MA) the female society was "*very low* since there has been so much said about women keeping in their 'appropriate sphere.' The hard times has without doubt done much to stop their efficient action, but not so much as the 'confounded woman question.'" The "hard times" were the lingering effects of the 1837 bank crashes and recession. As money continued to be tight, many women had to invest more time in darning socks, putting up food, and other household activities, which limited the time available for benevolent work. However, the continued debate about the proper role for women provided little encouragement for them to invest what free time they had in the antislavery cause.[12]

The rapid growth of cities may also have taken a toll on reformers' ability to hold an organization together. As the cities grew, people found it more difficult to maintain the social organizations and friendly interactions that worked well in small towns. There is some evidence that associations of all types—benevolent, reform, and simply social—declined in the 1840s. The growth of cities also sharpened ideological calls for a middle-class retreat to the privacy, safety, and sanctity of the home. A cultured retreat from the increasingly impersonal, dirty cities full of working-class people, home was to be a haven, free of politics and strife. Families became the appropriate site of woman's moral reformation of the world, rather than societies aimed at eliminating sin. This new incarnation of the separate spheres ideology continued to place women most properly in the home but elevated the home as a place of particular value to both men and women.[13]

Despite these factors, a few female antislavery societies managed to grow during the early 1840s. Growth thereafter was rare. A few of the new converts were pulled into the antislavery women's network through participation in antislavery fairs. These provided a highly structured and social arena for female action without requiring a commitment to weekly meetings. In 1842 and 1843 the calls for the Boston fair included instructions for "new friends at work." The ninth and tenth annual reports included a history and overview of the antislavery movement for "new converts." In 1844 women founded a new female antislavery society in Portsmouth (NH) that included a large number of women not previously active in the anti-slavery cause. One of the founders, a long-term abolitionist, lamented that she could rarely find articles in the antislavery press "suited to read to the novices who constitute our Ladies' Society."[14]

As Abby Kelley had worried in 1838, however, these new additions to the cause did not always have the same level of radical commitment as some earlier converts. While antislavery was not a popular reform, it no longer required a member to be willing to face a mob. As the women of Philadelphia noted: "the act of joining an Anti-Slavery Society was, in that day [1834], a test of character, which it is not now." While it was true that antiabolition violence declined after 1838, not to revive until the eve of the Civil War, the Philadelphia women were overstating the case. Abolitionists were still a tiny minority of the population, and antislavery was still not a popular cause. Yet the converts of the 1840s did seem far more comfortable in supportive, rather than leadership, roles and in activities that did not challenge conservative definitions of woman's role. In the Hallowell (ME) FASS the majority of the society rejected an 1843 annual report complimentary of William Lloyd Garrison. Most of these members were recent additions to the society. They claimed it was not proper for "any thing concerning *political* affairs to be said by a society of ladies." They also felt the report dealt too harshly with the Colonization Society, a highly conservative complaint not heard in abolitionist circles since the early 1830s. Thus few of these new converts could provide the leadership, public activism, or encouragement in the face of strife that longer-term abolitionists could.[15]

Changing Tactics and Strategies

The changing dynamics of female antislavery societies and the ideological atmosphere in which they worked led to changed tactics and strategies. Large national conventions became the province of woman's rights advocates after 1848. In that year abolitionists Lucretia Mott and Elizabeth Cady Stanton broadened their reform agenda to include demands for economic and political rights for women. Their Declaration of Sentiments was signed by both men and women and ended with the highly controversial call for female suffrage. This Seneca Falls (NY) convention was followed by an even larger national woman's rights convention in Worcester (MA) in 1850, sealing the association between conventions and women's rights.

Eastern antislavery women also ceased their large coordinated petition drives. A weariness with petitioning was already evident in 1839, when the Anti-Slavery Convention of American Women published a circular urging women to keep up the "same arduous work": the subject of petitions "has been presented to you again and again," the women wrote, "until, perhaps, some of you are as weary of it as of a 'twice told tale.'" Having seen few results for their previous efforts, the authors recognized that some activists, "are almost discouraged, and ready to say, 'We have labored in vain, we have spent our strength for naught.'"[16]

By 1840 the AAS seemed to agree. An editorial in the *National Anti-Slavery Standard,* the official newspaper of the AAS, noted: "In former years, much time, labor and money have been expended in procuring petitions. We cannot advise the same course to be pursued again, while there are other branches of the service, which yield a more prolific harvest. . . . We have thought that a useful purpose, and perhaps all that is necessary, might be answered by *societies* petitioning, as such." Over time, William Lloyd Garrison came to take a strong stand against petitioning, as being a useless interaction with a solidly proslavery government. By 1846 he felt the only petitions to Congress that had any use were ones petitioning to dissolve the Union.[17]

Many men and women disagreed with Garrison's stance. The acquisition of new Western territories excited and divided the nation, providing ample opportunities for antislavery petitions. In 1845 Texas declared its independence from Mexico and requested annexation to the United States with a proslavery constitution. Antislavery women and men promptly responded with hundreds of antiannexation petitions. The Mexican War produced another host of issues, as the United States acquired the vast Mexican Cession in the Treaty of Guadalupe Hidalgo in 1848. California's American settlers, many of whom had arrived as part of the 1849 gold rush, quickly petitioned for statehood. The application for statehood raised the question of whether California would be admitted as a free or a slave state, which would tip the balance of power in the evenly, and delicately, divided Senate.

Kentucky senator Henry Clay's attempts to maintain a working balance of power produced the Compromise of 1850. The Compromise admitted California as a free state, violating an imaginary extension of the Missouri Compromise line. It organized the other Mexican Cession territories under popular sovereignty, which allowed residents in those areas to decide whether to permit slavery when they applied for statehood. The compromise banned the slave trade, but not slavery itself, in the District of Columbia, the only area other than the territories over which Congress had direct control. In order to placate Southerners upset by these apparently antislavery moves, the Compromise of 1850 included a measure to strengthen the 1793 Fugitive Slave Law. The new act required Northerners to assist in the recapture of runaway slaves and provided financial incentives for judges to side with slaveholders who claimed Northern African Americans as fugitives.

Abolitionists were furious about many aspects of the Compromise of 1850. They were particularly angry at the continuance of slavery in the nation's capital and what they perceived as the coercive and dangerous implications of the Fugitive Slave Act. White Americans who had previously seen slavery as a Southern problem were now legally responsible to help reenslave fugitives who had made it to the North. For black Americans the Fugitive Slave Act meant freemen and slaves alike were more subject to being kidnapped and sent into slavery with a minimum of judicial proceeding. Abolitionists used petitions against the act as part of a widespread propaganda campaign to highlight Northern involvement in perpetuating slavery. The number of petitions further increased after the passage of the Kansas-Nebraska Act of 1854. This opened yet more Western territory to slavery and provided the possibility of slavery as far north as the Canadian border.

Most of these petitions, however, were no longer coordinated by female antislavery societies. The Boston FASS petitioned through 1843, and the women of the Philadelphia FASS petitioned at least every two years through 1854. As Western women formed female antislavery societies, they also petitioned in increasingly large numbers, occasionally outstripping male petitioners in the number of signatures sent in. Increasingly, however, individual women took responsibility for circulating petitions where female antislavery societies no longer existed, or they signed petitions circulated by men. With no national effort to circulate women's petitions, the overall number of female petitions to Congress and female signatures on mixed-sex petitions declined dramatically by 1850. It remained low until a new wave of female petitioning arose during the Civil War.[18]

The decline in petitions to Congress was balanced by an increase in female petitions to state legislatures regarding more local issues. The Philadelphia FASS petitioned for jury trials for black men in the state. They also circulated petitions calling for the repeal of a law that permitted slaveholders to keep their slaves in the state for six months before the slaves would be considered free. Salem FASS members petitioned the Eastern Railroad to eliminate "Jim Crow" or segregated seating arrangements. By 1844 their efforts had paid off. Massachusetts societies also continued to petition against the ban on interracial marriage in Massachusetts, despite the negative attention they received in the press and the legislature itself. They were successful in 1843, as the legislature admitted that the large number of petitioners, and their yearly persistence, helped to provoke the repeal. Rhode Island and Ohio women focused on eliminating restrictions on educational opportunities for black people. Without the national organization provided by the AAS or the Anti-Slavery Conventions of American Women, most female antislavery societies chose to refocus their petitioning on racial issues within their own states.[19]

The Growth and Influence of Antislavery Sewing Societies

In the 1840s and 1850s many women's organized contribution to the cause was not their name on paper but their stitches on cloth. Whereas in the 1830s the large petition drives had spread the antislavery message door-to-door and recruited women to the cause, in the 1840s sewing circles drew women together. As Elizabeth Chandler had pointed out in 1829: "ours is a busy fingered sex, and that society meeting merely to collect funds, and unconnected with employment of any kind, would not long be attended with interest." Sewing provided a less controversial focus for meetings than resolutions and debates, and the products of women's efforts kept the antislavery movement alive. By working together, women could aggregate their contributions into large enough amounts to make it financially and physically worthwhile to ship the goods to a fair or to a fugitive slave settlement. By contributing a discrete product and by receiving news that this product had aided a person or raised a set amount for the cause, women could maintain a stronger sense of engagement. In a period when the end of slavery seemed further away than ever, women could claim immediate returns for their efforts. In addition, sewing for the cause did not raise questions of woman's appropriate role as petitioning had done.[20]

Sewing had been an important aspect of female antislavery activism since the foundation of the first wave of societies. Members of the Lynn FASS, founded in 1835, included in their constitution the responsibility to meet *and* work, and they recorded the value of work done at each meeting in the meeting minutes. Often women founded sewing societies as adjuncts to female antislavery societies. The Ladies' Anti-Slavery Sewing Society of New York City formed just after the Ladies' New-York City Anti-Slavery Society in 1835, in order for women to devote part of their time to sewing for the cause. Like their sisters in the antislavery society, the sewing society members immediately opened correspondence with other sewing societies to share information and encouragement. They raised a third of the money donated by the Ladies' New-York City Anti-Slavery Society to the AAS in its first few years, leaving no record of any activity thereafter.[21]

In Fall River (MA) a sewing society also existed alongside the FASS and held its own meetings where women sewed, read antislavery publications, and discussed current antislavery events. Although the sewing society and FASS shared some members, the sewing society differentiated itself as a group of women "working" for the slave, presumably as opposed to simply passing resolutions. The women of Willimantic (CT) may have been attempting to emphasize the sewing aspect of their organization when they changed their name in the early 1840s. The Female Anti-Slavery Society of Willimantic began appearing in the newspaper as the Willimantic Female (Working) Anti-Slavery Society.[22]

The increasingly uncomfortable spotlight on women's public antislavery activities may have been what prompted women to found dozens of female antislavery sewing societies from 1839 onward. In that year the anti-Garrisonian women who controlled the Boston FASS suggested that the women of Massachusetts form sewing circles in all towns that lacked female antislavery societies. They hired Martha Ball as an agent to help form sewing societies in neighboring towns. The managers of the Boston fair, drawn primarily from Garrison-supporting women in the Boston society, also advocated the formation of sewing circles in 1844, as did Rhode Island and upstate New York women in their areas.[23]

This focus on sewing circles rather than antislavery societies, shared by women on both sides of the divide, may reflect the recognition that this domestic-based activity was more acceptable to a larger group of women than politically overtoned antislavery society meetings. Sewing societies may also have been more familiar and simply more fun. Gathering to sew together had long been a popular form of benevolence for churchwomen, and many women may have belonged to a church sewing circle as well as an antislavery one. This could cause conflict as women divided their time among causes that mattered to them. In early 1842 the Essex County Women's Anti-Slavery Conference felt it necessary to resolve: "That it is the duty of female aboli-tionists to encourage, by their punctual attendance, their anti-slavery soci-eties['] meetings, to the partial neglect, if need be of sectarian sewing soci-eties." But dual memberships could also result in the inclusion of antislavery work in church sewing circles, as particular members encouraged their sisters to include antislavery efforts amid their other benevolent commitments.[24]

The distinction between a female antislavery society and an antislavery sewing circle was often quite unclear. The Salem FASS had petitioned, had held lectures, and had been quite publicly active in the 1830s, but it did lit-tle except sew in the early 1840s, as it tried to figure out how best to serve the cause in the wake of the 1840 divisions. Sewing seems to have kept the women coming to meetings and working for the cause until another tactic emerged to replace it. The Hingham (MA) FASS apparently transformed into the Hingham Ladies Sewing Circle around 1843. The Portsmouth Ladies Anti-Slavery Society, founded in 1844, met weekly for "discussion and sewing." The Western New York State Anti-Slavery Society, a mixed-sex organization founded in 1842, seems to have contained within it a ladies' antislavery sewing circle. By 1848 a local newspaper noted that the West-ern New York "Ladies' Anti-Slavery Society" was meeting "to sew, knit, read, and talk for the cause" every Thursday evening. In 1851 another group of women in the same area would form the Rochester Ladies' Anti-Slavery Sewing Circle, and this too would transform into a Rochester Ladies' Anti-Slavery Society after four years of sewing and holding fairs.[25]

Many antislavery sewing societies did not limit themselves to sewing. The Boston FASS provided grants of books to women's sewing groups that wished to form an antislavery lending library. Sewing societies also occa-sionally served as sites of political engagement, since the Boston women also encouraged all "sewing and social circles, at work for the Fair, to take the opportunity to sign the petitions and memorials on slavery when they meet." The Hingham society seems to have held a public fair shortly after forming. The Loudon (NH) Anti-Slavery Sewing Society limited itself nei-ther to sewing nor to women, although women filled all the officer posi-tions and seem to have done all the actual sewing. Male members, includ-ing antislavery lecturer and debater Parker Pillsbury, presented and discussed resolutions, which may have been instrumental in the society's rapid demise only five months after it was founded in 1840.[26]

The ephemeral nature of many of these societies, which sometimes had neither constitutions nor membership lists, makes it difficult to ferret out why women chose this particular form of antislavery activity. While there are a few exceptions, most societies appear only in the donations columns of the antislavery newspapers, highlighting their important fund-raising role but giving us little information as to their motivations or meetings. In a few areas antislavery societies and antislavery sewing societies coexisted throughout the 1840s. In 1844 Worcester County (MA) had about a dozen female antislavery societies and an equal number of antislavery sewing societies. So what prompted women to favor one over the other?[27]

The founding of so many sewing societies in the wake of the antislavery divisions suggests that women may have found them to be a less controversial form of female antislavery activity. Sewing societies rarely had the formalized procedures, debates, and resolutions that had caused such dissension in female antislavery societies. Here women could concentrate their energies on making domestic goods to aid the antislavery cause. Changing the name of the organization did not necessarily mean women could *not* sign petitions, sponsor lectures, or in rare cases pass resolutions, but these were not necessarily *expected* of members of a sewing society. These different expectations may have made the groups more appealing to women eager to avoid the social abuse heaped on female antislavery societies in the 1830s.

While less formal than female antislavery societies, sewing societies did provide many of the same benefits: regular meetings, a chance to socialize, and a safe space in which to learn about and discuss political issues. Sewing societies met every week or month, thus members made a weekly or monthly commitment to work for the slave. This took greater dedication than simply putting one's name on a petition and required women to justify their efforts to friends and family who might judge their time ill-spent. The societies also gave women a sense of purpose, a sense that they were engaging in an action that made a difference in the world. Sewing societies may have appealed to women who simply wanted to do something for the cause. Producing a handmade item may have felt more fulfilling than debating the merits of political action or defending the abstract rights of women.

Sewing societies usually met in a woman's home or in a church. Both the location and the activity make sewing societies seem a world removed from the political battles of the 1840s and 1850s. Yet sewing provided women with an opportunity to bring politics into the home, as women's door-to-door petition efforts had tried to do. While their hands were busy sewing, women listened avidly to one member reading aloud about the slave child torn from its mother's arms for sale, the Southern congressman's defense of slavery, or William Lloyd Garrison's denunciation of the Constitution. Women also brought slavery into the domestic sphere when other women purchased the goods they were making. Many women sewed or stamped demands for the end of slavery directly onto their goods sold at antislavery fairs. When these items were purchased and then used in the home, they served as "tracts" to be read by the user. Women hoped these goods would not only raise money for the cause but slowly work the moral conversion that would spread a hatred of slavery and support for its eradication.[28]

The money raised by sewing societies supported antislavery tracts and lecturers. In this way sewing society members had a direct impact on the spread of antislavery information and thus helped develop an antislavery constituency. In Philadelphia the sewing society left few records, but it was central to the 1838 republication of Elizabeth Heyrick's influential free-produce pamphlet. In 1849 the Female Anti-Slavery Sewing Society of Plympton (MA) sent twelve dollars, "all we have," to reinstate Lucy Stone as a lecturer when other funds ran out. Although there were only six women in the society, they felt a deep connection between their sewing and the promulgation of the antislavery truth throughout the county. Women in Hallowell (ME) had a more direct impact on the creation of a political community, by "working with their hands" for "a political cause." They donated their fair goods to the A&FAS, which provided lecturers, pamphlets, and other support for the Liberty Party in that state.[29]

Sewing helped to build antislavery community, and the dual nature of sewing societies can be seen in how frequently they were also called "social circles." The 1846 notice of the Boston fair called on ministers to form "social circles," each of which would contribute a table of goods. The Boston women formed a "Sewing Circle," which soon became the "Social Sewing Circle" and then the "Social Circle" as it came to include men. The Boston women recognized the power of socializing to draw new workers into the cause. They suggested that sewing circles hold "working parties" for the fair, which could also be "reading-parties; tea parties; conversation parties; occasions of festivity and means of social improvement." Philadelphia women had the same insight. "Fair meetings," held every week at a different person's house, would consist of a full afternoon of sewing by the women, followed by a "picnic tea," and then social conversation when the gentlemen arrived in the evening. As one member noted: "Many young persons were induced to mingle in them, besides those who labored from love of the cause." Over time some were converted. Visiting among neighbors became an increasingly common aspect of middle-class life in the 1840s and 1850s, providing a social space to share information, conduct business, and engage in other community-strengthening activities. Sewing circles enabled women to mix moral duty, social responsibility, political engagement, and pleasure, all without challenging accepted roles for women.[30]

Antislavery Fairs

Enterprising women more comfortable with a public antislavery role built upon and encouraged the increase in sewing circles by drawing the production of these circles into antislavery fairs. As women moved away from other forms of antislavery activism after 1840, the number and variety of antislavery fairs increased dramatically. Societies that had previously held relatively small fairs held larger, more profitable events while areas that had not seen much antislavery activity in earlier periods held fairs for the first time. The coordination of women's efforts into fairs was absolutely crucial to the financial success of the antislavery movement. Women's fund-raising continued to make up a major portion of the operating funds of many societies. Yet antislavery sewing circles do not seem to have attracted as many women as other, usually church-based sewing societies. Therefore antislavery women had to raise larger sums of money per member, and they did so through diligent and coordinated effort.[31]

Many new fairs were the product of cooperation between women experienced in holding fairs and new recruits to the cause. This was the case with the 1841 New York City fair held during the AAS anniversary, which was a cooperative effort of the Manhattan Anti-Slavery Society (a mixed-sex society in New York City) and more experienced women from Boston. In 1843 Boston women also helped to run a fair in Lowell, and in 1848 Abby Kelley wrote to Maria Weston Chapman on behalf of abolitionist women in Worcester, asking if Chapman or other Boston women could come out and help Worcester women start up a fair there. Women in Rochester (NY) helped to organize an entire circuit of fairs in surrounding towns. They also opened stores in eleven villages to help dispose of goods not sold at the various fairs.[32]

In this period the strong societies and broad networks created during the 1830s helped to direct the efforts of weaker, less organized societies and the large numbers of unaffiliated women. In Boston and Philadelphia the female antislavery societies built their fairs into the central fund-raising effort in their state. In 1846 the Philadelphia fair drew most heavily on Pennsylvania women, with contributions from sixteen Pennsylvania towns, Boston, and various New England villages. The Boston fair drew more broadly, partly because of Maria Weston Chapman's incredibly prolific letter writing. By 1842, fifty-two towns were assisting the Boston fair, including three in New York, and one each in New Hampshire, Maine, Pennsylvania, and Connecticut. In 1845, fifty-three Massachusetts towns contributed, with other contributions coming from New York, New Hampshire, Maine, Connecticut, Rhode Island, Pennsylvania, Louisiana, and St. Louis, Missouri. Boston began to bill their fair as a "great national undertaking for humanity," emphasizing its nonpartisan nature, separation from politics, and sheer size. By the late 1840s the women changed its name from the Massachusetts Fair to the National Bazaar in order to emphasize its reach far beyond Massachusetts.[33]

While the larger fairs relied on contributions from smaller female societies, they also participated in a complicated circulation of goods that enabled smaller towns to hold grander fairs than they had previously thought possible. In Great Falls the divisions had seriously weakened the female antislavery society, and the women felt unable to hold a fair based solely on their own production. In 1841 they held a successful fair by combining the remnants of three other fairs. The women of Dover (NH) repeated the Great Falls' women's success with a second set of leftovers. The Rochester fair, which would eventually become quite large, began in style in 1843 with a large box of Boston fair leftovers contributed by British women in London, Cork, Dublin, Glasgow, and Liverpool. It then sputtered out, to be revived in 1846 after Rochester women again asked the women of Boston to help make the fair attractive by sending their leftovers. Women in Providence received old dresses from the Boston society to remodel into fair goods. They did so, sold many of them at the Providence fair, and then returned the remainder for sale in Boston. The Salem FASS was a crucial node in circulating goods throughout Massachusetts, ensuring that goods traveled from fair to fair until they had been sold.[34]

The uneven spread of the market revolution during this period meant that different articles sold better or worse in different places. This made the transfer of goods from one fair to another particularly useful, as long as women thought carefully about what they sent to which location. The women of Nantucket received some leftovers from the Boston fair but had to return many of them unsold. They were from Geneva, Switzerland, and were priced too high for the less affluent and more practically oriented Nantucket market. Goods could also become dirty or damaged by the constant handling they received at multiple fairs. Occasionally women noted that they could not get the price originally marked on the item because it no longer looked new. In general, though, the circulation of goods enabled women to squeeze as much money as possible out of the goods donated for any given fair.[35]

Antislavery women were justifiably proud of their financial contributions. In some years fair proceeds alone, not counting other forms of female fund-raising, provided from one-third to one-half of state society budgets, particularly in Rhode Island, Pennsylvania, Massachusetts, and New York. In New Hampshire antislavery women's fairs were wholly responsible for maintaining the antislavery weekly *Herald of Freedom*. In 1846 the Boston women stressed the importance of their fund-raising efforts by detailing the antislavery efforts funded by their fair. A tract that convinced a slaveholder to emancipate his slaves, a newspaper that convinced a politician to change his stand on slavery, a petition that produced congressional and public discussion of slavery, a corps of lecturers who undermined political opposition to slavery—all of these were funded by women's sewing, organizational labor, and fairs.[36]

Men were very aware of the financial importance of fairs. The New Hampshire *Herald of Freedom* argued that the divided men of New Hampshire had to hold a convention in 1840, "if for no other purpose than that the women may hold a Fair." The men needed the money to keep the state organization afloat. In Syracuse (NY), abolitionists wanted to extend their

1843 antislavery convention an extra day "to help the Fair along." In 1855 the Pennsylvania Anti-Slavery Society moved its annual meeting to the time of the fair "to take advantage of the extensive public interest in anti-slavery matters during this time of the year." The AAS regularly thanked women for contributing their labor and their goods to fairs, recognizing that without women the movement would be crippled for lack of funds.[37]

While fairs were primarily fund-raising events, they also served an important social role. Fairs enabled abolitionists to listen to lectures, shop for New Year's and Christmas presents, or have tea and cookies with friends. The Boston women called their fair "a social anti-slavery exchange," to which people came in order to feel a part of the larger community of anti-slavery, meeting people they had only corresponded with as well as long-time friends from the movement's earlier days. Woman's rights activist Susan B. Anthony attended the Worcester antislavery bazaar in 1855 eager to catch up with friends she had not seen in a while: "I suppose there were many beautiful things exhibited, but I was so absorbed in the conversation . . . that I really forgot to take a survey of the tables."[38]

Once divisions had split the antislavery movement, fairs provided an important unifying alternative to conventions. In 1843 the Boston FASS invited women interested in aiding the fair to come to the New England Anti-Slavery Convention. They suggested women could attend the convention for "consideration of principles" and then come to the fair-planning meetings for the practical application of those principles. In 1846 Garrison noted that fairs appealed to those "who cannot bear the severity of anti-slavery conventions." By this he may have meant the endless debates over tactics, attacks on the church, and other divisive issues. Fairs enabled antislavery women to meet, share strategies, and discuss their societies. They provided a regional replacement for the national conversations that had previously occurred at the Anti-Slavery Conventions of American Women in the 1830s.[39]

The role of the fair as a social counterpart to conventions may have grown out of women's common role of providing refreshments at antislavery conventions. In 1838 the men of Hingham thanked the ladies for serving refreshments at a convention in that town. They recommended that women in other towns take up the practice as an excellent way to engage in the cause without causing controversy. This aspect of female engagement became a little more common in the 1840s. At the same time women began to integrate soirees or tea parties into their fairs, often to provide a culminating event to a three- or four-day fair. When fairs were held at the same time as conventions, this provided a more informal and relaxed opportunity to meet friends and discuss the issues of the day. Soirees also enabled women to charge delegates admission to the fair and a price for the refreshments, turning what would have been a convention service into a fund-raising event.[40]

Fairs provided a chance for abolitionists to educate those not yet committed to the cause and reenergize those who needed encouragement. For people new to the cause, fairs provided organizers with a friendly opportunity to explain misconceptions about abolition and remove objections to it. Even the banners decorating the halls could impart the central beliefs of the movement and awaken sympathy for the slave. For older hands, fairs provided a focus for women's weekly meetings and a central event to help keep antislavery activism alive in an area. Boston women encouraged their collaborators to hold local fairs in order to "abolitionize" their townsmen. In 1843 the Boston women sent a letter to the Essex County Female Anti-slavery Conference asking each member to "make herself the nucleus of anti-slavery effort in her own town." They hoped that each woman's efforts would revive antislavery spirits "through the efforts to collect articles" for the fair. Recognizing that fairs were a source of funds, community spirit, energy, and education, numerous antislavery societies passed resolutions calling on women (or in some cases, women and men) to form sewing societies and organize fairs.[41]

The Transatlantic Women's Network

One of the major factors in the success of the fairs of the 1840s and 1850s was the financial and psychological power of the transatlantic network of female antislavery societies. English women had been an early inspiration to American female abolitionists, providing an example of how to organize and a language in which to defend female antislavery activity. In the 1840s American women returned the favor by encouraging the formation of at least a dozen new British female antislavery societies. In 1841 women in Glasgow created a FASS specifically to "obtain and transmit contributions of ladies' work to the Anti-Slavery Bazaar." Other societies rapidly emerged in Belfast, Ulster, Edinburgh, Perth, Cork, Bridgewater, and elsewhere.[42]

Women in these societies sewed and solicited thousands of dollars' worth of goods for the American fairs. Richly embroidered baby robes, caps, bonnets, ladies stockings, slippers, shirts, and aprons joined contributions of decorative, natural, and artistic items in boxes or barrels shipped to America. The quality and novelty of the British goods helped the antislavery fairs, particularly in Boston, attract a wealthier and more powerful class of people, spreading antislavery sentiment among those less likely to have attended an antislavery lecture or convention. Longtime fair worker Sarah Southwick believed that the fairs "became noted for having wares that were to be found in no Boston shops, and the first importation of many articles of merchandise was in the shape of gifts to our fairs." Chapman emphasized the impact of the British articles when she wrote to her Glasgow contributors: "The beauty and costliness of the articles drew great crowds. I could not say too much of the impression they produced. It really was an efficacious anti-Slavery instrumentality."[43]

British women's efforts also gave psychological support to American women, making them feel part of an international effort to eradicate slavery. In 1849 the Glasgow (Scotland) Female Anti-Slavery Society sent not only fair goods but also a memorial of forty-five thousand signatures urging the free women of America to exert themselves to abolish slavery. "The money is a most welcome aid to the cause," wrote Maria Chapman, "but the sympathy and encouragement operate for its benefit and advancement more strongly still."[44]

While crucial to the prominent women who organized and ran fairs, British financial support of American antislavery fairs may actually have undermined others' willingness to work for the cause. Rural American women found it difficult to value their contributions against the exotic and upper-class fashions being sent over from Great Britain. Lydia H. Earle of Worcester felt her society's contributions seemed particularly small and unimportant compared to the "variously beautiful and expensive articles, from so many different parts of the world, with which you are favor'd for the occasion." This type of letter may have prompted Maria Weston Chapman's opinion in 1847 that American women were "being dormant, & reposing upon the labours of others."[45]

The stability of the transatlantic network was challenged in the late 1840s, as the divisions that had wracked American abolitionist unity in the late 1830s finally made their way into British discussions. In 1846 the newly formed Ulster FASS put out a call for goods for both the Liberty Party and the Boston FASS fair, a call that raised eyebrows and tempers among the decidedly antipartisan Boston women. The Glasgow FASS, which had supported the Boston fair for almost a decade, found itself challenged by a splinter organization, the Glasgow Female Association for the Abolition of Slavery. This group rejected the Boston society fair as supporting the increasingly anticlerical William Lloyd Garrison. Instead they devoted their efforts to the support of the New York Vigilance Committee, which aided escaping slaves on their way to Canada. A similar division occurred in Edinburgh where the Edinburgh Ladies Emancipation Society withdrew support from Boston and focused their attention instead on the A&FAS efforts.[46]

These divisions among the British societies reflected the continuing divisions among American antislavery factions. As visitors from the various factions visited Britain, they advocated for their own cause and tried to direct women's efforts into particular channels. The power of personal visits is reflected in the number of female antislavery societies formed in the wake of Frederick Douglass's and William Lloyd Garrison's visits in 1846. It was also made clear by prominent English abolitionist Anna Richardson, in response to a request for help from the Philadelphia FASS bazaar committee. Richardson regretfully declined to support the Philadelphia women, explaining that she was already committed to the Boston and Rochester fairs. She made clear that preferential support of these two fairs was due to personal connections more than anything else. "The reason, my friends, that the Rochester and Boston bazaars have been helped more than your own, has been (I imagine) simply for their having been personal advocates of those bazaars in this country, who as they move about naturally gathered up friends and clients whom they set to work on behalf of an object immediately interesting them."[47]

As the Philadelphia women considered sending their own agent to Great Britain to drum up support for their fair, women in both Boston and Philadelphia began to think about uniting their efforts. Not since the Anti-Slavery Conventions of American Women had female abolitionists discussed a central committee or other form of bringing their efforts into closer coordination. However, the divisions were clearly confusing British women, and a united antislavery fair might mitigate the damage done by dissension, acrimony, and competition. United efforts might also dispel some of the misperceptions that were arising as female abolitionists worked in separate regional circles and did not come together as they once had. Maria Weston Chapman seems to have initiated the discussion, prompted partly by the desire for a united front and partly by the hope that she might thereby honorably relieve herself of the increasingly heavy burden of the Boston fair. She also hoped it would end what she thought of as jealousy on the part of the Philadelphia women. Chapman clearly thought the Boston fair far superior to what she termed the "provincial" Philadelphia fair, and her attitude may have undermined any cooperation from the beginning.

In the end both Boston and Philadelphia women rejected the potential merger. The Boston women reacted strongly against the proposal: "We do not think it will do at all," wrote Anne Warren Weston. "We all cried out with one voice that we should rather do all we did last year twice over than undertake it at Philadelphia." They felt it would be too hard to transfer local support for the fair to Philadelphia, and they were determined that the funds raised by any fair should go to the Massachusetts Anti-Slavery Society, the AAS, and William Lloyd Garrison. The Philadelphia women saw more clearly than those in Boston that Garrison turned off a number of potential donors, and they thus gave their support to free-labor efforts and the Pennsylvania Anti-Slavery Society. British women seem to have been under the inaccurate but useful impression that Philadelphia women were supporting the A&FAS or the Liberty Party, which made them an attractive alternative for those unwilling to donate to Boston. By mid-1852 the Philadelphia women would have their own agent, Sarah Pugh, in England. Soon thereafter Bostonians Maria Weston Chapman and her sister Anne Warren Weston would both visit that country to strengthen friendships and solicit new donations.[48]

Women in Rochester also created important transatlantic links among antislavery women. The Rochester Ladies' Anti-Slavery Sewing Society (RLASS) began in August 1851 to sew for fugitive slaves. There had previously been both black and white female antislavery societies in the town, but they had disbanded in the wake of the divisions and there was "no concert of action" among women from 1842 on. Hoping to avoid the divisiveness that had ended the previous societies, the Rochester ladies made clear they *"did not deem it a duty* to make an election between *old* and *new* organization,—'Liberty Party' or 'Free Soil,' but preferred to assume an independent position."[49]

Unlike most societies founded in the 1830s, the RLASS constitution drew far more heavily on the Declaration of Independence and the U.S. Constitution than on religious motivations for ending slavery. The political nature of slavery was far more clear now than it had been twenty years earlier. The women did not advocate political action, however. Rather, they committed themselves to fund-raising, fairs, and helping fugitive slaves. The women strongly advocated the formation of antislavery sewing societies in every "town, village and neighborhood" in western New York. They organized an extensive fair that drew together contributions from American sewing societies and from women in England. In their first year the Rochester women received contributions from Cork, Belfast, Manchester, Birmingham, Bridgewater, and Penkeith in Britain and Ireland.[50]

The Rochester women were able to solicit such wide support from Britain for two reasons. First, they had dedicated a portion of their funds to the support of Frederick Douglass's *North Star* newspaper. Douglass's 1846 tour of England had won him extensive support there, on which the Rochester women capitalized. The secretary of the society, Julia Griffiths, was herself an English woman. She had come to Rochester in 1849 and was soon Frederick Douglass's editorial assistant at the *North Star*. Her connections had brought beautiful items to the fairs run by the women of the mixed-sex Western New York State Anti-Slavery Society, until Griffith helped to found the RLASS in 1851. Over the next decade Griffith's extensive correspondence and travels in England would result in the formation of at least a half-dozen female antislavery societies there. She also secured donations from almost a dozen British female societies and another half-dozen mixed-sex organizations, making the Rochester fair a highly successful fund-raising enterprise.[51]

A New Focus: Assisting Fugitive Slaves

While fairs were the most public and well-documented aspect of female antislavery activity after 1840, care for fugitive slaves became increasingly important. In the 1830s many female antislavery societies had balanced a focus on the elimination of the institution of slavery with an attention to the direct and immediate needs of slaves and freed black people. This was particularly true of the few societies with black female members and officers. The female antislavery societies in Salem, Boston, and Philadelphia all donated some of the money they raised to the education or physical care of Northern black people.[52]

The divisions over woman's appropriate role in the movement prompted more white women to turn their attention to this aspect of antislavery activity. In 1840 the female antislavery societies of both Milford

(NH) and Dorchester (MA) sent funds directly to the fugitive slave communities in Canada, rather than supporting antislavery fairs. In 1841 the Boylston FASS members requested that the profits from their donations to the Boston fair be sent to the New York Vigilance Committee. They had read in the *Liberator* that the committee desperately needed funds to support fugitives in Canada. The Reading (MA) society appropriated money for Canada schools for fugitive slaves for the first time in July 1840 and sent the remainder of their treasury to the New York Vigilance Committee in December of that year. They continued to support both the Vigilance Committee and schools for fugitive slaves in Canada through 1849. The timing of these donations suggests that women were searching for an alternative to antislavery fairs in a period when donating to fairs was prompting harsh debate and internal divisions.[53]

Unfortunately women's donations prompted a new series of debates. The *National Anti-Slavery Standard* took the Milford women to task, claiming that "moneys contributed to aid the escape of fugitive slaves—or to buy slaves out of bondage—or to provide schools for those who have escaped into Canada, or the like, do not seem to come within the scope of our Society policy." A Canadian mission agent argued that the New Hampshire women had responded appropriately to a call on their benevolent nature as they provided care for the needy. The editor of the *Standard* maintained his insistence that, while women should individually support freed slaves, their organizational focus should be on ending slavery more broadly. Women in Weymouth and Braintree reinforced this opinion when they resolved in 1843 that aid to the Canada Mission provided only "collateral benefit" to the antislavery cause, and they protested "against the doctrine, that by laboring for this Mission, any portion of duty to the slave is discharged."[54]

Despite the debate, thank-you cards from Canadian Mission agents in the *Liberator* make clear that women continued to aid the Mission both individually and through society donations well into the 1850s. The Rochester Ladies' Anti-Slavery Society listed aid to fugitive slaves in their constitution. In 1854 they aided 50 fugitive slaves and by 1858 were aiding over 150 per year. This dramatic increase in support for fugitives suggests that, for a sizable number of societies, benevolent work for fugitives reemerged in this period as an important alternative to petitions, conventions, and even antislavery fairs.[55]

Black Women's Antislavery Agenda

Aid to fugitive slaves brought some white women closer to the goals black women had championed from their earliest antislavery activity. Black men and women had consistently articulated a more complex understanding of the relationship between free black people and slaves, partly out of recognition of the fine line that often separated the two. The 1793 Fugitive

Slave Law permitted masters to seize, without a warrant, any African American suspected of being a slave. If the master proved to the court's satisfaction that the person was in fact a slave, the judge would remand the person over to the master. The alleged slave could not testify on his or her own behalf, could not present witnesses, and could not demand a jury trial. This act—though never well enforced—technically put all free black people at risk of legalized kidnapping and made them much more sensitive to the need for antislavery activism than the white majority.

Beginning in the late 1830s African American men and women began to form vigilance associations, which provided food, shelter, and clothing to fugitive slaves as they blended into Northern free black communities or continued on their way to Canada. The New York Committee of Vigilance formed in 1835 and for four years aided approximately 335 fugitives a year. It would reorganize as a more interracial organization in 1847. The Philadelphia Vigilance Committee formed in 1838 and aided a similar number of fugitives during its six years, while its successor, the General Vigilance Committee, continued the work into the late 1850s. In 1842 the New England Freedom Association formed in Boston and the Colored Vigilance Committee formed in Detroit. After 1850 new societies formed in Cleveland, Albany, and Syracuse.[56]

Black women played central roles in these organizations. In Boston two of the seven directors of the organization were women, and in Cleveland women made up four of nine committee members. However, black women's major responsibility, like that of white women, was fund-raising. Black women's commitment to vigilance work may explain their absence from white sewing circles and fairs. In New York black women formed the Colored Female Vigilance Committee in 1841, held their own vigilance fairs, and participated in cent-a-week fund-raising programs. Philadelphia women formed the Female Vigilance Association to support the men's work. Founded by black members of the Philadelphia FASS in 1838, the Female Vigilance Association raised funds in the black community. In 1841 they also began to ask the Philadelphia FASS for support.

When black women asked their white counterparts for support of fugitives, two conflicting agendas became clear. The Philadelphia FASS returned a mixed response to the women's first query, resolving to "more efficiently . . . bear in mind the wants of the Vigilance Committee" but refusing to provide a general donation. They would only provide funds on a case-by-case basis. Despite this hesitancy, the Philadelphia FASS donated twenty dollars in 1841, fifty dollars in 1842, thirty-five dollars in 1843, and ten dollars in 1845, largely due to persistent requests from black Philadelphia FASS and Female Vigilance Association member Hetty Reckless.[57]

White Philadelphia women were quite divided over whether aid to the fugitives counted as true antislavery work. In 1842 they recommended that those "who are not numbered among abolitionists, whose sympathies are freely given to the flying captive" should give aid to the vigilance committee. They recognized that many women unwilling to support abolition generally could not withhold sympathy or aid after hearing the terrible stories of slaves who had chosen to run. In 1846 the women again debated the value of vigilance associations and "how far these mere branches of the Anti-Slavery cause had claims on abolitionists for their support." The wording makes clear that vigilance associations were still seen by Philadelphia's white female abolitionists as appendages to the true cause, potential distractions from the main goal of fighting slavery.[58]

This sense persisted into the 1850s, when general public sympathy for fugitives and anger at slaveholders dramatically expanded after the passing of the Fugitive Slave Act. Part of the Compromise of 1850, the act strengthened the 1793 Fugitive Slave Law while also implementing new procedures that made it easier to return slaves while making any assistance to those slaves highly illegal. Given this sympathy, Lucretia Mott felt it crucial to focus antislavery activity not on individual fugitives but on the system that permitted new potential fugitives to be born into slavery every day. The main goal of antislavery societies had to be "to destroy the system, root and branch, to lay the axe at the root of the corrupt tree." Everything else was "not proper anti-slavery work." Not everyone agreed with Mott. In 1846 longtime white activist Esther Moore resigned her membership in the Philadelphia FASS, since "she was much more interested in the Vigilance Com[mittee] operations and such like departments of the cause." Mott's views were echoed by Abby Kelley Foster, however, in the same year as Moore's departure. Foster wrote that many sewing societies in her area "aid fugitives and schools and asylums for the free," but these were not "the *real* work."[59]

Conflict between white and black women's organizational agendas and prejudice within interracial antislavery societies had led black women to form their own antislavery societies even prior to this period. Black Nantucket women formed a Female Colored Union Society in 1838, while black women long unwelcome in the Ladies' New-York City Anti-Slavery Society founded the Manhattan Abolition Society in 1840. Prejudice did not decrease in the 1840s. One of the founders of the Leominster (MA) FASS, founded in 1843, complained that fifty ladies would have joined the society but they disliked her relationship with local African Americans. "They thought the blacks should have their place and keep it," she wrote. The Rochester sewing circle lost numerous members when they chose to admit African Americans.[60]

By the end of the 1840s prominent black antislavery activist and escaped slave Frederick Douglass was denouncing the patronizing attitude of white abolitionists and staking out a position on political action that was quite opposed to that of his former mentor William Lloyd Garrison. This conflict, as well as rising nationalist sentiment in the African American community, prompted black women to take to their own road. In New York City black women founded the North Star Association in 1849 to support Frederick Douglass's Rochester newspaper, the *North Star.* In Philadelphia black women formed the Women's Association in 1849, which combined antislavery work, aid to the *North Star,* and assistance to fugitive slaves. Their first meeting was addressed by Martin Delaney, a prominent black nationalist, who focused on the "elevation of our people" as the women's most central goal. At least five of these women maintained dual membership in the Women's Association and the Philadelphia FASS. White Philadelphia FASS members did help the black women with a fund-raising fair for the *North Star* in 1851. This cooperation suggests that some divisions between black and white women were amiable differences of focus rather than unwillingness to cooperate. Similar cooperation occurred between the newly formed black female Union Anti-Slavery Society and white antislavery women in Rochester in 1850. The women collaborated to produce a vast antislavery festival in honor of George Thompson's return to the United States.[61]

The independent black women's organizations disappear from the historical record in both Rochester and Philadelphia after 1851. Yet white women in both those cities continued to support Douglass's *North Star* newspaper, and women elsewhere continued their contributions to fugitive slaves. White women in England stepped in to provide extensive funding to vigilance committees across the United States. The Glasgow Female New Association for the Abolition of Slavery, the Edinburgh Ladies' New Anti-Slavery Association, the Edinburgh Ladies Emancipation Society, and numerous others sent funds to vigilance associations in Philadelphia, New York, Rochester, Syracuse, and Delaware.[62]

Many of these donations were motivated not so much by black women's efforts to direct white women's antislavery activity but rather by the previous divisions within the antislavery movement. One of the most prominent white anti-Garrisonians, Charles Torrey, had been instrumental in founding the interracial Boston Committee of Vigilance. He traveled to England specifically to solicit female support for the endeavor. "New organization" or anti-Garrisonian women tended to support these organizations, seeing their work as part of women's traditional efforts to help the poor, neglected, or needy. However, black women's tireless efforts to combine antislavery activity with aid to fugitives provided a constant encouragement to white women on both sides of the Atlantic to broaden their vision of antislavery activity.

Western Female Antislavery Societies

While white Eastern women refocused their efforts on sewing, fairs, and fugitive slaves, Western antislavery women experienced an organizational boom in the 1840s. Sixteen new female societies were formed west of Ohio between 1841 and 1847, mirroring the dramatic Eastern growth of a decade before. Western women's experience seems to have paralleled that of Eastern women. Both had a short but highly productive period of organization and activism followed by a crisis over woman's appropriate role, and then a fading, but not complete loss, of women's independent organizations. However, Western women seem to have engaged in far more work for fugitive slaves from the beginning of their organizations and to have dealt with political antislavery earlier in their existence than their Eastern sisters.

Since 1800 New Englanders had been migrating to the Northwestern Territories in search of new opportunities. Ohio, Indiana, and Illinois received a steady influx of Yankee settlers for decades. The rate of emigration increased after the opening of the Erie Canal in 1825, which connected New England's burgeoning urban markets with the farmland of the Midwest. Michigan experienced tremendous population growth, particularly in the flush years just prior to the Panic of 1837. Minnesota's population tripled every decade from a lonely 103 people in 1800 to a respectable 42,203 in 1850. The Midwestern region as a whole added 4 million people between 1800 and 1860.[63]

While foreign immigrants made up a portion of that population growth, New Englanders dominated the area numerically and culturally. This gave the Midwest its nicknames of "Greater New England" and the "Yankee West." Communal institutions and market economics dominated the region, and most migrants continued to have family connections in the East. Like their New England counterparts, the majority of the settlers were Presbyterians, Congregationalists, and Baptists. Community development occurred as soon as an area had sufficient population to support churches, political parties, and social organizations.[64]

A few women were active in the antislavery cause prior to the major growth of the 1840s. In Prairie Village (WI) the female moral reform society, founded in 1834, raised funds to help free slaves as one of their benevolent activities. In Michigan women had been founding members of the Rum Raisin Anti-Slavery Society, one of the first Western antislavery societies. However, only in Indiana did women form female antislavery societies prior to 1840.[65]

The rapid rise in both male and female antislavery societies after 1840 may have resulted partially from the AAS support of numerous agents and conventions in the area. Turning away from the fractured and divided East, the AAS turned to the relatively untapped Western states in the 1840s, where agents and fund-raisers reported extensive antislavery sentiment among these transplanted New England freehold farmers. Between 1841 and 1847 women formed seven new societies in Illinois, two in Indiana, four in Michigan, and three in Wisconsin.

Western women's experiences seem to have been quite similar to those of Eastern women, while challenging the traditional chronology of women's antislavery activism. Western female antislavery activism grew out of the same religious enthusiasm that swept the East, with some female societies arising directly out of prayer meetings. The women justified their actions by reference to their religious responsibilities to pray for the oppressed and to speak for the silenced, as well as their responsibilities as women for the welfare of slave women. This gender-based rationale for women's involvement supported the desire for single-sex organizations, as did male exclusion. When women formed a society in Milwaukee in 1844 the men belatedly invited them to attend the men's society meetings but did not permit them to join the society itself. The women declined to join the men, meeting among themselves and corresponding with similar societies. In Illinois and Indiana men were more accommodating and numerous mixed-sex societies were formed, although these rarely if ever had female officers or female speakers. Women's clearest and freest participation came through female antislavery societies, even when these permitted male attendees. In Newport (IN) women formed an all-female antislavery society in the late 1830s. They began to permit men to attend their meetings in 1843, as did the Henry County FASS formed in 1841. However neither permitted men to be full members. Both societies retained "female" in their names, and women held all the officer positions.[66]

Western women circulated petitions, spread antislavery information through tracts and newspapers, and ran large fairs throughout the 1840s, often with contributions from women in the East. Yet many societies' major concern was to care for fugitive slaves. Western antislavery women seem to have paid closer attention to fugitive slaves than Eastern women, perhaps because they were geographically closer to slavery than women in New York and New England. Women in Indiana stressed that their work to "relieve the [fugitive's] tired and gloomy passage through our state" was equally important to their distribution of antislavery tracts and other materials. To facilitate work with fugitives, the Henry County FASS established a ten-member vigilance committee at their second meeting. In Milwaukee, the Ladies' Anti-Slavery Society formed specifically to raise funds for freed slaves. The first female antislavery society in Illinois, the Putnam County society, formed to correct public opinion, awaken public sympathy, and "befriend the outcast who flies from oppression." Other Illinois female antislavery societies, including Princeton County and Bureau County, also worked for both the end of slavery and the aid of fugitives passing through. An "Address to the Females of Putnam County" encouraged women to "welcome the homeless wanderer who seeks a shelter from oppression . . . and cheer him on his way from the house of bondage to a land of liberty."[67]

There seem to have been few organizational connections between Eastern and Western antislavery women in the 1840s. Western women were clearly aware of events going on in the East, particularly through subscriptions to the *Liberator* or the *National Anti-Slavery Standard*. Some of those subscriptions may actually have been supplied by Eastern female antislavery societies. The Salem FASS sent copies of the *Liberator* to subscribers in Illinois and Milwaukee in the 1850s and Dewitt (IA), Palmyra (WI), and Lawrence (KS) in 1860. While almost all these newspapers were sent to male subscribers, it was common for women to send mail to each other in care of their husbands, so this does not necessarily mean the recipients of the newspapers were male.[68]

Yet few Western women seem to have corresponded officially with Eastern female antislavery societies. The lack of connection may have been due to the skewed organizational chronology in the two regions. When Eastern women were most able to coordinate efforts across the country, Western women had not yet organized societies. No women from areas west of Ohio attended the Anti-Slavery Conventions of American Women, while Ohio women attended only the 1837 convention. Eastern women were aware that there were scattered supporters in the Midwest, and they attempted to include them in their 1837 petition campaigns. Women in New York took responsibility for contacting women in Michigan, while the Pennsylvania FASS accepted responsibility for Indiana, Illinois, and Ohio. However, Eastern women had plenty to do simply to organize women in their own areas, and there is no record that either organization sent a letter to women in the West.

Individual women did correspond with women in the West, usually with family members and friends. The records of Eastern organizations also hint at other links that individual women may have followed up. Lucy B. Williams, president of the Brooklyn (CT) Female Anti-Slavery Society notified the Philadelphia FASS that she was moving to Indiana in 1836. At least a dozen other active antislavery women removed west during the 1830s, leaving a tantalizing trail of possible East-West connections. Family connections may explain a letter from Mary H. Watson in Lakeland (Minnesota Territory) to the Boston FASS in 1857. Watson sent emotional support and a donation for the Boston fair. Letters from friends and family would have enabled Western women to keep up on the latest news in the East and to feel connected to the larger movement, but they did not result in extensive interregional cooperation. By the time Western women's societies were well organized enough to engage in extensive petition campaigns, Eastern women had refocused their petitioning efforts on local issues and lacked the coordinated organizational structures that might have integrated Western women into a national network.[69]

Networking among themselves proved crucial to Western women. Many found themselves one of very few in their county to support antislavery. Like women in the East, Western women used antislavery newspapers to publicize their efforts and recruit new members. Newspapers like the *Anti-Slavery Bugle* (OH), *Signal of Liberty* (MI), *Western Citizen* (IL), *Free Labor Advocate and Anti-Slavery Chronicle* (IN), and *Western Freeman* (WI) helped Western antislavery women find one another. The newspapers also enabled women to correspond across distance, spread tactics and strategies, and share arguments for women's involvement.

Illinois women took networking further than most. In 1844 they formed the only statewide women's antislavery society, which met concurrently with the male state society convention. Like their sisters in the East, the women faced some internal disagreement over the necessity or propriety of a female convention. One woman who was unable to attend expressed her concerns that a female convention might sacrifice "opportunities for home effort," a phrase that seems to have meant both local antislavery efforts and women's responsibilities within the home. Yet the "intelligence and consecration to the cause" of the women present quelled at least one other doubter. Women from twenty-two counties agreed to work together across the state.[70]

They focused their main efforts on the care of fugitive and freed blacks in Illinois, linking, as Eastern black women did, the condition of slave and free African Americans. They also resolved to spread antislavery sentiment among women, through the distribution of tracts and newspapers and by organizing female antislavery societies in every county where at least five abolitionists were known to live. Numerous members published letters in the *Western Citizen,* sharing ideas and information, and exhorting women to continued activity. Women drew on each other's strength to keep the cause moving forward.[71]

Despite their organizational success, Illinois women encountered many of the same organizational obstacles as Eastern women. Antislavery women faced a mob at their meeting in Bond County and women in McDonough County gave antislavery lectures to proslavery rioters. Attendees of the first women's convention in Illinois faced egg-throwing rowdies who later stole the wheels from a carriage, trapping some women at the convention site. Women in these situations seem to have drawn energy and enthusiasm from their ability to face down the rioters, an experience similar to that of the women of Boston, Concord, and other towns in the heyday of Eastern women's organizing. The women also suffered some of the same internal divisions that had plagued Eastern women's large-scale organizational efforts. When a resolution was presented to the Illinois women's state convention that abolitionists should dissolve their connections with churches that did not take an antislavery stance, heated discussion promptly ensued. The resolution did pass, but it made clear that not all women were united on this issue, which had divided their Eastern sisters only a few years before.[72]

The Illinois women's state society would only last two years before the divisions caught up with it. In 1845 women were still stressing their "gospel union" and attempting to smooth over their "sectarian differences," but it was not working. While the issue of woman's appropriate sphere does not seem to have been a crucial topic in the early days of Western antislavery organizing, the increasing prominence of the Liberty Party tightly linked antislavery and partisan politics. This left women few ways to justify their continued antislavery activism. Calls for female involvement in antislavery were understood as calls for female involvement in politics, which raised grave concerns about women overstepping their appropriate bounds. Women were invited to participate in Liberty Party gatherings, but their presence was mainly symbolic and their silence taken for granted. Women were forced to defend their right to engage in antislavery activism, turning the centre of discussion away from slaves and toward women's rights. This was not what had attracted most women to the cause, and they began to leave, as women in the East had done only slightly earlier. By 1846 the Illinois women's convention had become a series of occasional meetings, and even these ceased in 1847.[73]

The decline in public female activity in Illinois reflected a larger trend in Western antislavery. To a degree, the issues that had caused such division in the East caught up with Westerners in the late 1840s. Westerners had avoided controversy thus far mostly due to geography and disorganization. The large distances between Western and Eastern states had meant that few Western societies sent delegates to the divisive Eastern conventions, and few had close ties to the national societies in the 1830s. Once the AAS turned its attention west and Western abolitionists began to organize in large numbers, divisions over political action, church membership, and, ultimately, women's rights rapidly ensued.

One of the earliest references came in 1843, when the Union County (IN) FASS sympathized with "those members of different Christian churches, who have been obliged to abandon their old organizations, and to form new ones." They took to task those "professed abolitionists who have abandoned . . . associated action, for fear of censure, or in condescension to the wishes of those churches who have arrayed themselves against the present anti-slavery enterprise." Although the women made nine different resolutions at this April meeting, none dealt directly with the role of women in the movement. However, women in nearby Henry County asked later that year whether women must be "considered out of the proper spheres when remonstrating with the perpetrators of [slavery]."[74]

By 1846 Western women were facing serious complaints regarding their antislavery activities. While Illinois women had claimed political awareness as a female duty in 1842, four years later they faced an increasing number of calls for women to return to their sphere and not to presume to enter the arena of politics. In the same year Illinois women began to invite men to preside over their meetings and felt called upon to pass a resolution disavowing any ambition to public office. By late 1847 prominent abolitionist women were debating with men who felt antislavery women were "outside their sphere" and had no right to interfere in political topics. Some of the language of the debate was imported from the Eastern debates of the late 1830s. Ten years after the complaint had appeared in an Eastern newspaper, Western women read that they should be "shaking bed ticks, not politics."[75]

Abolitionists in Michigan also made an increasingly sharp distinction between political engagement and women's antislavery efforts. In 1846 male abolitionists suggested that women intent on holding an antislavery fair wait until after the election. At that time "political excitement will have subsided, and that calm, so favorable to moral influence, will succeed, and present to the Ladies every facility they may desire for their Christian effort." Caught up in Liberty Party enthusiasm, Michigan's male abolitionists gave women little support or encouragement. Michigan women responded by forming a number of Ladies Antislavery and Benevolent Associations, high-lighting in their name their close affiliation with the more accepted tradition of female benevolent association. These organizations stressed aid to the poor and needy rather than participation in political debate. By leaving partisan politics to the men and claiming their own work as moral Christian reform, Michigan women seem to have been able to maintain an antislavery sphere of their own longer than women in Illinois.[76]

In Indiana women had claimed political action as part of their moral ef-forts since 1841, urging women to use their moral influence to affect men's voting patterns. The Westfield (Hamilton County) FASS had even issued an address "To the Voters of Indiana." Organized female antislavery activism seems to have lasted there until 1849, at which point women faced contin-uous complaints that they were out of their sphere. The women seem to have disbanded, believing that their moral suasion efforts had succeeded. They had enabled male political antislavery campaigns to be far more suc-cessful than they had been in the past.[77]

As late as 1852 a major chronicler of the antislavery movement, William Goodell, did not think the issue of women's rights had affected Western so-cieties. In his grand history of the movement, he claimed: "The contention about women's acting in the Societies was, at the West, considered a frivo-lous one. There were differences of opinion, but the question would not have been pressed, on the one hand, nor have been made a ground of withdrawal, on the other." This may have been true in 1842, but by 1852 there were few if any female antislavery societies still in existence in Mid-western states. It is not clear whether women joined men in newly inte-grated mixed-sex societies or simply began to work as individuals. It is likely, however, that they continued to support the cause through dona-tions of goods and money and by working quietly to help speed fugitives on their way north.[78]

Conclusion: Organizations Fade, but Not Women's Commitment

In the late 1840s and early 1850s the majority of female antislavery soci-eties in both East and West dissolved, disbanded, or simply stopped their formal meetings. Few women recorded their reasons for ending their years of work together. Only the lack of further meeting records signals the end of their organizations. The Reading FASS, one of the first ever founded, ac-tually elected officers for 1850. That is the last entry in the minute book.

This trend was marked among both male and female organizations and resulted in part from changes within the antislavery movement. Starting in the mid-1840s, a few vocal activists denounced antislavery organizations as fettering the minds of individuals and limiting the range of action people could undertake. This was an understandable response to the continued factionalism within the movement. The regular publication of these diatribes against organization did not encourage the formation of new societies or the maintenance of those already in existence. The major antislavery organizations turned their attention to individual conversions rather than society formation. Fewer and fewer people felt the need to work in local societies, sending their money and membership directly to the national organization instead. The Boston fair committee recognized and accelerated this trend when they abandoned the National Anti-Slavery Bazaar in favor of a National Anti-Slavery Subscription in 1858. Rather than meeting together locally to create goods for sale, individuals could send cash to Boston. Those with the resources to come to Boston could gather for dinner, conversation, and celebration.[79]

The spread of antislavery sentiment to increasingly large segments of the American population also undermined the need for female antislavery societies. In a strange irony, at the moment that antislavery sentiment became most tolerated, though not wholly accepted, female antislavery society members found themselves a small remnant of a great organizational movement. Many of their peers had listened to the call for moral activism on behalf of the slave and were clothing, feeding, and housing fugitive slaves through the Underground Railroad or through donations of goods and cash to the American Missionary Association and other relief organizations. Antislavery newspapers record this change as they list donations from the Litchfield Medina County (OH) Female Benevolent Society or the Ladies Association of West Chester (NY). The Centre Missionary Sewing Circle of Worcester (MA) turned its attention from Christian foreign missions in 1839 to fugitive slaves, after the passing of the Fugitive Slave Act in 1850. In 1854 when the Kansas-Nebraska Act opened that territory to popular sovereignty and battles broke out between pro- and antislavery settlers, the women turned their benevolent eye westward to "meet the wants" of those caught up in the violence. It may be that women who left female antislavery societies "abolitionized" their churches and local benevolent organizations, or that their efforts to portray antislavery as a benevolent cause had finally succeeded.[80]

Other women had heard the message that women had the responsibility to affect national politics, and they were doing so in ways not anticipated by female antislavery societies. Some women were agitating for women's right to vote, and the female suffrage movement would expand dramatically during the Civil War. Others worked more indirectly through fairs, banners, and newspaper articles in support of the Liberty and Free Soil parties. Whig women had been active in political campaigns since 1840, when the Harrison campaign drew on the support of "moral" women to bolster the Whig Party's claim to be the party of moral reform. This enabled women in Boston to claim their own right to engage the political topic of slavery. In late 1840 they wrote, "Since men have proclaimed with pride how scarfs and handkerchiefs wave applause at whig and democratic gatherings, we feel no call to defend our interest in the anti-slavery cause from the charge of 'singular and unwomanly participation in things out of our sphere.'"[81]

However, the Boston women had scorned direct participation in partisan politics. By the 1850s this direct participation was more common. Jane Grey Swisshelm and Clarina Nichols edited political newspapers and regularly supported the antislavery efforts of the political parties. Abolitionist lecturer Lucy Stone campaigned for the Liberty Party in 1852 and for the Free Soil and Republican parties in 1856 and 1860. The formation of the Republican Party in 1854 provided yet more opportunities for politically minded women. Anna Dickinson gave antislavery lectures that were Republican Party rallies, and she helped to create Republican majorities in New York and Connecticut in 1863 and 1864.[82]

Women clearly did not disappear from antislavery in the 1850s. Rather they were everywhere. Antislavery women waved handkerchiefs at political rallies, edited national antislavery newspapers, gave lectures, assisted fugitives, held fairs, sewed goods, and advocated the cause in public and in private. But the independent female organizations that had provided women with a rationale for action, coordinated their efforts, and enabled them to carefully balance moral suasion with a sense of political engagement did mostly disappear. Those that remained provided an important network for continued action. The Rochester Ladies' Anti-Slavery Society met at least twenty-five times per year, and aided over seventy-five fugitives every year. Societies in Salem, Dover, and Philadelphia were equally active in their areas. The organizational legacy of these organizations, and of those that had recently faded away, would prove crucially important during and after the Civil War.

Civil War and Emancipation, 1861–1870

Ironies and Legacies

"In former years we found opportunity to help a few on their way to

freedom, now we may fit thousands to appreciate and enjoy its blessings."

—Rochester Ladies' Anti-Slavery Society, 1863

The election of Abraham Lincoln, the secession of seven Southern states, and the start of America's bloodiest conflict gave new urgency to antislavery women's work.[1] Although most women dreaded the horrors war could inflict, they recognized that it could be the means through which emancipation would finally come. War also gave all American women a stake in the political debates of the time, as they watched husbands, sons, lovers, brothers, fathers, and friends go off to fight. At first many found it hard to maintain their antislavery commitment as mobs threatened antislavery fairs, the economy contracted, and many women turned their attention to work for the soldiers rather than the slaves. However, as the Rochester women realized, war gave them a much larger field for their efforts. The remaining female antislavery societies provided escaped slaves with basic necessities while also petitioning for their civil rights of freedom, citizenship, and the vote. They hoped the end of the war would bring their thirty-year battle to a close.

Antislavery women's usual work was greatly disrupted even before the war began. Lincoln's election in November 1860 provoked numerous attacks on abolitionists. The members of the Rochester Ladies' Anti-Slavery Society were too nervous to hold their usual Christmas fair. Women in Philadelphia persevered with their fair despite the threat of mobbing and arranged for very prominent police protection, which may have deterred the promised riot. The outbreak of armed conflict in April 1861 galvanized women across America into action. Temporarily abandoning antislavery work, many women joined their friends and neighbors in "labor for the Army," "fitting out Volunteers," cutting bandages for soldiers, and making towels. Many antislavery women joined soldiers' aid societies, which helped to organize their relief work. Eventually women's efforts and their disgust at battlefield conditions for the wounded would result in the formation of the U.S. Sanitary Commission. This public-private partnership provided food, clothing, bandages, and nurses for Union soldiers.[2]

By 1863 so many slaves had escaped to freedom behind Union lines that the U.S. Sanitary Commission and the U.S. Army both had to concern themselves with fugitives. The Sanitary Commission, recognizing the organizational power of women, appealed directly to "the loyal women of the East to engage in the work." Thousands of white and black women responded. Sewing goods, sending donations, even traveling south to teach African Americans, many women went to great lengths to work for and with former slaves. Many formed Ladies' Freedmen's Aid Societies. That so many white women chose to cross racial lines to assist African Americans directly is a testament to antislavery women's decades of effort. They had finally succeeded in portraying assistance to African Americans as being part of women's moral responsibilities.[3]

The scattered female antislavery societies and antislavery sewing societies that continued to exist during the Civil War led the way in caring for fugitives. In Massachusetts the Salem FASS met regularly to "prepare articles of clothing for the use of Fugitives in Kansas or elsewhere." In New Hampshire, the Dover Female Anti-Slavery Sewing Circle collected funds and clothing to help slaves who had "freed themselves" by escaping behind Union army lines. Their membership grew rapidly, and they held working and reading meetings to learn about and assist freedmen. In 1863, the society changed its name to the Dover Anti-Slavery and Freedmen's Aid Society to better reflect its activities. By December 1864, the Dover women had created a fund-raising committee with members from each of the main religious denominations in town and held a grand festival to add to their almost two thousand dollars in donations. In 1865 they donated almost four thousand dollars in clothing and other goods and sponsored public lectures by Republican senator Charles Sumner and Republican Party activist and antislavery lecturer Anna Dickinson.[4]

In New York the Rochester Ladies' Anti-Slavery Society exceeded all others in their efforts, sponsoring one of their own officers, Julia Wilbur, as an agent in the freed black communities of Alexandria and Fredericksburg (VA). Beginning in 1863 Wilbur distributed goods made by the society and informed the government of the freedmen's needs. Her reports to the society galvanized the Rochester women's efforts, as well as those of women in New York, Massachusetts, and Philadelphia. The Rochester women continued to provide financial donations, handmade goods, secondhand clothing, and other necessities until 1868.[5]

While antislavery women cared for the immediate needs of fugitives, they continued to work for the end of slavery. Most were not encouraged by President Lincoln's 1861 inaugural address, which balanced his refusal to permit slavery in the territories with an unwillingness to interfere where it was already established. The Philadelphia FASS wrote: "Very efficient service in the anti-slavery cause cannot be reasonably expected of a President who vows his intention of restoring the fugitive slave to his master." Rochester women were similarly unimpressed. Congress took more radical action, however, and in 1862 abolished slavery in the District of Columbia and in the territories, after almost thirty years of antislavery petitioning. The Philadelphia women celebrated this victory but warned that further work was still necessary. Sustained "appeals to the conscience and heart of the nation" were the way to influence the Republican Party to continue toward the full emancipation of slaves. The women in Philadelphia, Dover, Salem, and Rochester all supported antislavery newspapers to keep their message before the public.

Lincoln surprised many in September 1862 when he announced the Emancipation Proclamation. The Proclamation freed slaves in all the states that had seceded from the Union and were not yet under Union control as of January 1, 1863. It was greeted with great joy among abolitionists, although they recognized that "full enforcement of the decree must depend, in great measure, on the future success of the United States armies." It also aroused them to new energies since its limited extent and the lukewarm public reception of it made clear the need for continued antislavery agitation.[6]

The Women's National Loyal League

Longtime abolitionists and women's rights activists Susan B. Anthony and Elizabeth Cady Stanton decided that the time for broad, united female action had come. In March 1863 Stanton published an address to the "Women of the Republic." She noted that, while many individual women had spoken out regarding the war, "we have, as yet, no means of judging how and where the majority of Northern women stand." Her address echoed the 1837 call for the Anti-Slavery Convention of American Women, which had gathered together hundreds of women to ascertain their views and to enable them to speak with a more national, collective voice. Stanton felt strongly that the "women of a nation mold its morals, religion, and politics" and that women needed to take a stand in support of the war for it to be successful. She reaffirmed the antislavery movement's early belief that a great cause could not be successful without woman's moral voice. Therefore she put out a "Call for a Meeting of the Loyal Women of the Nation" to take place in May 1863. Twenty-six years after the first Anti-Slavery Convention of American Women, women were being asked to meet once again in New York City in mid-May to discuss plans for uniting their actions and shaping the politics of their nation.[7]

The convention brought together seasoned abolitionists like Stanton, Angelina Grimké Weld, and Amy Post with newcomers from as far away as California. No list of delegates survives, but many of the women appear to have been members of Ladies' Aid Societies or other soldier relief groups. This may explain why Stanton and Weld gave speeches providing a little history of the antislavery movement and stressing that the war was a war for freedom. At least one woman was confused by this linkage. Mrs. E. O. Sampson Hoyt from Wisconsin, a convention officer, claimed that she and others had come hundreds of miles for a convention of the loyal women of the North and had accidentally found themselves at an antislavery meeting![8]

Despite this confusion the convention unanimously passed six resolutions. Four focused on the relationship between the war and slavery. In these, the women claimed the war was a battle between slavery and freedom. They praised the Emancipation Proclamation and called for further steps toward full emancipation of all slaves. Most radically, the women protested against all state and national laws that would limit the political and social rights of freemen. Two other resolutions focused on the relationship of women and war. The first excused Northern women's lack of enthusiasm for the war, claiming that women had not yet understood the just cause that required them to sacrifice their loved ones. The second pledged women's money, talents, and—if necessary—lives to ensure true freedom in America.[9]

Given that President Lincoln had only recently accepted the war as a war against slavery and had done so hesitantly and unwillingly, women's unanimity on these six resolutions is startling. None of the resolutions prompted any recorded debate. This may have been in part because the resolutions were read aloud to the delegates and are so linguistically complicated that some women may have missed their radical implications. Still they are remarkable resolutions for a convention of loyal, rather than antislavery, women. It is thus all the more striking that the one resolution that caused extensive debate called for the "civil and political equality" of African Americans and women. The women had no objection to political rights for African Americans, but a minority balked at demanding the vote for women. Although thirty-six years had passed since the Anti-Slavery Conventions of American Women, these delegates found themselves divided once again over woman's appropriate role.

Stanton had suggested that debate over woman's role would be a major aspect of the meeting when she wrote in the "Call": "To man, by common consent, is assigned the forum, camp and field. What is woman's legitimate work, and how she may best accomplish it, is worthy our earnest counsel one with another." Once a majority of delegates passed the disputed resolution, that earnest counsel turned into extensive debate. Susan B. Anthony, a prominent antislavery and women's rights lecturer, called on the women of the North to forget that they were women and go forward as independent human beings. "Forget conventionalisms," she urged the delegates, "forget what the world will say, whether you are in your place or out of your place." In the end, Anthony reminded the women, they were responsible only to "suffering humanity, your own conscience, and God." Another delegate declared that she recognized for herself "no narrow sphere." Multiple speakers objected to the suggestion that the resolution be passed simply with the removal of "women." Angelina Grimké Weld summed up their underlying rationale when she claimed: "I want to be identified with the Negro—until he gets his rights, we never shall have ours."[10]

A small minority of women vigorously dissented from the resolution. A California delegate disagreed with the resolution on principle. She argued: "We do not need to stand at the ballot-boxes and cast our votes," since "in our homes we have a great office." She felt that women did not need so large a sphere for action as the resolution proposed. Other women objected on more practical grounds. Mrs. Hoyt noted that the demand for women's rights "has not been received with entire favor by the women of the country." She did not want "thousands of earnest, loyal and able women" to avoid the Loyal League because they could not accept this linkage to women's rights.[11]

Yet even the minority accepted the mixing of morality and politics that antislavery women had shaped decades earlier. Mrs. Hoyt felt strongly that it was proper for women to "maintain . . . the integrity of our Government; to help vindicate its authority; to re-establish it upon a far more enduring basis than it is now." She felt women could best accomplish these aims if they did not involve themselves "in any purely political matter." Even for the more conservative women at the convention, reshaping the war aims of the country and agitating for the freedom and civil rights of African Americans were not defined as "political" matters. This changed understanding of politics makes clear how much the boundaries of woman's sphere had changed since antislavery women had begun their work.[12]

The women did not reach full agreement, but the grounds for that agreement were clearly laid out. One delegate argued that "the very term itself of forming a league . . . suggests . . . that we need not all of us profess the same politics." Another suggested: "Some of us have larger spheres than others, and we are necessarily different. . . . Our efforts should be to inspire each other with a unity of feeling. That inspiration going forth from the hearts of women, shall inspire the whole nation." All women could agree that they needed some "plan . . . in the form of practical action" around which women could unify and organize. The meeting then agreed to the formation of a Women's National Loyal League, which would make every practical effort to support the war and further its aims. Specific details of those efforts were left to the leaders to announce at a later date.[13]

Within weeks the women at the main office in New York City had organized a huge national antislavery petitioning campaign, the likes of which had not been seen since 1837. The correspondence networks created during the previous thirty years proved invaluable as women sent petitions to friends and acquaintances across the country. By February 1864, the League had circulated over twelve thousand petitions and collected over one hundred thousand signatures. By the summer the numbers had swelled to twenty thousand petitions and over four hundred thousand signatures, approximately two-thirds of which were by women. While the League did not reach its goal of one million signatures, it did keep the issue of antislavery in front of individual citizens, senators, and congressmen. Approximately one in every twenty-four Americans signed a League petition. The constant agitation at both the grassroots and the congressional levels placed intense pressure on the government to pass the Thirteenth Amendment. When the Amendment was finally ratified in late 1865, antislavery women had achieved what they had sought for almost thirty-five years—the abolition of legal slavery.[14]

The End of the Antislavery Societies

The Union victory and the passage of the Thirteenth Amendment vindicated antislavery activists' efforts. But the "long-awaited consummation" of their efforts also caused a crisis over whether they could justify retirement from the field or whether they should stay until full civil rights for former slaves had been assured. Economic depression, political infighting, and the seemingly bottomless needs of freedmen drained the energy of antislavery women. By 1864 donations from Britain were already decreasing, as the freedom of black slaves seemed assured. By 1866 women in Rochester were finding it difficult to keep their members' interest. The society continued to meet but attendance was "comparatively small." Women in Rochester, as in the rest of the country, were not inclined to use scarce resources to help black people in the South, when so many other pressing needs among the white community called closer to home. "[R]emoval from the city and death, have left very few members," the Rochester women wrote in 1867, and very few new women joined them in their efforts. The Dover Anti-Slavery Sewing Circle, which had achieved such heights of fund-raising and organization in 1865, died a rapid death in 1866. The women met in January and February but then paused until July. "The occasion was a very pleasant one but the attendance was small," wrote the secretary in the last entry in the society minutes.[15]

Some antislavery women felt that their fight was not over with the legal abolition of slavery. As the women of Salem noted in 1866, "there was much to be done before our country could be free from the curse of slavery." The Salem women debated whether to reorganize their society under a different name or dissolve it and work with the Salem Freedman's Association. The latter would entail a loss of autonomy; while the Freedmen's Association welcomed women both as ordinary members and as board members, there were no female officers. They decided to retain their original organization until 1869, when they finally disbanded. The Philadelphia women held on until 1870, focusing much of their energy on black Americans' political rights. However, their lament of "How long, O Lord! How long?" summed up their sense that the task was simply endless. With the dissolution of the American Anti-Slavery Society in 1870, and the passage of the Fifteenth Amendment guaranteeing black men the right to vote, the Philadelphia women agreed to disband. Women in Philadelphia, Rochester, Salem, Dover, and elsewhere turned their attention to other needs within their communities, providing staff and support for suffrage, temperance, missionary, and other organizations.[16]

Conclusions

On March 24, 1870, the only surviving female antislavery society met for the last time. The women of the Philadelphia FASS had joined the fight only days after the formation of the AAS, and they closed their minute book forever in the same year that organization disbanded. The women rejoiced that their main goal—the abolition of legalized slavery—had been accomplished, and they cheered the passage of the Fourteenth and Fifteenth Amendments, which went beyond legal freedom to provide African Americans with citizenship and black males with the right to vote.

While the tone of the report is highly celebratory, there is also a clear note of exhaustion. The women admitted there was much to do before the legacy of slavery was truly eradicated. Mary Grew, who had been the corresponding secretary for the organization for almost four decades, noted: "If we put off our armor here to-day, it is but for a moment's breathing space, to be resumed for other conflicts." Yet the women needed that breathing space. For thirty-seven years they had defended their right and responsibility to agitate against slavery. They had used lectures, sewing, fairs, petitioning, newspaper articles, abstinence from slave-made goods, personal conversations, and public conventions to maintain their own convictions and to change the hearts and minds of others. The women recognized that the organization they had created had "lived a life" at least as interesting as the lives of the women involved in it. They also recognized that their monthly meetings and annual fairs had enabled them to accomplish far more than they ever could have done as individuals.[17]

The story of female antislavery societies demonstrates the complexity and importance of these organizations. Far more numerous than has previously been recognized, these organizations ranged from the powerful, copiously documented, and long-lived Philadelphia society to the ephemeral societies mentioned only briefly in the antislavery newspapers. Each served an important role for the women who belonged to it, providing a space in which to learn about and take action against one of the largest social, economic, and political institutions in the country. Born in the religious and social ferment of the late 1820s and early 1830s, these societies took their shape from a long tradition of female benevolent organizing. They were based on the recognition that women tended to retain more power and influence in all-female organizations. Exclusion from the national male antislavery societies until 1839–1840 provided women with a particular incentive to organize their own networks, and many women remained active in those networks irrespective of whether they later worked with men. Handwritten letters and printed circulars spread advice, encouragement, strategies, and defenses of women's actions. Advice helped keep newer societies from replicating the mistakes made by their predecessors, while the shared strategies eventually enabled women to unite their efforts into huge petition campaigns and highly successful antislavery fairs. Encouragement helped hold together small societies where the members were the only known abolitionists for miles. The ability to write to a total stranger and address her as a friend solidified many women's sense that they belonged to a larger community. Through personal correspondence and printed reports, society members began to see that their daily (often tiny) efforts could, in conjunction with those of hundreds of other women, eventually accomplish such a distant, awe-inspiring, and morally imperative goal as the abolition of slavery.

While correspondence served as the lifeblood of the female antislavery network, the Anti-Slavery Conventions of American Women gave the network public form. Bringing together women from Maine to Ohio, the conventions gave women the chance to meet face-to-face, share meals as well as strategies, and cement friendships previously carried on only by letter. Twelve publications, lifelong friendships, and the largest female petition campaign to that date emerged out of these meetings. The conventions also produced a shared vision of women's antislavery activism, which at least temporarily helped women to stave off the divisions wracking the men's societies. The conventions forced women to confront, and overcome, not only their own diversity—particularly of race and religion—but also their differing visions of the proper role of women in the antislavery movement.

It has been said many times before, but it is worth saying again—not all abolitionist women were feminists. Not all believed that women should be equal to men. All did believe, however, that women had a right and a responsibility to agitate against slavery, and all believed that this fight began at home. Whether women should take the fight out of the home and into the public sphere caused more debate. This question would eventually divide both women from each other and the antislavery movement as a whole. But the compromises women tried to work out during the three Anti-Slavery Conventions of American Women provided women on all sides of the debate with an opportunity to understand each other's vision. They produced a shared understanding that placed women's moral power and influence at the center of the antislavery movement.

The life and death of many female antislavery societies revolved around this question of woman's appropriate role in the movement. From Elizabeth Chandler's earliest calls for female organization in the *Genius of Universal Emancipation* to the final Philadelphia FASS report, the question of whether antislavery was an appropriate field for women shaped the kinds of societies they formed and the activities they undertook. This is one of the factors that made the decade from 1829 to 1839 so unusual. During these years women were able to create independent female antislavery societies that took a clearly political stance against slavery. This stance was not political in the sense of any affiliation with a political party or any attempt to influence a particular election. Rather, women formed what would now be considered political action committees. They organized to encourage society to act upon widely shared moral beliefs.

Female antislavery societies were quite up-front about their desire to change the ways in which power was used and citizenship distributed in the United States. For a short period in the 1830s, women held onto a vision in which they had both the right and the responsibility to influence what their political representatives believed and how they voted. A small coalition of men agreed with them. The women's rights movement would take up parts of this vision, demanding political equality with men. But it would take women decades to regain the fusion of moral passion and political demands that antislavery women had shared, and to build the types of bridges between more radical and more conservative women that had existed among members of the female antislavery societies.

The legacy of these societies is long and varied. Many societies served as supports for and incubators of some of the most powerful antislavery lecturers of the antebellum period. Sarah and Angelina Grimké thought long and hard before taking a commission from the AAS in 1837. They were sustained in their choice and throughout their highly successful careers by the Philadelphia FASS, of which they had been early members. They also received both verbal and financial support from many other female antislavery societies, which saw the Grimkés as standing up for women's right to fight against slavery. Lucretia Mott was also sustained by the Philadelphia FASS, while Abby Kelley drew support, encouragement, and financial assistance from the Millbury, Lynn, and Worcester FASS. These lecturers in turn inspired other women, some of whom, like Sallie Holley, became antislavery lecturers, while others turned their efforts to women's rights and other causes.[18]

Female antislavery societies were fundamental to the success of the whole antislavery movement. Women provided many of the early antislavery voices, after the national male organizations of the eighteenth century had either died or proved ineffective. From black women's literary societies to free-produce organizations, Philadelphia women articulated a powerful and organized antislavery sentiment that may have pushed William Lloyd Garrison into a more activist antislavery stance. Women's societies preceded male societies in many areas, and the networks created by women provided structure to the early antislavery movement.

Throughout the course of the movement, women's societies did the vast majority of the fund-raising. Women's funds ensured that lecturers, newspapers, and pamphlets were kept in circulation and that the issue of slavery was kept before the American public. Without this basic grassroots work by women, the cause could not have gotten its message out to the American public to create a constituency for political activism. Women's sewn goods and antislavery fairs raised consciousness as well as funds. Women brought antislavery into the domestic sphere as they sewed political messages into their contributions and held elegant events at which people could be converted while they shopped. The network of female antislavery societies ensured that huge numbers of goods would be created for each fair, and goods that did not sell at a particular fair would be circulated until they were sold, maximizing the money raised by women's efforts.

The movement also could not have gotten its message in front of Congress as effectively without the network of women's organizations that coordinated the national petition campaign of 1837. Women's petitions had already been particularly visible in Congress, and the flood of petitions during that campaign eventually resulted in the annual Gag Rules. By forcing Congress to table all antislavery petitions, female antislavery societies helped expand abolition from an antislavery to a civil rights cause, as activists called for freedom of speech as well as freedom from slavery.

Female antislavery activism had been in part a fight for "the moral power of woman to be recognized in the politics of the nation." While Elizabeth Cady Stanton had suffrage in mind when she made this statement, by 1860 most women supported the general idea that women's moral concerns should help guide the politics of the country. This enabled the massive Women's National Loyal League petition in 1863. A few women saw the connection between women and politics more directly, creating a link between the antislavery movement and the woman's rights or suffrage movement. Many suffragists had been abolitionists and relied heavily on the language, strategies, and networks that had been created by antislavery women.

It is not surprising that the debates faced by abolitionists over the proper role for women would continue to haunt the suffrage movement. In 1869 this movement would divide into two competing organizations, split over whether to support the Fifteenth Amendment, which would extend the right to vote to black males but not to women. The division focused in part on whether the Amendment was the most tactically appropriate place to demand women's right to vote. Echoing the Women's National Loyal League Convention, some women argued that this was the best chance women had to get the right to vote, while others argued it was the freedman's hour. Equally important, the two groups differed over whether they should stress women's equality with men or women's moral influence over and difference from men. The legacies of abolitionist women's inability to find a middle ground on that issue lived on for generations.[19]

The example of female antislavery societies is an important one for our own time, when individuals find it difficult to have an impact on the political system and when many claims to political power are made in the name of moral responsibility. Antislavery women drew inspiration from the example of those who came before them. They drew on previous benevolent organizations and English antislavery societies for practical organizational advice and psychological encouragement. Many antislavery women took pride in turning over their efforts to another generation. They recognized that they had not fully accomplished their goals, particularly for those who saw black equality as a crucial aspect of antislavery work. Yet they left a powerful example of how a politically excluded group could organize and demand change in society.

Examining the ways in which antislavery women built their network makes clearer the power of organization to motivate and facilitate change. Antislavery women did not fully succeed in overcoming the divisions that continue to limit female organizing. Interracial societies were relatively rare and a shared gender identity could not always overcome religious and ideological differences. The power of association, however, enabled women to challenge the limits of their time and define new roles for themselves. It helped keep them busy doing weekly and monthly tasks that built friendships and a sense of belonging. It brought them together in national conventions. It gave them the power of numbers. Together antislavery women faced down mobs, chastised politicians, and funded a mass movement. They helped force a nation to make fundamental political and economic change.

Appendix

The following tables include all of the female antislavery societies encountered during the research for this book. Previous examinations of female antislavery societies have not made clear the full extent of women's organizing, in part because they relied heavily on the AAS annual reports. Although these included extensive lists of antislavery societies, the editors of these lists made clear that they were incomplete, and in fact they often left out societies whose formation was prominently announced in the major antislavery papers. The list here is far more complete, but it still significantly underrepresents the total number of female societies. For example, the first annual report of the Ladies Anti-Slavery Society of Concord (NH) claims there were sixty-five female antislavery societies in New England and New York by the close of 1835. I can find records for only fifty-three (see report in *Herald of Freedom,* January 9, 1836, p. 89, cols. 2–4).

Table A1 also underrepresents the number of societies created after 1840, due to inadequate sources. The AAS stopped listing new societies in 1839. Also in 1839 the *Liberator* stopped printing the annual reports of antislavery societies, except in special instances, because of lack of space (see Editorial, *Liberator,* April 5, 1839, p. 55). The packed nature of its columns may also have had an impact on the recording of new societies.

Societies that were not friendly to the AAS or the *Liberator*—that is, those affiliated with the new A&FAS—were not mentioned in the *Liberator,* except to deride them. Thus, tracking down these women's organizations requires turning elsewhere for information. The *National Anti-Slavery Standard,* founded by the AAS as a unifying, neutral paper, and the *Emancipator,* the A&FAS publication, both should serve as better sources for these women, yet both tended to avoid the particulars of individual societies in favor of the larger issues that would interest a broader readership. This means that notices of A&FAS-affiliated female societies probably fell through the cracks. The only other sources of information are the religious periodicals of the time, which might mention female antislavery societies for their charitable work, particularly if they cooperated with moral reform societies, or the papers of the women involved, many of which were not saved.

Three other groups are also underrepresented. Western female antislavery societies often announced their organization in local Western papers rather than in the antislavery papers. I did not examine any Western papers as thoroughly as those from the East. Antislavery sewing societies are not consistently included; they appear only if they evolved into or out of female antislavery societies. Black women's antislavery activities were often undertaken in organizations not specifically dedicated to antislavery. Black women's organizations are not included unless antislavery made up the main focus of their efforts.

Founding years without a question mark are based on a definitive statement—a constitution, annual report, letter, and so on. A founding year with a question mark is based on the first appearance of the society in the sources. Disbanding years without qualification are based on a definitive statement—final annual report, or final entry in minute book, or such. A disbanding year with a question mark indicates that the ending date is unclear. A disbanding year that states "after" a certain year indicates the final year in which that society appeared in the sources. I have not consistently checked disbanding dates after 1846.

The following tables are not presented as being definitive but provide a more complete starting point than the sources consulted below. Researchers with information that would improve these charts are invited to contact the author.

Main Sources

Newspapers: *Free Labor Advocate and Anti-Slavery Chronicle,* 1843; *Genius of Universal Emancipation,* 1821–1839; *Herald of Freedom,* 1835–1841; *Liberator,* 1831–1855; *National Anti-Slavery Standard,* 1840–1850; *Signal of Liberty,* 1846.

Also: American Anti-Slavery Society Annual Reports 1834–1839; American Anti-Slavery Society, *The American Anti-Slavery Almanac for 1836* (Boston: Webster and Southard, 1835); Massachusetts Anti-Slavery Society, *Sixth Annual Report of the Board of Managers of the Mass. Anti-Slavery Society* (Boston: Isaac Knapp, 1838); Massachusetts Anti-Slavery Society, *Seventh Annual Report* (Boston: Isaac Knapp, 1839); New England Anti-Slavery Society, *Second Annual Report of the Board of Managers of the New England Anti-Slavery Society* (Boston: Garrison and Knapp, 1834); Boston Female Anti-Slavery Society, *Fifth Annual Report of the Boston Female Anti-Slavery Society* (Boston: Isaac Knapp, 1838); Peggy Brase Seigel, "Moral Champions and Public Pathfinders: Antebellum Quaker Women in Eastcentral Indiana," *Quaker History* 81.2 (1992): 87–106; Mary Van Vleck Garman, "'Altered tone of expression': The Anti-Slavery Rhetoric of Illinois Women, 1837–1847" (Ph.D. diss., Northwestern University Garrett-Evangelical Theological Seminary, 1989); Genevieve G. McBride, *On Wisconsin Women: Working for Their Rights from Settlement to Suffrage* (Madison: University of Wisconsin Press, 1993); Marion C. Miller, *The Anti-Slavery Movement in Indiana* (Ph.D. diss., University of Michigan, 1938).

Table A—Female Antislavery Societies by Year of Founding

State	Town	Name	Founded	Disbanded
MA	Salem	FASS of Salem	1832	1834?
RI	Providence	Providence FASS	1832	
MA	Amesbury/ Amesbury Mills	FASS of Amesbury	1833	
MA	Boston	Boston FASS (evolves into Boston Social/Sewing Circle in late 1845)	1833	after mid-1846
MA	Reading	Reading FASS	1833	1850
NY	Hudson		1833	
PA	Philadelphia	Philadelphia FASS (added a sewing society in 1837)	1833	1870
CT	Brooklyn	FASS of Brooklyn & Vicinity	1834	
CT	Middletown		1834	
CT	Norwich	Ladies ASS of Norwich CT	1834	
MA	Haverhill	Haverhill FASS	1834	
MA	Lowell		1834	
MA	Newburyport	Newburyport FASS	1834	after 1843
MA	Salem	Salem FASS (had a related sewing society)	1834	1866
MA	Sudbury		1834	after 1839
ME	Portland	Portland FASS	1834	after 1838
NH	Concord	Concord Ladies, later Female	1834	after 1840
NH	Plymouth		1834	
NY	NYC	FASS of Chatham St. Chapel	1834	
NY	Rochester	Union Anti-Slavery Society (women of the African Methodist Episcopal Zion Church)	1834	
NY	Whitesboro		1834	
RI	Natick		1834?	
VT	Bellingham		1834?	
VT	Weybridge	Weybridge FASS	1834	

State	Town	Name	Founded	Disbanded
NH	Great Falls		early 1830s	
MA	Boxborough (Boxboro)		1835	
MA	Dorchester		1835	after mid-1840
MA	Fall River	FASS of Fall River	1835	after 1839; sewing society continued through 1845
MA	Lynn	Lynn FASS (Lynn Women's as of 1839)	1835	after early 1846; parallel sewing circle 1844–46
MA	Plymouth		1835?	1835?
MA	South Reading	FASS South Reading	1835	after 1839
MA	South Weymouth		1835	after late 1841
MA	Weymouth (also Weymouth and Braintree)	Weymouth & Braintree Female Emancipation Society (FASS as of late 1840)	1835	after 1846 (1842 –46 as sewing circle)
NH	Dover	Dover FASS; then Dover A-S Sewing Circle; then Dover Anti-Slavery and Freedman's Aid Society	1835	1866?
NH	Grantham		1835	
NH	Pittsfield	Pittsfield Ladies	1835	
NY	Buffalo		1835	
NY	Clinton		1835?	
NY	NYC	Ladies' New-York City Anti-Slavery Society	1835	after 1838
NY	Peru		1835	after 1838
NY	Rochester	Rochester FASS	1835	1842 at latest
NY	Sanquoit		1835	
NY	Sherburne		1835	
NY	Troy		1835	
NY	Utica		1835	after 1838
NY	Warsaw		1835	
OH	Ashtabula Co.		1835	after 1846

Female Antislavery Societies by Year of Founding

State	Town	Name	Founded	Disbanded
OH	Granville		1835	
OH	Muskingham Co.		1835	
OH	Oberlin		1835	
OH	Vernon		1835	
RI	Kent Co.		1835	around 1840
RI	Pawtucket		1835	after 1838
RI	Providence	Providence Ladies (later Female)	1835	after mid-1846
CT	Greenville		1836	
CT	Willimantre (Willimantic)	FASS of Willimantic until 1842; then Willimantic Female (Working) ASS	1836	after 1843
MA	Amesbury & Salisbury		1836	after early 1840
MA	Andover		1836	after 1839
MA	Ashburnham		1836	after 1839
MA	Cambridgeport	Cambridgeport FASS	1836	1841
MA	East Bradford		1836	after early 1840
MA	Groton	Groton Ladies ASS	1836	after 1838
MA	Haverhill East		1836	after 1839
MA	Millville		1836	after 1838
MA	New Bedford	New Bedford FASS; became New Bedford Female Union Socy. 1839	1836	after early 1845
MA	North Leicester		1836	
MA	Uxbridge	Uxbridge FASS	1836	after 1838
MA	West Bradford		1836	after 1837
NH	New Market		1836	
NH	Portsmouth	Portsmouth FASS	1836	
NH	Rochester		1836	1836?
NH	Sandwich		1836	
NY	NYC	Female Wesleyan ASS	1836	after 1842
OH	Abbyville	Abbyville OH FASS	1836	

Female Antislavery Societies by Year of Founding

State	Town	Name	Founded	Disbanded
OH	Andover	Andover State Road Female Anti-Slavery Society	1836	
OH	Canton		1836	
OH	Cherry Valley	CV Township	1836	
OH	Elyria		1836?	
OH	Geneva		1836?	
OH	Harpersfield and Austinburg		1836	
OH	Madison		1836?	
OH	Morgan	Morgan Township	1836	
OH	New Lyme	New Lyme FASS	1836	
OH	Portage Co.		1836?	
OH	Rome	Rome Township	1836	
OH	St. Albans		1836?	
OH	Wayne	Wayne Township	1836	
OH	Windsor	Windsor Township	1836	
PA	Buckingham	Buckingham FASS	1836	after 1837
PA	Germantown		1836?	
PA	Lower Wakefield		1836	
PA	Pittsburgh	Pittsburgh (later Pittsburgh & Allegheny)	1836	
RI	Smithfield (Upper)		1836	after 1838
VT	Waitsfield		1836	
CT	New Haven		1837	
MA	Abington		1837	after early 1842
MA	Barnstable		1837	after late 1838
MA	Brookline		1837	after 1839
MA	Concord	Concord FASS	1837	after late 1846
MA	Danvers	Danvers FASS	1837	after late 1843
MA	Fairhaven	Fairhaven Ladies	1837	after 1839

Female Antislavery Societies by Year of Founding

State	Town	Name	Founded	Disbanded
MA	Fitchburg		1837	after 1838
MA	Franklin	Franklin Ladies	1837	after 1839
MA	Holliston	Ladies ASS	1837	after early 1843
MA	Leicester		1837?	after 1838
MA	North Bridgewater	North Bridgewater FASS	1837	after late 1838
MA	North Danvers		1837	after early 1840
MA	North Marshfield		1837	after 1839
MA	Plymouth		1837	after mid-1840
MA	Roxbury	Roxbury Ladies	1837	after early 1840
MA	South Danvers	South Danvers FASS	1837	after early 1839
MA	Upton		1837?	1846?
MA	West Hampton		1837	
MA	West Newbury		1837	after late 1843
MA	Worcester Co.	Worcester Co. FASS (added a sewing circle from 1839 on)	1837	after 1841
MA	Wrentham		1837	after early 1843
ME	Bangor		1837	late 1843
ME	Hallowell	Hallowell ME FASS	1837	after late 1843
ME	Winthrop	Winthrop FASS	1837	
NH	Canaan		1837	
NH	Dunbarton		1837	
NH	Durham		1837	
NH	Haverhill	Haverhill FASS	1837	after early 1843
NH	Newark		1837	
NH	Wakefield		1837	
NH	Weare		1837	
NJ	Bloomfield		1837	
NY	Champlain		1837	after 1838
NY	Farmington		1837	after 1839

Female Antislavery Societies by Year of Founding

State	Town	Name	Founded	Disbanded
NY	Knowlesville		1837	
NY	Lockport		1837	
NY	Palmyra		1837	
NY	Pompey		1837	
OH	Bloomingburgh		1837	
OH	Cadiz	Cadiz FASS	1837?	after mid-1841
RI	Providence	Providence FASS	1837	after 1838
VT	Cornwall		1837	
??	Massillon	Massillon FASS	1837?	
CT	Hartford	Hartford Female	1838	
MA	Athol		1838?	after 1839
MA	Boylston		1838?	after 1842
MA	Braintree and Salisbury		1838	
MA	Dedham	Dedham FASS (later Ladies)	1838	after 1840
MA	Duxbury		1838	1839/1841
MA	East Bridgewater		1838	after 1839
MA	Hingham	Hingham FASS (later Hingham Ladies Sewing Circle)	1838?	after mid-1840
MA	Millbury	Millbury Women's	1838	after 1843
MA	Nantucket	Nantucket FASS (became Women's in 1839)	1838	1839
MA	Nantucket	Female Colored Union Society	1838	after 1839
MA	Provinceton	Provincetown FASS	1838	after mid-1839
MA	Stoneham	Stoneham FASS	1838	after early 1846
MA	West Amesbury	West Amesbury FASS	1838	
MA	West Boylston		1838?	after late 1838
MA	West Brooksfield	West Brooksfield FASS	1838?	after 1838
NY	Madison		1838	
OH	Cincinnati	Cincinnati Women's (also Ladies ASS of Cincinnati?)	1838	after early 1840

Female Antislavery Societies by Year of Founding

State	Town	Name	Founded	Disbanded
OH	Concord	Ross Co. Female	1838	
OH	Unionville		1838?	
PA	Philadelphia	Female Vigilance Association	1838	
PA	Philadelphia	Female Wesleyan	1838?	
VT	Randolph		1838?*	
IN	Economy, Wayne Co.	Economy Wayne Co. FASS	late 1830s	
IN	Newport, Wayne Co.	Newport FASS	late 1830s	after 1845
IN	Union County	FASS Union Co.	late 1830s	after 1843
IN	Westfield, Hamilton Co.		late 1830s	after 1847
MA	Andover	Andover FASS	1839	after late 1843
MA	Anisquam Point		1839	
MA	Byfield	FASS of Byfield	1839	
MA	Dighton		1839	after early 1842
MA	Georgetown		1839?	after mid-1843
MA	Glouster Harbor		1839	
MA	Greenfield		1839?	
MA	Ipswich		1839?	
MA	Marblehead		1839	
MA	Methuen	Methuen Ladies	1839?	1846
MA	Newton Upper Falls	FASS of Newton Upper Falls	1839?	after 1839
MA	Northampton	Northampton FASS	1839?	after 1839
MA	Shrewsbury	Ladies Abolition Society	1839?	
MA	Southboro	Southboro FASS	1839	after 1840
MA	West Bridgewater		1839?	after 1839

---

* There may have been an earlier society in 1834.

Female Antislavery Societies by Year of Founding

State	Town	Name	Founded	Disbanded
NY	NYC	Female Wesleyan ASS of the Methodist Episcopal Church	1839?	after 1840
MA	Boston	Mass. Female Emancipation Society	1840	1845?
MA	Boxford	Boxford FASS	1840?	
MA	Dedham	Dedham FASS	1840	after 1843
MA	Essex Co.	Essex Co. FASS	1840	early 1844
MA	New Ipswich	New Ipswich FASS	1840?	
MA	North Andover	Female Charitable Anti-Slavery Society	1840	
MA	North Andover	North Andover FASS	1840	
NH	Milford	Milford FASS	1840?	
NY	Manhattan	Manhattan Abolition Society	1840	1841?
CT	Bloomfield	Ladies ASS Bloomfield CT	1841?	
IN	Henry Co.	Henry Co. FASS	1841	summer 1849
IN	Wayne Township, Wayne Co.		1841	
MA	Hanover	Hanover FASS	1841?	
MA	Hyannis	FASS	1841?	
MA	Mansfield	Mansfield Sewing Circle	1841?	
MA	Nantucket	Nantucket Female Union	1841?	after 1844
MA	Sterling	FASS of Sterling	1841?	
NY	NYC	Colored Female Vigilance Cmte	1841	
IL	Elk Grove	Elk Grove FASS	1841 to 1844	
IL	Bureau Co.		1842 or 1843	
IL	Peoria		1842 or 1843	
IL	Princeton Co.		1842 or 1843	
??	New London	FASS of New London	1842?	

Female Antislavery Societies by Year of Founding

State	Town	Name	Founded	Disbanded
CT	Prospect	Prospect CT FASS	1843?	
IL	Putnam Co		1843	
MA	Essex	Essex FASS	1843?	
MA	Leominster	Garrisonian Society	1843	
MA	West Boxford	West Boxford FASS	1843?	
MA	West Reading	West Reading FASS	1843?	after 1846
IL		Illinois State FASS	1844	1847
IL	Jerseyville	FAS Dorcas Society	1844?	
NH	Portsmouth	Portsmouth Ladies	1844	after 1850
WI	Milwaukie	Ladies' Anti-Slavery Society	1844	
MA?	Princeton	Princeton AS Sewing Circle	1845?	
MA	Hopkinton	Ladies ASS (also known as sewing circle)	1846?	
MA	Salem	Female Emancipation Society of Salem	1846?	
MI	Highland Township	Female Anti-Slavery and Benevolent Society	1846	
MI	Lenawee County	FASS of Lenawee County	1846	
MI	Paw Paw and Lawrence	Van Buren Co. Ladies ASS	1846	
MI	Salem Township	Female Anti-Slavery and Benevolent Society	1846	
OH?	Orwell	Orwell FASS	1846?	
WI	Prairieville	FASS	1846	
WI	Milwaukee	Women's Anti-Slavery Society	1847	
MA	Plympton	Female Anti-Slavery Sewing Society of Plympton	1849?	
NY	Rochester	Union Anti-Slavery Sewing Society	1850	1851?
NY	Rochester	Ladies' A-S Sewing Society; then Ladies' ASS; then Freedmen's Aid Society	1851	1868
NY	Livonia	Livonia Ladies Anti-Slavery Society	1855?	1855?

State	Town	Name	Founded	Disbanded
OH	Delaware	Delaware Ladies ASS	1855?	
PA	Philadelphia	Philadelphia Women's Assoc.	1859	

Table B—Female Antislavery Societies by State

State	Town	Name	Founded	Disbanded
CT	Bloomfield	Ladies ASS Bloomfield CT	1841?	
CT	Brooklyn	FASS of Brooklyn & Vicinity	1834	
CT	Greenville		1836	
CT	Hartford	Hartford Female	1838	
CT	Middletown		1834	
CT	New Haven		1837	
CT	Norwich	Ladies ASS of Norwich CT	1834	
CT	Prospect	Prospect CT FASS	1843?	
CT	Willimantre (Willimantic)	FASS of Willimantic until 1842; then Willimantic Female (Working) ASS	1836	after 1843
IL	Bureau Co.		1842 or 1843	
IL	Elk Grove	Elk Grove FASS	1841 to 1844	
IL	Jerseyville	FAS Dorcas Society	1844?	
IL	Peoria		1842 or 1843	
IL	Princeton Co.		1842 or 1843	
IL	Putnam Co		1843	
IL		Illinois State FASS	1844	1847
IN	Economy, Wayne Co.	Economy Wayne Co. FASS	late 1830s	
IN	Henry Co.	Henry Co. FASS	1841	summer 1849
IN	Newport, Wayne Co.	Newport FASS	late 1830s	after 1845

State	Town	Name	Founded	Disbanded
IN	Union County	FASS Union Co.	late 1830s	after 1843
IN	Wayne Township, Wayne Co		1841	
IN	Westfield, Hamilton Co.		late 1830s	after 1847
MA	Abington		1837	after early 1842
MA	Amesbury/ Amesbury Mills	FASS of Amesbury	1833	
MA	Amesbury & Salisbury		1836	after early 1840
MA	Andover		1836	after 1839
MA	Andover	Andover FASS	1839	after late 1843
MA	Anisquam Point		1839	
MA	Ashburnham		1836	after 1839
MA	Athol		1838?	after 1839
MA	Barnstable		1837	after late 1838
MA	Boston	Boston FASS (evolves into Boston Social/Sewing Circle in late 1845)	1833	after mid-1846
MA	Boston	Mass. Female Emancipation Society	1840	1845?
MA	Boxborough (Boxboro)		1835	
MA	Boxford	Boxford FASS	1840?	
MA	Boylston		1838?	after 1842
MA	Braintree and Salisbury		1838	
MA	Brookline		1837	after 1839
MA	Byfield	FASS of Byfield	1839	
MA	Cambridgeport	Cambridgeport FASS	1836	1841
MA	Concord	Concord FASS	1837	after late 1846

Female Antislavery Societies by State

State	Town	Name	Founded	Disbanded
MA	Danvers	Danvers FASS	1837	after late 1843
MA	Dedham	Dedham FASS (later Ladies)	1838	after 1840
MA	Dedham	Dedham FASS	1840	after 1843
MA	Dighton		1839	after early 1842
MA	Dorchester		1835	after mid-1840
MA	Duxbury		1838	1839/1841
MA	East Bradford		1836	after early 1840
MA	East Bridgewater		1838	after 1839
MA	Essex	Essex FASS	1843?	
MA	Essex Co.	Essex Co. FASS	1840	early 1844
MA	Fairhaven	Fairhaven Ladies	1837	after 1839
MA	Fall River	FASS of Fall River	1835	after 1839; sewing society continued through 1845
MA	Fitchburg		1837	after 1838
MA	Franklin	Franklin Ladies	1837	after 1839
MA	Georgetown		1839?	after mid-1843
MA	Glouster Harbor		1839	
MA	Greenfield		1839?	
MA	Groton	Groton Ladies ASS	1836	after 1838
MA	Hanover	Hanover FASS	1841?	
MA	Haverhill	Haverhill FASS	1834	
MA	East Haverhill		1836	after 1839
MA	Hingham	Hingham FASS (later Hingham Ladies Sewing Circle)	1838?	after mid-1840
MA	Holliston	Ladies ASS	1837	after early 1843
MA	Hopkinton	Ladies ASS (also known as sewing circle)	1846?	

State	Town	Name	Founded	Disbanded
MA	Hyannis	Female Anti-Slavery Society	1841?	
MA	Ipswich		1839?	
MA	Leicester		1837?	after 1838
MA	Leominster	Garrisonian Society	1843	
MA	Lowell		1834	
MA	Lynn	FASS of Lynn (Lynn Women's ASS as of 1839)	1835	after early 1846
MA	Lynn	Lynn Anti-Slavery Sewing Circle	1844	1846
MA	Marblehead		1839	
MA	Methuen	Methuen Ladies	1839?	1846
MA	Millbury	Millbury Women's	1838	after 1843
MA	Millville		1836	after 1838
MA	Nantucket	Nantucket FASS (became Women's in 1839)	1838	1839
MA	Nantucket	Female Colored Union Society	1838	after 1839
MA	Nantucket	Nantucket Female Union	1841?	after 1844
MA	New Bedford	New Bedford FASS; became New Bedford Female Union Socy. 1839	1836	after 1845
MA	New Ipswich	New Ipswich FASS	1840?	
MA	Newburyport	Newburyport FASS	1834	after 1843
MA	Newton Upper Falls	FASS of Newton Upper Falls	1839?	after 1839
MA	North Andover	Female Charitable Anti-Slavery Society	1840	
MA	North Andover	North Andover FASS	1840	
MA	North Bridgewater	North Bridgewater FASS	1837	after late 1838
MA	North Danvers		1837	after early 1840
MA	North Leicester		1836	

State	Town	Name	Founded	Disbanded
MA	North Marshfield		1837	after 1839
MA	Northampton	Northampton FASS	1839?	after 1839
MA	Plymouth		1835?	1835?
MA	Plymouth		1837	after mid-1840
MA	Plympton	Female Anti-Slavery Sewing Society of Plympton	1849?	
MA?	Princeton	Princeton AS Sewing Circle	1845?	
MA	Provinceton	Provincetown FASS	1838	after mid-1839
MA	Reading	Reading FASS	1833	1850
MA	Roxbury	Roxbury Ladies	1840	after early 1837
MA	Salem	FASS of Salem	1832	1834?
MA	Salem	Salem FASS (had a related sewing society)	1834	1866
MA	Salem	Female Emancipation Society of Salem	1846?	
MA	Shrewsbury	Ladies Abolition Society	1839?	
MA	South Reading	FASS South Reading	1835	after 1839
MA	South Weymouth		1835	after late 1841
MA	South Danvers	South Danvers FASS	1837	after early 1839
MA	Southboro	Southboro FASS	1839	after 1840
MA	Sterling	FASS of Sterling	1841?	
MA	Stoneham	Stoneham FASS	1838	after early 1846
MA	Sudbury		1834	after 1839
MA	Upton		1837?	1846?
MA	Uxbridge	Uxbridge FASS	1836	after 1838
MA	West Amesbury	West Amesbury FASS	1838	
MA	West Boxford	West Boxford FASS	1843?	
MA	West Boylston		1838?	after late 1838

State	Town	Name	Founded	Disbanded
MA	West Bradford		1836	after 1837
MA	West Bridgewater		1839?	after 1839
MA	West Brooksfield	West Brooksfield FASS	1838?	after 1838
MA	West Hampton		1837	
MA	West Newbury		1837	after late 1843
MA	West Reading	West Reading FASS	1843?	after 1846
MA	Weymouth (also Weymouth and Braintree)	Weymouth & Braintree Female Emancipation Society (W&B FASS as of late 1840)	1835	1846 (1842-46 as sewing circle)
MA	Worcester Co.	Worcester Co. FASS (added a sewing circle from 1839 on)	1837	after 1841
MA	Wrentham		1837	after early 1843
ME	Bangor		1837	late 1843
ME	Hallowell	Hallowell ME FASS	1837	after late 1843
ME	Portland	Portland FASS	1834	after 1838
ME	Winthrop	Winthrop FASS	1837	
MI	Highland Township	Female Anti-Slavery and Benevolent Society	1846	
MI	Lenawee County	FASS of Lenawee County	1846	
MI	Paw Paw and Lawrence	Van Buren Co. Ladies ASS	1846	
MI	Salem Township	Female Anti-Slavery and Benevolent Society	1846	
NH	Canaan		1837	
NH	Chester		1836 or 1839?	
NH	Concord	Concord Ladies, later Female	1834	after 1840
NH	Dover	Dover FASS; then Dover A-S Sewing Circle; then Dover Anti-Slavery and Freedmen's Aid Society	1835	1866?
NH	Dunbarton		1837	

State	Town	Name	Founded	Disbanded
NH	Durham		1837	
NH	Grantham		1835	
NH	Great Falls		early 1830s	
NH	Haverhill		1837	after early 1843
NH	Milford	Milford FASS	1840?	
NH	New Market		1836	
NH	Newark		1837	
NH	Pittsfield	Pittsfield Ladies	1835	
NH	Plymouth		1834	
NH	Portsmouth	Portsmouth FASS	1836	
NH	Portsmouth	Portsmouth Ladies	1844	after 1850
NH	Rochester		1836	1836?
NH	Sandwich		1836	
NH	Wakefield		1837	
NH	Weare		1837	
NJ	Bloomfield		1837	
NY	Buffalo		1835	
NY	Champlain		1837	after 1838
NY	Clinton		1835?	
NY	Farmington		1837	after 1839
NY	Hudson		1833	
NY	Knowlesville		1837	
NY	Lockport		1837	
NY	Livonia	Livonia Ladies Anti-Slavery Society	1855?	1855?
NY	Madison		1838	
NY	Manhattan	Manhattan Abolition Society	1840	1841?

State	Town	Name	Founded	Disbanded
NY	NYC	FASS of Chatham St. Chapel	1834	
NY	NYC	Ladies' New-York City Anti-Slavery Society	1835	after 1838
NY	NYC	Female Wesleyan ASS	1836	after 1842
NY	NYC	Female Wesleyan ASS of the Methodist Episcopal Church	1839?	after 1840
NY	NYC	Colored Female Vigilance Cmte	1841	
NY	Palmyra		1837	
NY	Peru		1835	after 1838
NY	Pompey		1837	
NY	Rochester	Union Anti-Slavery Society (women of the African Methodist Episcopal Zion Church)	1834	
NY	Rochester	Rochester FASS	1835	1842 at latest
NY	Rochester	Union Anti-Slavery Sewing Society	1850?	1851?
NY	Rochester	Ladies' Anti-Slavery Sewing Society; then Ladies' A-S Society; then Freedmen's Aid Society	1851	1868
NY	Sanquoit		1835	
NY	Sherburne		1835	
NY	Troy		1835	
NY	Utica		1835	after 1838
NY	Warsaw		1835	
NY	Whitesboro		1834	
OH	Abbyville	Abbyville OH FASS	1836	
OH	Andover	Andover State Road Female Anti-Slavery Society	1836	
OH	Ashtabula Co.		1835	after 1846
OH	Bloomingburgh		1837	

State	Town	Name	Founded	Disbanded
OH	Cadiz	Cadiz FASS	1837?	after mid-1841
OH	Canton		1836	
OH	Cherry Valley	CV Township	1836	
OH	Cincinnati	Cincinnati Women's (also Ladies ASS of Cincinnati?)	1838	after early 1840
OH	Concord	Ross Co. Female	1838	
OH	Delaware	Delaware Ladies ASS	1855?	
OH	Elyria		1836?	
OH	Geneva		1836?	
OH	Granville		1835	
OH	Harpersfield and Austinburg		1836	
OH	Madison		1836?	
OH	Morgan	Morgan Township	1836	
OH	Muskingham Co.		1835	
OH	New Lyme	New Lyme FASS	1836	
OH	Oberlin		1835	
OH?	Orwell	Orwell FASS	1846?	
OH	Portage Co.		1836?	
OH	Rome	Rome Township	1836	
OH	St. Albans		1836?	
OH	Unionville		1838?	
OH	Vernon		1835	
OH	Wayne	Wayne Township	1836	
OH	Windsor	Windsor Township	1836	
PA	Buckingham	Buckingham FASS	1836	after 1837
PA	Germantown		1836?	

State	Town	Name	Founded	Disbanded
PA	Lower Wakefield		1836	
PA	Philadelphia	Philadelphia FASS (added a sewing society in 1837)	1833	1870
PA	Philadelphia	Female Vigilance Association	1838	
PA	Philadelphia	Female Wesleyan	1838?	
PA	Philadelphia	Philadelphia Women's Assoc.	1859	
PA	Pittsburgh	Pittsburgh (later Pittsburgh & Allegheny)	1836	
RI	Kent Co.		1835	around 1840
RI	Natick		1834?	
RI	Pawtucket		1835	after 1838
RI	Providence	Providence FASS	1832	
RI	Providence	Providence Ladies (later Female)	1835	after mid-1846
RI	Providence	FASS	1837	after 1838
RI	Smithfield (Upper)		1836	after 1838
VT	Bellingham		1834?	
VT	Cornwall		1837	
VT	Randolph		1838?*	
VT	Waitsfield		1836	
VT	Weybridge	Weybridge FASS	1834	
WI	Milwaukee	Women's Anti-Slavery Society	1847	
WI	Milwaukie	Ladies' Anti-Slavery Society	1844	
WI	Prairieville	FASS	1846	
??	Massillon	Massillon FASS	1837?	
??	New London	Female Anti-Slavery Society of New London	1842?	

---

* There may have been an earlier society in 1834 as well.

Notes

Abbreviations Used

In the interests of space, the following abbreviations are used throughout the notes and text to designate particular newspapers, archives, libraries, collections, or organizations.

ACS	American Colonization Society.
AAS	American Anti-Slavery Society.
AASW	American Antiquarian Society, Worcester, Massachusetts.
AKF Papers	Abby Kelley Foster Papers (in AASW).
ASCAW	Anti-Slavery Convention of American Women.
Boston FASS Letterbook	Boston Female Anti-Slavery Society Letterbook, MHS. Entries dated from April 9, 1834, to January 7, 1838.
BPL	Boston Public Library/Rare Books Department. All citations courtesy of the Trustees.
Cowles Papers	Betsy Mix Cowles Papers, Department of Special Collections and Archives, Kent State University Libraries and Media Services, Kent, Ohio.
Genius	*Genius of Universal Emancipation.*
HSP	Philadelphia Female Anti-Slavery Society Records, reel 31, incoming correspondence. Pennsylvania Abolition Society Collection, Historical Society of Pennsylvania, Philadelphia.
MFES	Massachusetts Female Emancipation Society.
MGF	Maloney Collection of the McKim-Garrison Family Papers, Manuscripts and Archives Division, NYPL, Astor, Lenox and Tilden Foundations.
MHS	Massachusetts Historical Society, Boston.
NHHS	New Hampshire Historical Society, Concord.
NYHS	New York Historical Society, New York.
NYPL	New York Public Library, New York.
OSV	Research Library at Old Sturbridge Village, Sturbridge, Massachusetts.
PEM	Peabody Essex Museum, Salem, Massachusetts.

RUL   Department of Rare Books and Special Collections, Rochester University Library, Rochester, New York.

Salem FASS   Salem Female Anti-Slavery Society Records, mss. 34. Phillips Library, PEM.

Introduction—The Power of Association

1. The epigraph is taken from Boston Female Anti-Slavery Society (Boston FASS), *Ten Years of Experience: Ninth Annual Report of the Boston Female Anti-Slavery Society, presented October 12, 1842* (Boston: Oliver Johnson, 1842), 9 (italics deleted).

2. "Riots, Muzzling the Press, &c." and "The Mob at Concord," *Liberator,* December 13, 1834, pp. 197, 198; "Female Courage," *Liberator,* December 6, 1834, p. 193; New Hampshire Anti-Slavery Convention, *Proceedings of the New Hampshire Anti-Slavery Convention, held in Concord, on the 11th and 12th of November, 1834* (Concord, NH: Eastman, Webster and Co., 1834); "Constitution of the Concord Female Anti-Slavery Society," *Herald of Freedom,* June 24, 1837, p. 67, cols. 3–4.

3. "Franklin" to Miss Lucy W. Allen and the 188 Ladies of Muskingham County, Ohio, March 9, 1841, under "Sphere of Woman," in *National Anti-Slavery Standard,* April 29, 1841; Eli Potter, *Remarks of Eli Potter, Esq. At the Trial of Two Individuals for A Breach of the Peace, in Disturbing a Meeting, In Which a Female Was Lecturing, Upon the Subject of Abolition* (Litchfield, CT: C. E. Moss & Co., 1840).

4. Rochester Ladies' Anti-Slavery Society, *Thirteenth Annual Report* (Rochester, NY: Rochester Democrat Steam Printing House, 1864), 2.

1—Antecedents, 1760–1831

1. The epigraph is taken from "Opinions," Ladies' Repository, *Genius of Universal Emancipation* (hereafter *Genius*), December 11, 1829, p. 108.

2. According to the Pennsylvania census, slavery continued in that state through at least 1820, and possibly 1830, while Connecticut did not grant freedom to its last slaves until 1848. Arthur Zilversmit, *The First Emancipation: The Abolition of Slavery in the North* (Chicago: University of Chicago Press, 1967), 202, 207.

3. Richard S. Newman, *The Transformation of American Abolitionism: Fighting Slavery in the Early Republic* (Chapel Hill: University of North Carolina Press, 2002), 16–59; Alice Dana Adams, *The Neglected Period of Anti-Slavery in America, 1808–1831* (1908; Gloucester, MA: Peter Smith, 1964).

4. Gary B. Nash and Jean R. Soderlund, *Freedom by Degrees: Emancipation in Pennsylvania and Its Aftermath* (New York: Oxford University Press, 1991), 68–69; Shane White, *Somewhat More Independent: The End of Slavery in New York City, 1770–1810* (Athens: University of Georgia Press, 1991), 134–38.

5. Margaret Hope Bacon, "By Moral Force Alone: The Antislavery Women and Nonresistance," in *The Abolitionist Sisterhood: Women's Political Culture in Antebellum America,* ed. Jean Fagan Yellin and John C. Van Horne (Ithaca, NY: Cornell University Press, 1994), 277.

6. Donald G. Mathews, "The Second Great Awakening as an Organizing Process, 1780–1830: An Hypothesis," *American Quarterly* 21.1 (1969): 23–43; Carol Sheriff, *The Artificial River: The Erie Canal and the Paradox of Progress, 1817–1862* (New York: Hill and Wang, 1996), 138–71; Robert H. Abzug, *Cosmos Crumbling: American Reform and the Religious Imagination* (New York: Oxford University Press, 1994), 3–8.

7. Nancy F. Cott, "Young Women in the Second Great Awakening in New England," *Feminist Studies* 3 (Fall 1975): 15–29; Mary P. Ryan, "A Women's Awakening: Evangelical Religion and the Families of Utica, New York, 1800–1840," *American Quarterly* 30.5 (Winter 1978): 602–23; Mary P. Ryan, *Cradle of the Middle Class: The Family in Oneida County, New York, 1790–1865* (Cambridge: Cambridge University Press, 1981), 60–104; Suzanne Lebsock, *The Free Women of Petersburg: Status and Culture in a Southern Town, 1784–1860* (New York: W. W. Norton, 1984), 215–16.

8. Anne M. Boylan, "Benevolence and Antislavery Activity among African American Women in New York and Boston, 1820–1840," in Yellin and Van Horne, *Abolitionist Sisterhood*, 121–25; Anne Firor Scott, "Most Invisible of All: Black Women's Voluntary Associations," *Journal of Southern History* 56.1 (1990): 3–22.

9. "Colored People of Salem," *Liberator*, January 7, 1832, p. 3.

10. Boylan, "Benevolence and Antislavery Activity," 125, 130; Dorothy Sterling, ed., *We Are Your Sisters: Black Women in the Nineteenth Century* (New York: W. W. Norton, 1984), 110–12.

11. "Female Benevolence," *Genius* 1.6, December 1821, p. 95.

12. *Liberator,* October 1, 1836.

13. Philip J. Staudenraus, *The African Colonization Movement, 1816–1865* (New York: Columbia University Press, 1961); Douglas R. Egerton, "'Its Origin Is Not a Little Curious': A New Look at the American Colonization Society," *Journal of the Early Republic* 5.4 (Winter 1985): 463–67; William Lloyd Garrison, *Thoughts on African Colonization* (Boston: Garrison and Knapp, 1832; rpt., New York: Arno Press, 1968); Newman, *American Abolitionism*, 117.

14. Staudenraus, *African Colonization Movement*, 123, 127, 149; Elizabeth Varon, *We Mean to Be Counted: White Women and Politics in Antebellum Virginia* (Chapel Hill: University of North Carolina Press, 1998), 41–70; "More Female Patriotism," *Genius,* February 18, 1826, p. 197; "Female Philanthropy," *Genius,* January 3, 1829, p. 94.

15. I have been unable to locate any other materials regarding the Norwich Society and thus am unable to verify the women's reasons for their odd affiliation choice. *Liberator,* July 26, 1834, p. 117.

16. Benjamin Quarles, *Black Abolitionists* (New York: Oxford University Press, 1969), 7; Maria W. Stewart, "An Address, Delivered at the African Masonic Hall, Boston, Feb. 27, 1833," in Sue E. Houchins, *Spiritual Narratives* (New York: Oxford University Press, 1988), 69.

17. *Liberator,* December 10, 1836, p. 199; Mary Clark to Anne Warren Weston, June 13, 1837, Concord, NH (BPL Ms.A.9.2.9.40).

18. Judith Wellman, "Women and Radical Reform in Antebellum Upstate New York: A Profile of Grassroots Female Abolitionists," in *Clio Was a Woman: Studies in the History of American Women,* ed. Mabel E. Deutrich and Virginia C. Purdy (Washington, DC: Howard University Press, 1980), 121; Nancy A. Hewitt, *Women's Activism and Social Change: Rochester, New York, 1822–1872* (Ithaca, NY: Cornell University Press, 1984), 38–68.

19. Maria Stewart, "Religion and the Pure Principles of Morality, the Sure Foundation on Which We Must Build," from *Productions of Mrs. Maria Stewart* (Boston: Published by the Friends of Freedom and Virtue, 1835), in Houchins, *Spiritual Narratives,* 4, 13; James O. Horton, "Freedom's Yoke: Gender Conventions among Antebellum Free Blacks," *Feminist Studies* 12.1 (Spring 1986): 51–76.

20. "Female Literary Association [of Philadelphia]," Miscellaneous section, *Liberator*, December 3, 1831, p. 196; "Constitution of the Afric-American Female Intelligence Society of Boston," Ladies' Department, *Liberator*, January 7, 1832; Dorothy B. Porter, "The Organized Educational Activities of Negro Literary Societies, 1828–1846," *Journal of Negro Education* 5.4 (October 1936): 556–76; Julie Winch, "'You Have Talents—Only Cultivate Them': Philadelphia's Black Female Literary Societies and the Abolitionist Crusade," in Yellin and Van Horne, *Abolitionist Sisterhood*, 101–19.

21. Ladies' Department, *Liberator*, February 16, 1832, p. 26; Ann C. Smith, President, and Susan Paul, Secretary, to William Lloyd Garrison, November 23, 1833, Boston (BPL Ms.A.1.2.v3.p87).

22. Porter, "Negro Literary Societies," 575. The Sarah M. Douglass Literary Circle in Philadelphia held its first meeting on September 22, 1859. Quarles, *Black Abolitionists*, 105.

23. Porter, "Negro Literary Societies," 569.

24. Bacon, "By Moral Force Alone," 277.

25. Ruth Nuermberger, *The Free Produce Movement: A Quaker Protest against Slavery* (Durham, NC: Duke University Press, 1942), 12–19.

26. See "What Shall Be Done?" *Liberator*, July 30, 1831.

27. Clare Midgley, "Slave Sugar Boycotts, Female Activism and the Domestic Base of British Anti-Slavery Culture," *Slavery and Abolition* 17.3 (December 1996): 137–62; Charlotte Sussman, *Consuming Anxieties: Consumer Protest, Gender, and British Slavery, 1713–1833* (Stanford, CA: Stanford University Press, 2000).

28. Nuermberger, *Free Produce Movement*, 59, 113–15; Norman B. Wilkinson, "The Philadelphia Free Produce Attack upon Slavery," *Pennsylvania Magazine of History and Biography* 64 (1942): 294–313.

29. T. H. Breen, "Narrative of Commercial Life: Consumption, Ideology, and Community on the Eve of the American Revolution," *William and Mary Quarterly*, 3rd ser., 50.3 (July 1993): 471–501; Ruth Bloch, "The Gendered Meanings of Virtue in Revolutionary America," *Signs* 13.1 (1987): 37–58.

30. Mary S. Lloyd, Wood Green near Wednesbury, Staffordshire, [September] 9, 1825 (Miscellaneous Manuscripts, Friends Historical Library, Swarthmore College); Clare Taylor, *Women of the Anti-Slavery Movement: The Weston Sisters* (New York: St. Martin's Press, 1995), 19.

31. Clare Midgley, *Women against Slavery: The British Campaigns, 1780–1870* (London: Routledge, 1992); Clare Midgley, "'Remember Those in Bonds, As Bound with Them': Women's approach to anti-slavery campaigning in Britain, 1780–1870," in *Women, Migration, and Empire*, ed. Joan Grant (Staffordshire, England: Trentham Books, 1996), 73–102; Karen I. Halbersleben, *Women's Participation in the British Anti-slavery Movement, 1824–1865* (Lewiston, ME: E. Mellen Press, 1993).

32. Elizabeth Heyrick, *Immediate, Not Gradual Abolition; or, An Inquiry into the Shortest, Safest, and Most Effectual Means of Getting Rid of West Indian Slavery* (London, 1824).

33. Elizabeth Heyrick, *Apology for Ladies' Anti-Slavery Associations* (London: J. Hatchard and Son, 1828); [Elizabeth Heyrick], *Appeal to the Hearts and Consciences of British Women* (Leicester: A. Cockshaw, 1828).

34. In 1838 the Philadelphia Female Anti-Slavery Society (Philadelphia FASS) reprinted Heyrick's work, giving it a new and more expanded circulation in America. Philadelphia FASS, *Fifth Annual Report of the Philadelphia Female Anti-Slavery Society, January 10, 1839* (Philadelphia: Merrihew and Thompson, 1839).

35. "Temple of the Muses and Ladies' Literary Cabinet," *Genius* 1.1, July 1821; "Anti-Slavery Ladies' Association," *Genius* 2.27, May 12, 1827, p. 213.

36. H.C., "Forty-Sixth Anniversary of American Independence," *Genius* 2.5, November 1822, p. 69; "From a Female Pen," *Genius* 3.5, September 1823, pp. 40–41; "Temple of the Muses and Ladies' Literary Cabinet," *Genius* 1.1, July 1821; "The Empire of Woman," *Genius* 1[5].20, January 14, 1826; "Female Philanthropists," *Genius,* November 17, 1827, p. 159.

37. "Associations," *Genius,* January 22, 1830, p. 156, June 1831, p. 28; Merton L. Dillon, "Elizabeth Chandler and the Spread of Antislavery Sentiment in Michigan," *Michigan History* 39 (December 1955): 481–94.

38. "Opinions," *Genius,* December 11, 1829, p. 108.

39. Females of Philadelphia, unsigned, Philadelphia, November 3, 1831 (BPL Ms.A.1.2.v1.p44).

40. "A Noble Example," *Liberator,* December 17, 1831, p. 203; "Petitioning Congress," *Genius,* December 1831; "The District of Columbia," *Genius,* January 1833, p. 44.

41. *Liberator,* March 23, 1833, p. 45; Winch, "'You Have Talents,'" 112.

42. Linda K. Kerber, *Women of the Republic: Intellect and Ideology in Revolutionary America* (Chapel Hill: University of North Carolina, 1980), 85–87, 98, 112.

43. Mary Hershberger, "Mobilizing Women, Anticipating Abolition: The Struggle against Indian Removal in the 1830s," *Journal of American History* 86.1 (June 1999): 15–40.

2—Organizational Beginnings, 1832–1837

1. The epigraph is taken from L., "Address to the Women of New Hampshire on the Importance of Forming Female Anti-Slavery Societies," Dunbarton, July 10, 1837, *Herald of Freedom,* July 15, 1837, p. 82, cols. 3–4.

2. "Constitution of the Female Anti-Slavery Society of Salem, Formed February 22, 1832," *Liberator,* November 17, 1832.

3. See Appendix Table A for a complete list of societies by year of founding.

4. Bylaws and meeting minutes, Record of the Lynn Female Anti-Slavery Society (Lynn Museum, Lynn, MA).

5. *Herald of Freedom,* June 24, 1837, p. 67, cols. 1–2.

6. H. E. Guzzam, Pittsburgh Female Anti-Slavery Society, to Mary Grew, December 26, 1836, Pittsburgh (HSP).

7. "Female Anti-Slavery Society of Hudson, N.Y.," *Genius,* January 1834, p. 11.

8. "Another Female Anti-Slavery Society," *Genius,* November 1832, p. 12; "Female Anti-Slavery Society," *Liberator,* July 14, 1832, p. 111.

9. Horace P. Wakefield seems to have attended as the delegate of the FASS of Reading, Massachusetts, but he seems to have been the only representative of female societies. "Female Anti-Slavery Associations," *Genius,* March 1834, p. 49; entry dated December 16, 1833, in the Reading FASS Records (Reading Historical Commission, Reading, MA).

10. Quotation from L. H., "The Duty of Females," *Liberator,* May 5, 1832, p. 70. The other three women who attended the AAS Convention were Sidney Ann Lewis, Esther Moore, and Lydia White. Lucretia Mott's reminiscences of the 1833 meeting can be found in *Proceedings of the American Anti-Slavery Society at its Third Decade, held in the City of Philadelphia, Dec. 3d and 4th, 1863* (New York: AAS, 1864),

41–43, and Anna Davis Hallowell, ed., *James and Lucretia Mott: Life and Letters* (1884; Boston: Houghton, Mifflin, 1890), 111–16. For details of the constitutional articles related to membership, voting, and delegates, see AAS, *Proceedings of the Anti-Slavery Convention, assembled at Philadelphia, December 4, 5 and 6, 1833* (New York: Dorr and Butterfield, 1833), 3, 7, 8, 18. The wording of these articles would become the subject of controversy beginning in 1838.

11. For the Limington Society, see *Liberator*, July 2, 1836. The Clarkson Anti-Slavery Society had all male officers at its founding in 1834 but had a female officer by 1836. Clarkson Anti-Slavery Society to Mary Grew, May 26, 1836, Pennsgrove, PA (HSP); *Liberator*, September 13, 1834, p. 145.

12. Carroll Smith-Rosenberg, "The Female World of Love and Ritual: Relations between Women in Nineteenth-Century America," *Signs* 1.1 (1975): 1–30.

13. These societies were Abington, Dorchester, Fall River, South Reading, and Uxbridge. In Abington women were a tiny minority of the members; in Fall River they made up fully half of the society.

14. *Liberator*, May 7, 1836, p. 74; L., "Address to the Women of New Hampshire on the Importance of Forming Female Anti-Slavery Societies," July 10, 1837, Dunbarton, *Herald of Freedom*, July 15, 1837, p. 82, cols. 3–4.

15. See L. M. Child to Mrs. Phelps, n.d. [Jan. 2, 1834] (BPL Ms.A.21.4.p4).

16. AAS, *Proceedings . . . Third Decade*, 41–43. A similar "push-pull" relationship fueled female organization and institution building between 1870 and 1920. Estelle Freedman, "Separatism as Strategy: Female Institution Building and American Feminism, 1870–1930," *Feminist Studies* 5.3 (Fall 1979): 512–29.

17. For AAS resolutions, see *Proceedings . . . Convention* (New York: Dorr and Butterfield, 1833): 16–18, and *Liberator*, December 21, 1833, p. 202. New-England Anti-Slavery Convention, *Proceedings of the New-England Anti-Slavery Convention, held in Boston on the 27th, 28th and 29th of May, 1834* (Boston: Garrison and Knapp, 1834), 18; New Hampshire Anti-Slavery Convention, *Proceedings . . . Convention*, 8; Rhode Island Anti-Slavery Convention, *Proceedings of the Rhode Island Anti-Slavery Convention held in Providence, on the 2d, 3d and 4th of February, 1836* (Providence: H. H. Brown, 1836); and "Minutes of the Fifth Annual Convention for the Improvement of the Free People of Color in the U.S.," *Liberator*, August 1, 1835.

18. Weld commission in Dwight L. Dumond and Gilbert H. Barnes, eds., *The Letters of Theodore Dwight Weld, Angelina Grimké Weld and Sarah Grimké, 1822–1844* (New York: D. Appleton-Century, for the American Historical Association, 1934), 1:124–28; "Particular Instructions," 1836 American Antislavery Society Agency Commission for James McKim (Maloney/McKim/Garrison Papers, box 2, MGF 11, NYPL).

19. James A. Thome to Theodore Weld, March 31, 1836, Wellsville [Ohio], in Dumond and Barnes, *Letters*, 1:281–86; Charles Burleigh to Samuel J. May, April 8, 9, 1835 (BPL), quoted in Newman, *American Abolitionism*, 169; George Thompson, *Letters and Addresses by George Thompson during his Mission to the United States, from October 1, 1834, to November 27, 1835* (Boston: Isaac Knapp, 1837), 62.

20. "Mission to the U.S.," *Liberator*, October 11, 1834, p. 162; George Thompson, *Substance of an Address to the Ladies of Glasgow and its Vicinity upon the Present Aspect of the Great Question of Negro Emancipation* (Glasgow: David Robertson, 1833), 36–39; Glasgow Ladies' Auxiliary Emancipation Society, *Three Years' Female Anti-Slavery Effort in Britain and America: Being a Report of the Proceedings of the Glasgow Ladies' Auxiliary Emancipation Society, Since its Formation in January, 1834* (Glasgow: Published by the Society, 1837).

21. Thompson, *Letters and Addresses,* 4–5, 15, 39, 62; *Liberator,* April 18, 1835, p. 63, October 11, 1834, p. 163; Ladies' New-York City Anti-Slavery Society, *First Annual Report of the Ladies' New-York City Anti-Slavery Society* (New York: William S. Dorr, 1836; rpt. Louisville: Lost Cause Press, 1962), 5.

22. Letter from Miss Elizabeth Dudley "To the Ladies forming the Anti-Slavery Association at Reading, in Massachusetts," *Liberator,* February 15, 1834, p. 26.

23. "First Annual Report of the Concord (NH) Female Anti-Slavery Society," *Herald of Freedom,* January 9, 1836, p. 39, cols. 2–4; Anna Purinton, Corresponding Secretary, Lynn, June 17, 1835, as printed in the *Liberator,* June 20, 1835, p. 99; Juliana Tappan to "Dear Madam," April 13, 1835, in Glasgow Ladies' Auxiliary Emancipation Society, *Three Years' . . . Effort.*

24. Amy Swerdlow, "Abolition's Conservative Sisters: The Ladies' New York City Anti-Slavery Societies, 1834–1840," in Yellin and Van Horne, *Abolitionist Sisterhood,* 34; Anne M. Boylan, *The Origins of Women's Activism: New York and Boston, 1797–1840* (Chapel Hill: University of North Carolina Press, 2002), 39–47.

25. Hewitt, *Women's Activism.* For an excellent account of this problem, see Mrs. A. H. L. Phelps, "Female Associations," *Herald of Freedom,* October 29, 1836, p. 140, cols. 2–3.

26. Debra Gold Hansen, *Strained Sisterhood: Gender and Class in the Boston Female Anti-Slavery Society* (Amherst: University of Massachusetts Press, 1993), 13.

27. Hallowell, *James and Lucretia Mott,* 121. See also AAS, *Proceedings . . . Third Decade,* 41–43.

28. Bruce Dorsey, "Friends Becoming Enemies: Philadelphia Benevolence and the Neglected Era of American Quaker History," *Journal of the Early Republic* 18.3 (Fall 1998): 395–428.

29. Emma Lapsansky, "Feminism, Freedom, and Community: Charlotte Forten and Women Activists in Nineteenth-Century Philadelphia," *Pennsylvania Magazine of History and Biography* 113.1 (January 1989): 13; Gerda Lerner, *The Grimké Sisters from South Carolina: Rebels against Slavery* (Boston: Houghton Mifflin, 1967), 132–33.

30. Carolyn Williams, "The Female Antislavery Movement: Fighting against Racial Prejudice and Promoting Women's Rights in Antebellum America," in Yellin and Van Horne, *Abolitionist Sisterhood,* 168; Hallowell, *James and Lucretia Mott,* 121; Carolyn Luverne Williams, "Religion, Race, and Gender in Antebellum American Radicalism: The Philadelphia Female Anti-Slavery Society, 1833–1870" (Ph.D. diss., University of California–Los Angeles, 1991), 565, 456–66, 480–81, 303.

31. William Lloyd Garrison to the Ladies Anti-Slavery Society, April 9, 1834, Boston. See also reply from Mary Grew, April 11, 1834, and Mary Grew to Mrs. Amos A. Phelps, April 11, 1834, Boston (all in Boston FASS Letterbook, MHS).

32. Hansen, *Strained Sisterhood,* 64. The discussion of race in the Boston FASS (and elsewhere) is complicated by the difficulties researchers face in determining the race of individuals in previous historical periods. In addition to the simple problem of "discovering" the race of a name on the page, race as a social construct was often more fluid than we tend to admit. Martha and Lucy Ball, daughters of a Jamaican planter, were considered "women of slight color" by a delegate to the 1838 Anti-Slavery Convention of American Women. However, their death certificates noted their race as white, and they seem to have been considered such by the other members of the Boston FASS. By contrast Susan Paul, whom most Boston FASS members did see as black, was considered "not very dark." Debra Gold Hansen, "The Boston

Female Anti-Slavery Society and the Limits of Gender Politics," in Yellin and Van Horne, *Abolitionist Sisterhood,* 56, n. 37; Sarah H. Southwick, *Reminiscences of Early Anti-Slavery Days* (Cambridge, MA: Riverside Press, 1893), 29.

33. Elizabeth Buffum Chase, *Anti-Slavery Reminiscences* (Central Falls, RI: E. L. Freeman and Son, 1891), 16 (AASW).

34. Shirley Yee, *Black Women Abolitionists: A Study in Activism, 1828–1860* (Knoxville: University of Tennessee Press, 1992), 108–9; Sterling, *We Are Your Sisters,* 117–18; Gretchen W. Cohen, "Clip Not Her Wings: Female Abolitionists in Rochester, New York, 1835–1868" (master's thesis, City College of the City University of New York, 1994), 22.

35. Louisa Phillips to Mrs. Chapman, July 31, 1837, North Marshfield (BPL Ms.A.9.2.9.58, Weston Sisters microfilm reel 2); S. Arnold to Betsy Mix Cowles, 5 April [year unclear], New Lyme (Cowles Papers, box 2, folder 9); Abby Kelley to Hudsons, April 12, 1841, quoted in Dorothy Sterling, *Ahead of Her Time: Abby Kelley and the Politics of Anti-Slavery* (New York: W. W. Norton, 1991), 119.

36. John Hayward, *A Gazetteer of Massachusetts,* rev. ed. (Boston: J. P. Jewett, 1849), 328–29.

37. Lynn Manring and Jack Larkin, eds, *Women, Anti-Slavery, and the Constitution in Rural New England: A Sourcebook of Interpretation,* vol. 2 (Massachusetts: Old Sturbridge Village, [1984]), particularly the section on "The Abolitionist Activities of Mary A. White," by Lynn Manring, July 15, 1983 (OSV Collection).

38. Anne Warren Weston to the New York Female Anti-Slavery Society, July 21, 1835, Boston (Boston FASS Letterbook, MHS); Mary Clark to Miss A. E. Grimké, November 1836, Concord, NH, Mary P. Rogers to Miss [Margaretta] Forten, August 2, 1834, Plymouth, NH (both in HSP).

39. Lucy B. Williams and Samuel J. May to Lucretia Motte [sic], June 25, 1834, Brooklyn, Conn[ecticut] (HSP). The Boston FASS also received a letter from the Ladies of Brooklyn. Olive Gilbert and Sarah Benson to the Boston Female Anti-Slavery Society, June 29, 1834, Brooklyn (Boston FASS Letterbook, MHS).

40. Ann Buckman to Lucretia Mott, June 11, 1836, per HSP documentation, but actually [November] 13, [1836] (HSP).

41. Ashtabula County Anti-Slavery Society Records (Ms 387, Western Reserve Historical Society, Cleveland, Ohio); Lucy M. Wright to Betsy Mix Cowles, March 5, 1836, Tallmadge, Ohio (Cowles Papers, box 1, folder 3).

42. M. Grew to the Female Anti-Slavery Society at Amesbury Mills [Mrs. Howarth, President], May 17, 1834, Boston; Mary Grew to the Reading Female Anti-Slavery Society [Mrs. Reid, President], May 17, 1834, Boston; Anne Warren Weston to the Concord Female Anti-Slavery Society, July 22, 1835, Boston; and Anne Warren Weston to Mrs. Hesekiah Sturges, Corresponding Secretary for the Putnam, Ohio Female Anti-Slavery Society, July 22, 1835, Boston (all in Boston FASS Letterbook, MHS).

43. C. C. Burleigh to William Lloyd Garrison, March 17, 1835, Groton, in the *Liberator,* March 28, 1835, p. 50; "First Annual Report of the Boston Female Anti-Slavery Society," *Liberator,* January 3, 1835; Anne [Weston] to Debora [Weston], April 18, 1837, Boston (BPL Ms.A.9.2.9.28); Anne Warren Weston to Miss Elisa [Elvira?] Mason, Corresponding Secretary of the Bangor Female Anti Slavery Society, January 7, 1838, Boston (Boston FASS Letterbook, MHS); Appendix to *Immediate Abolition Vindicated. An Address, delivered June 26, 1838 before the Randolph Female Anti-Slavery Society, at their Annual Meeting. By Elderkin J. Boardman, A.B., Pastor of the First Church in Randolph, Vt. Published by Request* (Montpelier, VT: E. P. Watson and Son, 1838).

44. Louisa Phillips to Maria Weston Chapman, July 31, 1837, August 6, [1837], North Marshfield (BPL Ms.A.9.2.9.58, Ms.A.9.2.10.p46, Weston Sisters microfilm reel 2).

45. *Liberator,* December 28, 1833, p. 207, February 8, 1834, p. 23; Mary Bosworth Truedley, "The 'Benevolent Fair': A Study of Charitable Organization among American Women in the First Third of the Nineteenth Century," *Social Service Review* 16 (September 1940): 509–22.

46. "Anti-Slavery Ladies—Attention!" *Liberator,* November 22, 1834, p. 187.

47. See the inflation calculator at www.westegg.com/inflation, or John J. Mc-Cusker, *How Much Is That in Real Money? A Historical Commodity Price Index for Use as a Deflator of Money Values in the Economy of the United States,* 2nd ed. (Worcester, MA: American Antiquarian Society, 2001).

48. Louisa Phillips to Mrs. Chapman, July 31, 1837, North Marshfield (BPL Ms.A.9.2.9.58).

49. S. H. Earle to Maria W. and Mary Gray Chapman, [December] 21, 1841, Worcester (BPL Ms.A.4.6A.v.1.no.18).

50. *Liberator,* December 20, 1834, p. 203.

51. *Liberator,* January 2, 1837, p. 3.

52. New-England Anti-Slavery Society, *Third Annual Report of the Board of Managers of the New-England Anti-Slavery Society, presented January 21, 1835* (Boston: Garrison and Knapp, 1835), 6 (PEM); Andrea M. Atkin, "'When Pincushions Are Periodicals': Women's Work, Race, and Material Objects in Female Abolitionism," *American Transcendental Quarterly,* n.s., 11.2 (June 1997): 93–113.

53. Caroline Weston to Samuel J. May, October 21, 1871, Weymouth (BPL Ms.B.1.6.v13.p93).

54. "Vanity Fairs," *Liberator,* April 16, 1831, p. 63. Also see "Fairs for Benevolent Objects," *Genius,* January 29, 1830, pp. 165–66.

55. *Herald of Freedom,* May 16, 1835, p. 23, col. 4, May 28, 1836; *Liberator,* May 16, 1835, p. 79.

56. Female Anti-Slavery Society of Chatham-Street Chapel, *Constitution and Address of the Female Anti-Slavery Society of Chatham Street Chapel* (New York: William S. Dorr, 1834; rpt. Louisville: Lost Cause Press, 1965), 8.

57. AAS, "Declaration of Sentiments," in *The Abolitionists,* ed. Louis Ruchames (New York: Putnam, 1963), 78.

58. Boston FASS, *Right and Wrong in Boston. Report of the Boston Female Anti-Slavery Society; with a Concise Statement of Events, Previous and Subsequent to the Annual Meeting of 1835* (Boston: Published by the Society, 1836), 48–49; Chatham-Street Chapel FASS, *Constitution and Address,* 10; Concord FASS, *First Annual Report of the Ladies' Anti-Slavery Society of Concord, December 25, 1835* (Concord, NH: Elbridge G. Chase, 1836).

59. Ladies' New-York City Anti-Slavery Society, *First Annual Report,* 7–9; Swerdlow, "Abolition's Conservative Sisters."

60. *Liberator,* June 13, 1835, p. 95, June 11, 1836, p. 95, November 14, 1835, p. 183.

61. Leonard Richards, *"Gentlemen of Property and Standing": Anti-Abolition Mobs in Jacksonian America* (New York: Oxford University Press, 1970); David Grimsted, *American Mobbing, 1828–1861: Toward Civil War* (New York: Oxford University Press, 1998).

62. Susan Zaeske, *Signatures of Citizenship: Petitioning, Antislavery and Women's Political Identity* (Chapel Hill: University of North Carolina Press, 2003), 49; Ryan, *Cradle of the Middle Class,* 112–15; James A. Thome to Theodore Weld, Newark, May 2, 1836, Licking Co. [Ohio], in Dumond and Barnes, *Letters,* 1:298–302; Edward

Beecher, *Narrative of riots at Alton: in connection with the death of Rev. Elijah P. Lovejoy* (Alton, IL: G. Holton, 1838); Bertram Wyatt-Brown, "The Abolitionists' Postal Campaign of 1835," *Journal of Negro History* 50.2 (1965): 227–38.

63. "Female Courage," *Liberator,* December 6, 1834, p. 193; Michael Feldberg, *The Turbulent Era: Riot and Disorder in Jacksonian America* (New York: Oxford University Press, 1980), 34–44.

64. From the Boston *Courier,* quoted in Boston FASS, *Right and Wrong in Boston, 1835,* 16 ("running after" Thompson); "Thompson—The Abolitionist," *Boston Commercial Gazette,* reprinted in *Liberator,* October 17, 1835, p. 167 (one writer); Boston FASS, *Right and Wrong in Boston, 1835,* 10–11 (owner of hall).

65. "To the Editor of the Courier," *Liberator,* October 24, 1835.

66. Boston FASS, *Right and Wrong in Boston, 1835,* 29–39.

67. Ibid.; *Liberator,* Extra, November 7, 1835; *Herald of Freedom,* November 28, 1835, p. 79, col. 5.

68. Hansen, *Strained Sisterhood,* 16; Anne Warren Weston to the Uxbridge FASS, April 12, 1836, Boston (Boston FASS Letterbook, MHS).

69. "Riots, Muzzling the Press, &c.," *Liberator,* December 13, 1834, p. 197. See also "Female Courage," *Liberator,* December 6, 1834, p. 193; "The Mob at Concord," *Liberator,* December 13, 1834, p. 198.

70. "Mr. Thompson at Lowell" and "Cowardice and Ruffianism," *Liberator,* December 6, 1834, pp. 195–96. The Lowell society did not last past 1839. See A. Farnsworth to Mrs. Chapman, November 1, 1839, Groton (BPL Ms.A.9.2.12.74).

71. "Another Gallant Interruption," *Liberator,* December 31, 1835.

72. Theodore Lyman, III, ed., *Papers relating to The Garrison Mob* (Cambridge: Welch, Bigelow, and Company, 1870).

73. Boston FASS, *Right and Wrong in Boston, 1835,* 24 ("When before"), 6 (*"Those* ladies"), 18 (Moral Reform Society), 26 ("We must").

74. Ibid., 48–49 (quotation); "To the Editor of the Courier," *Liberator,* October 24, 1835.

75. Boston FASS, *Right and Wrong in Boston, 1835,* 31–32.

76. Nathaniel P. Rogers, *An Address Delivered Before the Concord Female Anti-Slavery Society, at its annual meeting 25 December 1837* (Concord, NH: William White, 1838), 25 (OSV).

77. George W. Benson to N. C. Benson, October 26, 1835, Providence (BPL Ms.A.1.2.v5.p65).

78. "Another Gallant Interruption," *Liberator,* December 19, 1835, p. 203.

79. Lydia Maria Child, *An Appeal in Favor of that Class of Americans Called Africans* (Boston: Allen and Ticknor, 1833).

80. "First Annual Report of the South Reading FASS," *Liberator,* December 17, 1836, p. 202; S. Judson, Corresponding Secretary, to the Boston Female Anti-Slavery Society, May 7, 1836, Uxbridge (Boston FASS Letterbook, MHS); "Preamble and Constitution of the Groton Ladies Anti-Slavery Society," *Liberator,* April 9, 1836, p. 59; Debora Weston to Anne Warren Weston, Monday 6th, 1836, Boston, and Debora Weston to Dear Aunt Mary [Weston], Thursday noon, October 22, 1835 (BPL Ms.A.9.2.8.4, Ms.A.9.2.7.70, Weston Sisters microfilm reel 2).

81. "Cowardice and Ruffianism," *Liberator,* December 6, 1834, p. 195; Helen E. Garrison to Caroline Weston, October 31, 1835, Brooklyn (BPL, Weston Sisters microfilm reel 2); Ladies' New-York City Anti-Slavery Society, *First Annual Report,* 6; Frances Harriet Whipple, in *Liberator,* May 21, 1836.

82. Silvan Tomkins, "The Psychology of Commitment: The Constructive Role of Violence and Suffering for the Individual and for His Society," in *The Antislavery Vanguard: New Essays on the Abolitionists,* ed. Martin Duberman (Princeton, NJ: Princeton University Press, 1965), 270–98.

3—United amid Differences, 1836–1837

1. The epigraph is taken from M. W. Chapman to the Philadelphia Ladies A. S. Society, January 12, 1837, Boston (HSP).

2. Ibid.

3. AAS, *Second Annual Report of the American Anti-Slavery Society* (New York: William S. Dorr, 1835).

4. Lucy B. Williams to Philadelphia Female Anti-Slavery Society [Mary Grew], April 9, 1836, Brooklyn (HSP).

5. Mary Clark to Mary Grew, April 20, 1836, Boston (HSP).

6. Melanie Ammidon to Mary Grew, April 15, 1836, Boston (HSP).

7. Lindley Coates to Mary Grew, [February] 21, 1837, Salisbury, Lancaster County (HSP).

8. Elizur Wright, Jr., to Mary Grew, April 18, 1836, New York (HSP).

9. Maria Weston Chapman to the Secretary of the Philadelphia Female Anti-Slavery Society, August 4, 1836, Boston (HSP). Chapman also wrote a letter to the Ladies' New-York City Anti-Slavery Society to obtain their opinion. This letter has been lost but is referenced in Angelina E. Grimké to Jane Smith, [September] 18, [1836], Shrewsbury, in Larry Ceplair, ed., *The Public Years of Sarah and Angelina Grimké: Selected Writings, 1835–1839* (New York: Columbia University Press, 1989), 81–82.

10. African American men faced a similar issue during the same period, as they debated whether to organize along single-race lines, with all black conventions, or to work in interracial cooperation with white men. See Jane H. Pease and William H. Pease, "Negro Conventions and the Problem of Black Leadership," *Journal of Black Studies* 2.1 (1971), 30–33.

11. A. A. Cox to the Female Anti-Slavery Society of Boston, November 19, 1836, New York (BPL Ms.A.9.2.8.72).

12. Ibid.

13. Mary Grew to the Secretary of the Boston Female Anti-Slavery Society, September 9, 1836, Philadelphia (BPL Ms.A.9.2.8.48).

14. M. W. Chapman to the Philadelphia Ladies A. S. Society, January 12, 1837, Boston (HSP). Entire second quotation is underlined in the original.

15. M. W. Chapman to the Philadelphia Ladies A. S. Society, January 12, 1837, Boston (HSP). The Boston women noted later in 1837 that, shortly after they proposed the conference, they received a letter from Lewis Tappan suggesting a very similar idea. See Boston FASS, *Right and Wrong in Boston. Annual Report of the Boston Female Anti-Slavery Society, with a Sketch of the Obstacles thrown in the way of Emancipation by certain Clerical Abolitionists and Advocates for the Subjection of Woman, in 1837* (Boston: Isaac Knapp, 1837), 32.

16. M. W. Chapman to the Philadelphia Ladies A. S. Society, January 12, 1837, Boston (HSP).

17. Anti-Slavery Convention of American Women (ASCAW), *Proceedings of the Anti-Slavery Convention of American Women, Held in the City of New-York, May 9th, 10th, 11th, and 12th, 1837* (New York: William S. Dorr, 1837), 3–4.

18. A. E. Grimké to Dear Sister [Abby Kelley], [April] 15 [1837], New York (AKF Papers, box 1, folder 2, AASW); Call for Convention in *Herald of Freedom,* March 18, 1837, p. 11, col. 5.

19. Harriet B. Guzzam to Mary Grew, April 18, 1837, Pittsburgh (HSP); Mary Clark to Francis Jackson, April 15, 1837, Concord (BPL Ms.A.1.2.6.52); Mary Clark to Mary Grew, May 2, 1838, Concord, NH (HSP); Lee Chambers-Schiller, "The Single Woman Reformer: Conflicts between Family and Vocation, 1830–1860," *Frontiers* 3.3 (1978): 41–48; Lee Chambers-Schiller, "The Single Woman: Family and Vocation among Nineteenth-Century Reformers," in *Woman's Being, Woman's Place: Female Identity and Vocation in American History,* ed. Mary Kelley (Boston: G. K. Hall, 1979), 334–50.

20. Mary Clark to Francis Jackson, April 15, 1837, Concord (BPL Ms.A.1.2.6.52); Lucy W. Foster to My friend Abby [Kelley], [March] 27, 1837, Uxbridge (AKF Papers, box 1, folder 2, AASW); Harriet B. Guzzam to Mary Grew, April 18, 1837, Pittsburgh (HSP). The depression also took a heavy toll on male abolitionists; some of them went bankrupt while others curtailed their activities for a time. John Stauffer, *The Black Hearts of Men: Radical Abolitionists and the Transformation of Race* (Cambridge: Harvard University Press, 2002), 14–15, 95–133.

21. Maria [Child] to Lydia B. Child, April 2, 1837, South Natick, and L. M. Child to Henrietta Sargent, April 17 [1837], South Natick, in Milton Meltzer and Patricia G. Holland, eds., *Lydia Maria Child: Selected Letters, 1817–1880* (Amherst: University of Massachusetts Press, 1982), 64–68.

22. *Herald of Freedom,* May 27, 1837, p. 51, cols. 2–4; Southwick, *Reminiscences,* 22–23, 25 (AASW).

23. Sarah M. Grimké to My dear sister [Ann Warren Weston], [April] 7, 1837, New York (BPL Ms.A.9.2.9.25).

24. Anne Weston to Debora Weston, April 18, 1837, Boston (BPL Ms.A.9.2.9.28); Sarah L. Forten to Angelina Grimké, April 15, 1837, Philadelphia, cited in Margot Melia, "The Role of Black Garrisonian Women in Anti-Slavery and Other Reforms in the Antebellum North, 1830–1865" (Ph.D. diss., University of Western Australia, 1991), chap. 5, p. 2. Susan Paul does not appear to have attended the convention or at least is not listed among the delegates or corresponding members.

25. ASCAW, *Proceedings, 1837,* 15.

26. Lois E. Horton, "Community Organization and Social Activism: Black Boston and the Antislavery Movement," *Sociological Inquiry* 55.2 (Spring 1985): 182–99; Sharon Harley, "Northern Black Female Workers: Jacksonian Era," in *The Afro-American Woman: Struggles and Images,* ed. Sharon Harley and Rosalyn Terborg-Penn (Port Washington, NY: Kennikat Press, 1978), 5–16.

27. Jean R. Soderlund, "Priorities and Power: The Philadelphia Female Anti-Slavery Society," in Yellin and Van Horne, *Abolitionist Sisterhood,* 74; Horton, "Freedom's Yoke."

28. William Lloyd Garrison to Helen Garrison, May 6, 1837, New York, in Louis Ruchames and Walter Merrill, eds., *The Letters of William Lloyd Garrison* (Cambridge, MA: Belknap Press of Harvard University Press, 1971), 2:260–61.

29. *Liberator,* May 24, 1839; Southwick, *Reminiscences,* 29.

30. ASCAW, *Proceedings, 1837,* 3–4; "Ladies Anti-Slavery Convention," *Genius,* July 1837, p. 17; "To the Anti-Slavery Women of Great Britain" by the Convention, printed in *Genius,* July 1837, p. 18.

31. ASCAW, *Proceedings, 1837,* 3–4.

32. *Herald of Freedom,* May 27, 1837, p. 51, cols. 2–4.

33. ASCAW, *Proceedings, 1837,* 9–10.

34. Ten of the dissenting women were from New York City, one was from Pittsburgh, and one was from Peru, Massachusetts (ASCAW, *Proceedings, 1837,* 9–12, 17).

35. ASCAW, *Proceedings, 1837,* 10–11, 13.

36. ASCAW, *Proceedings, 1837,* 14; Swerdlow, "Abolition's Conservative Sisters," 41. My numbers differ slightly from hers.

37. ASCAW, *Proceedings, 1837,* 18 (original emphasis).

38. Boston FASS, *Right and Wrong in Boston, 1837,* 40; S. M. and A. E. Grimké to Brother [Henry C.] Wright, August 27, 1837, Brookline (BPL Ms.A.1.2.v6.p64); Dorothy C. Bass, "The Best Hopes of the Sexes: The Woman Question in Garrisonian Abolitionism" (Ph.D. diss., Brown University, 1980), 254–55.

39. A. E. Grimké to Jane Smith, [March] 22, 1837, New York, in Ceplair, *Sarah and Angelina Grimké,* 125–26.

40. "Ladies Anti-Slavery Convention," *Genius,* July 1837, p. 17.

41. Ibid.

42. A. W. Weston [?] [no signature] to Debora Weston, Saturday April 29, 1837 (BPL Ms.A.9.2.9.30). This occurred again in 1838. M. C. Pennock [signature unclear] to Abby Kelley, [March] 18, 1838, Philadelphia (AKF Papers, microfilm, AASW); Mary Clark to Mary Grew, May 2, 1838, Concord, NH (HSP); "Letter from a Member of the Convention," *Herald of Freedom,* June 2, 1838, p. 54, cols. 3–5.

43. Juliana Tappan to Anne W. Weston, May 26, 1837, New York (BPL Ms.A.9.2.9.37); Anne Warren Weston to the Providence Female A. S. Society, June 6, 1837, Boston (Boston FASS Letterbook, MHS); Sarah M. Grimké to My dear sister [Ann Warren Weston], [April] 7, 1837, New York (BPL Ms.A.9.2.9.25).

44. *Herald of Freedom,* May 27, 1837, p. 51, cols. 2–4; ASCAW, *Proceedings, 1837,* 13.

45. ASCAW, *An Address to Free Colored Americans* (New York: William S. Dorr, 1837; rpt. Lost Cause Press, 1962), 8.

46. ASCAW, *An Appeal to the Women of the Nominally Free States,* 2nd ed. (Boston: Isaac Knapp, 1838), 58–63; "Circular, Addressed by the Convention of Women assembled in New York, in May last, to the Societies of Anti-Slavery Women in the United States," *Herald of Freedom,* July 8, 1837, p. 75.

47. ASCAW, *Proceedings, 1837,* 8, 12–13.

48. Ibid., 17; Juliana Tappan to Anne Warren Weston, May 18, 1837, New York (BPL Ms.A.9.2.9.35).

49. "Petition of the Female Citizens of the County of Fluvanna to the General Assembly of the Commonwealth of Virginia," *Liberator,* February 25, 1832; "A Noble Example," *Liberator,* December 17, 1831, p. 203; *Liberator,* February 18, 1832; *Liberator,* August 10, 1833, p. 127; Zaeske, *Signatures of Citizenship,* 44.

50. Ladies' New-York City Anti-Slavery Society, *First Annual Report,* 10–11; Philadelphia FASS minutes of August 6, 1835, as cited in Williams, "Religion, Race, and Gender," 225–26; Zaeske, *Signatures of Citizenship,* 43; *Liberator,* March 14, 1835, p. 43.

51. *Liberator,* August 13, 1836; Lucy M. Wright to Beloved Sister [Betsy Mix Cowles], May 20, 1836, Aurora, Ohio (Cowles Papers, box 1, folder 3).

52. Lucy M. Wright to Beloved sisters [Boston FASS], August 11, 1836, Tallmadge, and Anne Warren Weston to The Portage County Female A. S. Society, August 27, 1836, Boston (Boston FASS Letterbook, MHS); "Address of the Boston

Female Anti-Slavery Society to the Women of Massachusetts," *Liberator,* August 13, 1836, p. 130; "Address of the Ladies Anti-Slavery Society of Concord to the Women of New Hampshire," *Herald of Freedom,* September 17, 1836, p. 115, cols. 2–3; "Female Anti-Slavery Society of Philadelphia," *Herald of Freedom,* October 22, 1836, p. 135, cols. 2–3; "Address to Females," *Herald of Freedom,* July 30, 1836, pp. 85–86, cols. 2–3.

53. Zaeske, *Signatures of Citizenship,* 69; *Liberator,* April 28, 1837; *Herald of Freedom,* May 6, 1837, p. 29, col. 3. Any study of antislavery petitions must deal with the fact that some large proportion of antislavery petitions are not available in the congressional archives. In some cases, antislavery petitions were not sent to Congress in time for presentation, or an overzealous circulator decided to recopy all the signatures in order to make them look better, thus raising the question of forgery and invalidating the petition. More often, valid antislavery petitions sent to unsympathetic legislators were simply never presented. Of the petitions that were presented only a fraction have been saved. See Gilbert Barnes, *The Antislavery Impulse, 1830–1844* (New York: Harcourt, Brace and World, 1933), 266 n. 40.

54. Barnes, *Antislavery Impulse,* 122–29.

55. Ibid., 141; *Liberator,* January 2, 1836, p. 3.

56. "Circular, Addressed by the Convention of Women assembled in New-York," *Herald of Freedom,* July 8, 1837, p. 75, cols. 2–4.

57. List of Worcester County (MA) town names, contact names, and dates, with the number of petition signatures received, plus a list of towns and secretaries with fair donations received (BPL Ms.A.4.6A.2.107).

58. *Herald of Freedom,* July 1, 1837, p. 71, cols. 4–5, June 24, 1837, p. 67, cols. 3–4; Mary Clark to Anne W. Weston, June 13, 1837, Concord, NH (BPL Ms.A.9.2.9.40).

59. Ladies' New-York City Anti-Slavery Society, *Third Annual Report of the Ladies' New-York City Anti-Slavery Society* (New York: William S. Dorr, 1838), 8–9; Juliana Tappan to Susan Porter Benson, cited in Cohen, "Clip Not Her Wings," 19; Juliana A. Tappan to Mary Grew, June 22, 1837, New York, and J. A. Tappan to My dear friend [Mary Grew], June 7, 1837, New York (HSP).

60. Philadelphia FASS, *Fourth Annual Report of the Philadelphia FASS, Jan. 11, 1838* (Philadelphia: Merrihew and Gunn, 1838), 5–6, and *Fifth Annual Report,* 8–9; Female Anti Slavery [Society] of Pittsburgh and Alleghany to Mary Grew, July 15, [1837], Pittsburgh, J. A. Tappan to My dear friend [Mary Grew], June 7, 1837, New York, and Abby Goodwin to Mary Grew, [June] 20, 1837, Salem [County, NJ] (all in HSP).

61. "Circular, Addressed by the Convention of Women assembled in New-York," *Herald of Freedom,* July 8, 1837, p. 75, cols. 2–4; Mary P. Cook for Anna P. Cook to Maria Weston Chapman, December 25, 1839, Hadley (BPL Ms.A.9.2.12.125); Ladies' New-York City Anti-Slavery Society, *Third Annual Report,* 9; "Extracts from a Young Lady's Journal," *Genius,* August 4, 1837, p. 127.

62. Juliana A. Tappan to Anne W. Weston, July 21, 1837, New York (BPL Ms.A.9.2.9.49).

63. "Notice," *Liberator,* September 8, 1837, p. 147; Susan Zaeske, "Petitioning, Antislavery, and the Emergence of Women's Political Consciousness" (Ph.D. diss., University of Wisconsin–Madison, 1997), 248; Dorchester FASS, *First Annual Report of the Dorchester Female Anti-Slavery Society, December 1837* (Boston: D. Clapp, Jr., 1838), 17.

64. Williams, "Religion, Race, and Gender," 537; Richard H. Sewell, *Ballots for Freedom: Antislavery Politics in the United States, 1837–1860* (New York: Oxford University Press, 1976), 3–23.

65. Wellman, "Women and Radical Reform," 113–27; Patricia Heard, "'One Blood All Nations': Anti-Slavery Petitions in Sandwich," *Annual Excursion of the Sandwich Historical Society* 59 (1978): 26–31; Gerda Lerner, "The Political Activities of Antislavery Women," in *The Majority Finds Its Past*, ed. Gerda Lerner (New York: Oxford University Press, 1979), 112–28.

66. Quoted in Barnes, *Anti-Slavery Impulse*, 141; "Hon. John Reed's Letters," *Liberator*, August 13, 1836.

67. A. A. Cox to the Philadelphia Female Anti-Slavery Society, February 15, 1837, New York (HSP); "Angelina E. Grimké," *Herald of Freedom*, February 25, 1836, p. 207, cols. 3–4.

68. "Pastoral Letter," *Genius*, August 11, 1837; Boston FASS, *Right and Wrong in Boston, 1837*, 45–48.

69. "Pastoral Letter," *Genius*, August 11, 1837 (italics removed); Ann Douglas, *The Feminization of American Culture* (New York: Knopf, 1977). I am grateful to Carolyn Lawes for a thoughtful discussion of these issues.

70. "Clerical Appeal" of the faculty of the Andover Theological Seminary, cited in Alma Lutz, *Crusade for Freedom: Women of the Antislavery Movement* (Boston: Beacon Press, 1968), 116; Sterling, *Ahead of Her Time*, 53; ASCAW, *Proceedings, 1837*, 10; *Liberator*, August 4, 1837, p. 126; Theodore D. W[eld] to Sarah and Angelina Grimké, Oct. 1 [September 1,] 1837, [New York], in Dumond and Barnes, *Letters*, 442–45.

71. "To the Female Anti-Slavery Societies throughout New England," *Herald of Freedom*, June 17, 1837, p. 63, cols. 3–4; "Andover Female Antislavery Society," *Genius*, August 25, 1837, p. 139; extract from *Third Annual Report of Philadelphia FASS* in the *Herald of Freedom*, February 25, 1836, p. 207, cols. 3–4.

72. Buckingham Female Anti-Slavery Society to Sarah and Angelina Grimké, July 27, 1837 (S. M. Grimké Papers, Center for American History, University of Texas at Austin), as quoted in Anna M. Speicher, "'Faith Which Worketh By Love': The Religious World of Female Antislavery Lecturers" (Ph.D. diss., George Washington University, 1996), 70; *Liberator*, March 23, 1838, p. 47, January 12, 1838, p. 6, January 19, 1838.

73. Dorchester FASS, *First Annual Report*, 10; Philadelphia FASS, *Fourth Annual Report*, 5; editorial article by William L. Stone, *New York Commercial Advertiser*, May 17, 1837, reprinted as "Billingsgate Abuse," *Herald of Freedom*, May 27, 1837, p. 51.

74. "To the Women of New Hampshire," *Herald of Freedom*, June 24, 1837, p. 66, cols. 2–4; Resolution by John G. Whittier, *Herald of Freedom*, June 3, 1837, p. 55, col. 4; H. C. Wright speech, *Herald of Freedom*, May 20, 1837, p. 46, col. 4.

75. *Religious Magazine and Family Miscellany*, quoted in the Boston FASS, *Right and Wrong in Boston, 1837*, 57–58; Lydia Maria Child to [Lucretia Mott], [March] 5, 1839, Northampton (Mott MSS, Friends Historical Library, Swarthmore College); "Female Petitioners," *Liberator*, September 15, 1837, p. 152; "Congress. Husbands for Female Abolitionists," *Liberator*, October 20, 1837, p. 171.

76. Correspondent of the *Providence Journal*, "Female Politicians," *Liberator*, September 8, 1837.

77. Elizabeth Chandler, "Opinions," *Genius*, December 11, 1829, p. 108.

78. "The District of Columbia," *Genius*, January 1833, p. 44 (1831); "A Noble Example," *Liberator*, December 17, 1831, p. 203 (Garrison).

79. Thompson, *Letters and Addresses*, 4–5; Angelina Grimké, *Appeal to the Christian Women of America* (New York: William S. Dorr, 1836), 4–5.

80. "Speech of Mr. Dickson," *Herald of Freedom*, March 21, 1835, p. 1, col. 2; Juliana A. Tappan to Mary Grew, June 22, 1837, New York (HSP); "To the Members of the Ladies' Anti-Slavery Society of Concord, N.H.," *Herald of Freedom*, October 15, 1836, p. 130, cols. 4–5.

81. ASCAW, *An Appeal*, 59, 63, 69.

82. Ibid., 10–11, 5–6.

83. Boston FASS, *Right and Wrong in Boston, 1837*, 95 (italics removed); "Female Anti-Slavery Society of Philadelphia," *Herald of Freedom*, October 22, 1836, p. 135, cols. 2–3; Adams quoted from "The Petitions of Females," *Herald of Freedom*, August 6, 1836, p. 91, col. 1.

84. Kerber, *Women of the Republic*, 85–98; Ruth Bogin, "Petitioning and the New Moral Economy of Post-Revolutionary America," *William and Mary Quarterly*, 3rd ser., 45.3 (July 1988): 420–21.

85. "Father and Rulers petition," Dumond and Barnes, *Letters*, 1:175–76; short-form petition, "Address of the Ladies' Anti-Slavery Society of Concord to the Women of New Hampshire," *Herald of Freedom*, September 17, 1836, p. 115, cols. 2–3; Zaeske, *Signatures of Citizenship*, 55–59; Zaeske, "Petitioning, Antislavery," 198–201.

86. ASCAW, *An Appeal*, 10–13.

87. ASCAW, *Proceedings, 1837*, 16; "To the Honorable John Q. Adams," *Genius*, June 9, 1837, p. 95.

88. *Proceedings of the Fourth New-England Anti-Slavery Convention* (Boston: Isaac Knapp, 1837), 42; Philadelphia FASS, *Fourth Annual Report*, 7, and *Fifth Annual Report*, 5; *Liberator*, September 1, 1837, p. 144; "Report of the Groton Female Anti-Slavery Society, Presented May 10, 1837," *Genius*, June 9, 1837, p. 95.

89. Dorchester FASS, *First Annual Report*, 16; Anne [Weston] to Debora [Weston], April 18, 1837, Boston (BPL Ms.A.9.2.9.28); Deborah Bingham Van Broekhoven, "'A Determination to Labor...': Female Antislavery Activity in Rhode Island," *Rhode Island History* 44.2 (1985): 40, 45; Anne Warren Weston to the Providence Female A. S. Society, June 6, 1837, Boston (Boston FASS Letterbook, MHS).

90. Boston FASS, "Address to the Women of Great Britain," reprinted in Angelina Grimké, *Slavery in America. A Reprint of An Appeal to the Christian Women of the Slave States of America. By Angelina Grimké, of Charleston, South Carolina. with Introduction, Notes, and Appendix by George Thompson. Recommended to the Special Attention of the Anti-Slavery Females of Great Britain* (Edinburgh: William Oliphant and Son, 1837), appendix 2; ASCAW, *Proceedings, 1837*, 23; "Letter to the Women of Great Britain," *Genius*, July 1837, p. 18.

91. Grimké, *Slavery in America*, xvi, xviii, xix.

92. "Circular, Addressed by the Convention of Women assembled in New York," *Herald of Freedom*, July 8, 1837, p. 75, col. 2–4; *Genius*, July 1837, pp. 53–55; editorial, *Herald of Freedom*, September 30, 1837, p. 122, cols. 2–3; "Ladies' Petition to the Queen," *Liberator*, November 3, 1837, p. 178.

4—Internal Divisions, 1837–1840

1. The epigraph is from Juliana A. Tappan to Anne W. Weston, July 21, 1837, New York (BPL Ms.A.9.2.9.49).

2. *Liberator*, January 31, 1835; editorial, *Liberator*, August 22, 1836.

3. *Liberator,* September 22, 1837, p. 155, October 6, 13, 20, 27, November 3, 1837, and January 19, 1838, p. 11.

4. Excerpt from the *Friend of Man* in *Liberator,* September 15, 1837, p. 150, cols. 1–3; call for new organization in *Liberator,* November 17, 1837; William Smith letter in *Liberator,* January 12, 1838; *Liberator,* February 23, 1838.

5. "Circular Addressed to Female Anti-Slavery Societies," *Genius,* January 1838, pp. 155–56; J. A. Tappan to Anne Warren Weston, April 20, 1838, New York (BPL Ms.A.9.2.10.24); Abby Kelley to the Philadelphia F.A.S. Society, [March] 16, 1838, Lynn (HSP).

6. ASCAW, *Proceedings of the Anti-Slavery Convention of American Women, Held in Philadelphia, May 15th, 16th, 17th and 18th, 1838* (Philadelphia: Merrihew and Gunn, 1838), 12–14, now on-line at http://memory.loc.gov in the "Votes for Women: Selections from the National American Woman Suffrage Association Collection, 1848–1921" section.

7. Melia, "Black Garrisonian Women," chap. 5, p. 7. Melia's numbers seem more accurate than Dorothy Sterling's unsupported claim that one of every ten women was black. Sterling, *Ahead of Her Time,* 45.

8. ASCAW, *Proceedings, 1838,* 5–9; [Laura H. Lovell,] *Report of a Delegate to the Anti-Slavery Convention of American Women, Held in Philadelphia, May, 1838* (Boston: J. Knapp, 1838), 23–24.

9. ASCAW, *Proceedings, 1838,* 6.

10. Ibid., 5.

11. [Lovell,] *Report of a Delegate,* 10; *The History of Pennsylvania Hall, Which Was Destroyed by a Mob, on the 17th of May, 1838* (1838; New York: Negro Universities Press, 1969), 117 (Mott).

12. *History of Pennsylvania Hall,* 127 (Mott); Mary Grew to Anne Warren Weston, December 25, 1838, Philadelphia (BPL Ms.A.9.2.10.p87, Weston Sisters microfilm reel 3); Angelina [Grimké] to Anne Warren Weston, [October] 14, [1838], Fort Lee (BPL Ms.A.9.2.10.58); [Lovell,] *Report of a Delegate,* 12 (Grimké).

13. ASCAW, *Proceedings, 1838,* 5–6.

14. Ibid., 6–7.

15. ASCAW, *Proceedings, 1837,* 13; ASCAW, *Proceedings, 1838,* 8.

16. ASCAW, *Proceedings, 1838,* 8; James Mott to Anne Warren Weston, June 7, 1838, Philadelphia (BPL Ms.A.9.2.v10.p29); L. Mott to Edward Davis, [June] 18, 1838, Philadelphia (Mott MSS, Friends Historical Library, Swarthmore College; original at Harvard College Library).

17. [Lovell,] *Report of a Delegate,* 14 (black woman); Sarah M. Douglass to Abby Kelley, May 18, 1838, and March 19, 1839, Philadelphia (AKF Papers, box 1, folders 2, 3, AASW).

18. Phillip Lapsansky, "Graphic Discord: Abolitionist and Antiabolitionist Images," in Yellin and Van Horne, *Abolitionist Sisterhood,* 226–28; numerous newspaper excerpts in *Liberator,* May 25, 1838; Ira V. Brown, "Racism and Sexism: The Case of Pennsylvania Hall," *Phylon* 37 (June 1976): 126–36.

19. [Lovell,] *Report of a Delegate,* 10–12; L[ouisa] W[hipple], "Letter from a member of the Convention," *Herald of Freedom,* June 2, 1838, p. 54, cols. 3–5.

20. [Lovell,] *Report of a Delegate,* 13, 15; Boston FASS, *Fifth Annual Report of the Boston Female Anti-Slavery Society* (Boston: Isaac Knapp, 1838), 13–14; "Extract of a letter from a lady of this city," *Liberator,* May 25, 1838, p. 82.

21. ASCAW, *Proceedings, 1838,* 5; John Runcie, "'Hunting the Nigs' in Philadelphia:

The Race Riot of August 1834," *Pennsylvania History* 39 (April 1972): 187–218; [Lovell,] *Report of a Delegate*, 15–16; Boston FASS, *Fifth Annual Report*, 14–15; [Lovell,] *Report of a Delegate*, 16 (Mott).

22. L[ouisa] W[hipple], "Letter from a member of the Convention," *Herald of Freedom*, June 2, 1838, p. 54, cols. 3–5; [Lovell,] *Report of a Delegate*, 17; "Extract of a letter from a lady of this city, now in Philadelphia," *Liberator*, May 25, 1838, p. 82.

23. Philadelphia FASS, *Fifth Annual Report*, 6.

24. [Lovell,] *Report of a Delegate*, 20–21.

25. Ibid., 21; Boston FASS, *Fifth Annual Report*, 18–19; ASCAW, *Proceedings, 1838*, 10.

26. ASCAW, *Proceedings, 1838*, 7–11.

27. Sarah Baker to the Lynn Female Anti-Slavery Society, May 31, 1838, Dorchester (AKF Papers, box 1, folder 2, AASW); Philadelphia FASS, *Fifth Annual Report*, 5–8.

28. Grimké quoted from *History of Pennsylvania Hall*, 124.

29. Lydia Maria Child to Caroline Weston, August 13, 1838, Northampton, in Meltzer and Holland, *Lydia Maria Child*, 83; L. M. Child to A. W. Weston, July 27, 1838, Northampton, in *Selected Letters*, 79–80, 80 n. 1. See also FRANKLIN letter, *Herald of Freedom*, June 9, 1838, p. 59, cols. 3–4.

30. *New York Commercial Advertiser* article, *Liberator*, May 25, 1838, p. 82.

31. *Boston Centinel and Gazette* article, *Liberator*, May 25, 1838, p. 82.

32. Lapsansky, "Graphic Discord," 229; *Liberator*, March 1, 1839, p. 33.

33. Louis Ruchames, "Race, Marriage, and Abolition in Massachusetts," *Journal of Negro History* 40 (1955): 250–73; *Liberator*, February 8, 1839, p. 23, February 15, 22, March 1, 29, 1839, April 26, 1839, p. 66; "Interesting Reports," *Liberator*, May 24, 1839, p. 83.

34. New-England Anti-Slavery Society, *Constitution of the New-England Anti-Slavery Society with an Address to the Public* (Boston: Garrison and Knapp, 1832); New-England Anti-Slavery Convention, *Proceedings of the New-England Anti-Slavery Convention, held in Boston, May 24, 25, 26, 1836* (Boston: Isaac Knapp, 1836), 5, 22, 53 (both in AASW).

35. Massachusetts Anti-Slavery Society, *Seventh Annual Report of the Board of Managers of the Mass. Anti-Slavery Society, presented January 24, 1839. With an appendix* (Boston: Isaac Knapp, 1839), 31–32; New England Anti-Slavery Society Reports (PEM).

36. Samuel J. May, *Some Recollections of our Antislavery Conflict* (Boston: Fields, Osgood, and Co., 1869), 237–38 (first two quotes; italics removed); *Christian Mirror* quoted in Massachusetts Anti-Slavery Society, *Seventh Annual Report* (Boston: Isaac Knapp, 1839), 35–36. See also Maria Weston Chapman, *Right and Wrong in Massachusetts* (Boston: Henry L. Devereaux, 1840), 52–54 (General Reading Room Collection, IIR p. v. 16, NYPL).

37. Louisa S. Wilcox, President, to Friend Garrison, [February] 23, 1839, Amesbury, as printed in the *Liberator*, March 22, 1839, p. 48; "East Haverhill Female A. S. Society," *Liberator*, November 15, 1839, p. 182; Sarah Baker to the Lynn Female Anti-Slavery Society, May 31, 1838, Dorchester (AKF Papers, box 1, folder 2, AASW; emphasis mine). See also Dorchester FASS, *First Annual Report*, 10.

38. Lydia Maria Child to Lucretia Mott, [March] 5, 1839, Northampton (Mott MSS, Friends Historical Library, Swarthmore College); Abby Kelley to the Philadelphia F.A.S. Society, [March] 16, 1838, Lynn (HSP); Angelina Grimké to Theodore Weld and John Greenleaf Whittier, [August] 20, 1837, in Dumond and Barnes, *Letters*, 1:428.

39. Lucretia Mott to Abby Kelley, [March] 18, 1839, Philadelphia (AKF Papers, box 1, folder 3, AASW).

40. ASCAW, *Proceedings of the Third Anti-Slavery Convention of American Women, Held in Philadelphia May 1st, 2d and 3d, 1839* (Philadelphia: Merrihew and Thompson, 1839), 13–14.

41. Ibid., 3, 13–14.

42. Ibid., 4–5.

43. Ibid., 5–12.

44. Sarah M. Grimké, *Letters on the Equality of the Sexes and the Condition of Woman, addressed to Mary S. Parker, President of the Boston Female Anti-Slavery Society* (Boston: Isaac Knapp, 1838); Angelina E. Grimké, *Letters to Catherine E. Beecher, in Reply to An Essay on Slavery and Abolitionism, Addressed to A. E. Grimké. Revised by the Author* (Boston: Isaac Knapp, 1838).

45. ASCAW, *Proceedings, 1839,* 10–12.

46. Ibid., 12.

47. AAS, *Sixth Annual Report of the Executive Committee of the American Anti-Slavery Society, with the Speeches delivered at the Anniversary Meeting held in the city of New-York, on the 7th of May, 1839, and the minutes of the meetings of the Society for business, held on the evening and the three following days* (New York: William S. Dorr, 1839), 27–30.

48. Ibid., 30.

49. The scheduling of the two meetings one after the other may help explain why there were no female delegates from Philadelphia at the AAS meeting, despite its quite active female antislavery society and its earlier enthusiasm for opening the AAS to female delegates. It may be that the women did not wish to travel all the way to New York only days after hosting the women's convention, and housing many of its delegates.

50. I thank Anne Boylan for locating information on these two women.

51. AAS, *Sixth Annual Report,* 44–46.

52. Douglas M. Strong, *Perfectionist Politics: Abolitionism and the Religious Tensions of American Democracy* (Syracuse, NY: Syracuse University Press, 1999), 78–83.

53. Anne (Weston) to Maria Weston Chapman, May 23, 1840, New York (BPL Ms.A.9.2.v13.p74); Aileen S. Kraditor, *Means and Ends in American Abolitionism: Garrison and His Critics on Strategy and Tactics, 1834–1850* (New York: Pantheon Books, 1969), 52.

54. Parker Pillsbury, *Acts of the Anti-Slavery Apostles* (Concord, NH: Clague, Wegman, Schlicht, and Co., 1883), 98–99; *Liberator,* February 10, 1843.

55. Salem FASS, "Eighth Annual Report of the Salem Female Anti-Slavery Society," [1842], no publication information ("Charter, Resolves, and Annual Reports, 1840–1845," Salem FASS, box 1, folder 1, PEM); Boston FASS, *Ten Years of Experience,* 16–17.

56. Massachusetts Female Emancipation Society (MFES), *First Annual Report of the Massachusetts Female Emancipation Society* (Boston: James Loring, 1841), 8–11, 16–17 (original emphasis).

57. Hansen, *Strained Sisterhood,* 66–68; M. Clark to "Respected & dear Mrs. R" [Mary Rogers], Tuesday Morning [June 4, 1839] (Nathaniel P. Rogers Collection, no. 806, box 1, Mary Clark folder, Treasure Room, Haverford College); Kathryn Kish Sklar, "'Women Who Speak for an Entire Nation': American and British Women Compared at the World Anti-Slavery Convention, London, 1840," *Pacific Historical Review* 59 (November 1990): 453–99.

58. *Liberator* May 29, 1840; *Colored American,* May 30, 1840; Boylan, "Benevolence and Antislavery Activity," 133.

59. Hansen, "Boston Female Anti-Slavery Society," 59; Yee, *Black Women Abolitionists,* 102–3, 143–46; Willie Mae Coleman, "Keeping the Faith and Disturbing the Peace: Black Women, from Anti-Slavery to Women's Suffrage" (Ph.D. diss., University of California–Irvine, 1982), 18–20; Quarles, *Black Abolitionists,* 54–55.

60. Hansen, *Strained Sisterhood,* 80–88, 114; Hansen, "Boston Female Anti-Slavery Society," 61; Hewitt, *Women's Activism,* 38–68, tables 10, 17; Blanche Hersh, "To Make the World Better: Protestant Women in the Abolitionist Movement," in *Triumph over Silence: Women in Protestant History,* ed. Richard L. Greaves (Westport, CT: Greenwood Press, 1985), 173–74; Nancy A. Hewitt, "The Perimeters of Women's Power in American Religion," in *The Evangelical Tradition in America,* ed. Leonard I. Sweet (1984; Macon, GA: Mercer University Press, 1997), 233–56.

61. Hansen, "Boston Female Anti-Slavery Society," 61; Hansen, *Strained Sisterhood,* 69–88, 97; Wellman, "Women and Radical Reform," 113–27; Hewitt, "Perimeters of Women's Power," 233–56.

62. Eleanor A. Jewett to Maria [Weston] Chapman, January 5, 1840, Byfield (BPL Ms.A.9.2.13.14).

63. Alvan Ward to Maria Weston Chapman, July 23, 1840, Ashburnham (BPL Ms.A.9.2.13.106, Weston Sisters microfilm reel 4); Anna M. Speicher, *The Religious World of Antislavery Women: Spirituality in the Lives of Five Abolitionist Lecturers* (Syracuse, NY: Syracuse University Press, 2000).

64. Boston FASS, *Right and Wrong in Boston, 1837,* 4; Hansen, *Strained Sisterhood,* 93–123; Hansen, "Boston Female Anti-Slavery Society," 45–66; Taylor, *Women of the Anti-Slavery Movement,* 31–42.

65. Lucretia Mott to Maria Weston Chapman, [May] 29, 1839, Philadelphia (BPL Ms.A.9.2.11.14, Weston Sisters microfilm reel 3); Bass, "Best Hopes of the Sexes," 254.

66. *Liberator,* May 11, 1838, p. 74; "Report of the Groton FASS," *Genius,* June 9, 1837, p. 95.

67. Hansen, *Strained Sisterhood,* 112–13.

68. Charlotte Austin to Maria Weston Chapman, [July] 12, 1839, Nantucket (BPL Ms.A.9.2.11.136); *Liberator,* December 6, 1839, and *Liberator,* July 17, 1840, p. 115.

69. M. Dye to Beloved Sisters [Ladies Philadelphia Antislavery Society], January 6, 1840, New York (HSP).

70. Charlotte Austin to Maria Weston Chapman, [October] 4, 1839, Nantucket (BPL Ms.A.9.2.12.47, Weston Sisters microfilm reel 3); MFES, *First Annual Report,* 5–6.

71. Salem FASS, *Sixth Annual Report of the Salem Female Anti-Slavery Society, presented Jan 15 1840* (Salem FASS, box 1, folder 1, PEM); E. Quincy to Maria Weston Chapman, June 17, 1840, Dedham (BPL Ms.A.9.2.13.87).

72. Mary Clark to Maria Weston Chapman, June 4, 1840, Concord (BPL Ms.A.9.2.13.78); *Liberator,* February 5, 1841.

73. Maria Weston Chapman to Elizabeth Pease, April 20, 1840, Boston (BPL Ms.A.1.2.v9.p27). Newspapers continued to be sloppier about names than the women themselves. The *National Anti-Slavery Standard* for July 29, 1841, contains a notice of the Millbury Female Anti-Slavery Society fair and the Millbury Women's Anti-Slavery Society collation, in the same column.

74. Harry L. Watson, *Liberty and Power: The Politics of Jacksonian America* (New York: Noonday Press, 1990), 205–6.

75. *Liberator,* December 21, 1838, p. 203.

76. *Liberator,* November 29, 1839.

77. Hansen, *Strained Sisterhood,* 124–39.

78. "The Appeal of the Mass. Female Emancipation Society, to the Lovers of Freedom Throughout the World," in MFES, *First Annual Report.* Massachusetts Abolition Society, *Second Annual Report of the Massachusetts Abolition Society* [cover and printing information missing]: 4–5 (Uncatalogued Collection, Massachusetts Institutions, Massachusetts Abolition Society, AASW).

79. Maria [Child] to Lydia B. Child, Nov. 18, 1839, Boston, in Meltzer and Holland, *Lydia Maria Child,* 125–26; C. Bartlett to Maria Weston Chapman, July 24 [?], [1840?], Worcester (BPL Ms.A.9.2.13.108, Weston Sisters microfilm reel 4); Lee Chambers-Schiller, "'A Good Work Among the People': The Political Culture of the Boston Antislavery Fair," in Yellin and Van Horne, *Abolitionist Sisterhood,* 249–74.

80. Pauline Gerry to Mrs. Chapman, July 6, 1839, Stoneham, and Eliza Boyer to Respected Friend [Maria Weston Chapman], [October] 1839, Lynn (BPL Ms.A.9.2.11.131, Ms.A.9.2.12.44); Melania A. Parker to Mrs. Chapman, April 22, 1839, Cambridge (BPL Ms.A.9.2.11.88, Weston Sisters microfilm reel 3); Debora Weston to Maria W. Chapman, April 28, [1839?], New Bedford (BPL Ms.A.9.2.3.p60); "Dorchester Female Anti-Slavery Society," *Liberator,* June 12, 1840, p. 95.

81. Mary White to Maria Weston Chapman, December 2, 1839, and March 16, 1840, Boylston (BPL Ms.A.9.2.12.103, Ms.A.9.2.13.41); Lucretia Richardson to Mrs. Chapman, September 30, also November 12, 1839, Andover (BPL Ms.A.9.2.12.42, Weston Sisters microfilm reel 3, also Ms.A9.2.12.86).

82. Elizabeth B. Chase to Maria W. Chapman, [March] 1840, Pawtucket, and [D. Weston?] to Anne Warren Weston, November 25, 1839, New Bedford (BPL Ms.A.9.2.13.32, Ms.A.9.2.12.94); Experience Billings to Oliver Johnson, June 27, 1840, Foxborough (BPL Ms.A.9.2.13.94a and b, Weston Sisters microfilm reel 4).

83. M. P. Rogers to My Dear Mrs. [Maria Weston] Chapman, February 21, [1839?], Concord (BPL Ms.A.9.2.11.45); Mary C.[lark] to Dear Mrs. R.[ogers], February 10, 1840, Boston, and M[ary] C[lark] to Respected Friend [N. P. Rogers], January 28, 1840, Boston (Nathaniel P. Rogers Collection, no. 806, box 1, Mary Clark folder, Treasure Room, Haverford College).

84. Lydia Dean and Harriet Foster to the Women of Essex County, June 10, 1839, Salem; Ann C. Brown to Miss Harriet Foster, August 31, 1839, West Newbury; A. B. Ordway to the Board of the Salem FASS, August 25, 1839, West Newbury (all in Salem FASS, box 1, folder 3, PEM, except Lydia Dean, in folder 1).

85. A. B. Ordway to the Board of the Salem FASS, August 25, 1839, West Newbury; Mary P. Wade to Miss Harriet Foster, August 15, 1839, Ipswich (both in Salem FASS, box 1, folder 3, PEM).

86. A. B. Ordway to the Board of the Salem FASS, August 25, 1839, West Newbury (Salem FASS, box 1, folder 3, PEM).

87. "Women's Anti-Slavery Conference," *Liberator,* November 15, 1839, p. 181; "Women's Convention," *Liberator,* January 31, 1840, p. 19; "Essex Co. Women's Anti-Slavery Conference," *Liberator,* October 30, 1840, p. 174.

88. Abby Kelley to the Philadelphia Female Anti-Slavery Society, [March] 16, 1838, Lynn (HSP).

89. E. Quincy to Caroline Weston, July 9, 1840, Dedham, and Rachel A. Hunt to Maria Weston Chapman, March 9, 1840, Southboro (BPL Ms.A.9.2.13.99, Ms.A.9.2.13.35).

90. "Particular Instructions," 1836 American Antislavery Society Agency Commission for James McKim, and 1839 "Commission and Instructions" (Maloney/McKim/Garrison Papers, box 2, MGF 11, 12, NYPL); Hannah H. Smith to Miss Abby Kelley, July 25, 1839, Glastenbury (AKF Papers, box 1, folder 3, AASW). See Appendix Table A for a complete list of female antislavery societies founded during this period.

91. Ronald Walters, *The Antislavery Appeal: American Abolitionism after 1830* (Baltimore: Johns Hopkins University Press, 1976); Kraditor, *Means and Ends.*

5—Transition and Transformation, 1841–1855

1. The epigraph and subsequent quotation come from *Signal of Liberty,* July 25, 1846.

2. Miss Harriet Minot to Rev. A. A. Phelps, November 22, 1838, Haverhill (BPL Ms.A.21.8[88]); Eliza Boyce, Corresponding Secretary for the Lynn Women's Anti-Slavery Society to Mrs. Maria Weston Chapman, [December] 1, 1839, Lynn (BPL Ms.A.9.2.12.100).

3. Hannah Wilbur to N. P. Rogers, January 27, 1841, as cited in Stephen Lawrence Cox, "Power, Oppression and Liberation: New Hampshire Abolitionism and the Radical Critique of Slavery, 1825–1850" (Ph.D. diss., University of New Hampshire, 1980), n. 72; *National Anti-Slavery Standard,* April 29, 1841, p. 157.

4. MM [Mary Moses?] to Sister Abby [Kelly], August 1, 1841, Great Falls (AKF Papers, box 1, folder 4, AASW); Abel Tanner to Mrs. Chapman, July 6, [1841?], Great Falls (BPL Ms.A.9.2.18.70); Harriet Hale to the Phila. Ladies Anti-Slavery So'y [Philadelphia FASS], February 12, 1841, Providence (HSP).

5. L.M.C. to Ellis Gray Loring, March 6, 1843, New York, and L. Maria Child to Maria [Weston] Chapman, May 19, [1843], New York, in Meltzer and Holland, *Lydia Maria Child,* 192–97 (italics deleted); L.M.C. to Ellis Gray Loring, March 9, 1842, New York (Lydia Maria Child Personal Miscellaneous Collection, NYPL).

6. Harriet N. Webster to Dear friend [Harriet Foster], November 26, 1840, Danvers (Salem FASS, box 1, folder 4, PEM).

7. "Women's Anti-Slavery Conference," *Liberator,* February 16, 1844, p. 26; "Boston Female Anti-Slavery Society," *Liberator,* April 22, 1842, p. 62.

8. Boylan, *Origins of Women's Activism,* 215; Cohen, "Clip Not Her Wings," 30; Hewitt, *Women's Activism,* 105, 110.

9. Melia, "Black Garrisonian Women," chap. 7, p. 9 (Susan Paul and Grace Douglass); *Herald of Freedom,* May 14, 1841 (Mary Clark); Harriet N. Webster to Dear friend [Harriet Foster], November 26, 1840, Danvers (Salem FASS, box 1, folder 4, PEM); "Anti-Slavery in Maine," *Liberator,* September 8, 1843, p. 126.

10. Soderlund, "Priorities and Power," 67–88; Boylan, *Origins of Women's Activism,* 72.

11. Elizabeth L. B. Wright to Miss Foster, May 24, 1839, Newburyport (Salem FASS, box 1, folder 3, PEM); Frances H. Drake, Secretary Leominster Garrisonian Society to Mrs. Chapman, August 6, 1843, Leominster (BPL Ms.A.4.6a.1.86).

12. Alvan Ward to Maria Weston Chapman, July 23, 1840, Ashburnham (BPL Ms.A.9.2.13.106).

13. Hewitt, *Women's Activism;* Ryan, *Cradle of the Middle Class,* 142–43, 150.

14. "Tenth Massachusetts Anti-Slavery Fair," *Liberator,* September 22, 1843; Boston FASS, *Ten Years of Experience;* "Tenth Annual Meeting of the Boston FASS,"

Liberator, October 20, 1843; C.H.L.C. to Maria Weston Chapman, December 20, 1844, Portsmouth (NH) (BPL Ms.A.9.2.20.129).

15. Philadelphia FASS, *Tenth Annual Report of the Philadelphia Female Anti-Slavery Society, January 11, 1844* (Philadelphia: Merrihew and Thompson, 1844), 5; *Liberator,* September 8, 1843, p. 126; Charles Sellers, *The Market Revolution: Jacksonian America, 1815–1846* (New York: Oxford University Press, 1991), 386–91.

16. "Circular of the Anti-Slavery Convention of American Women," contained in ASCAW, *Proceedings, 1839,* 25–28.

17. *National Anti-Slavery Standard,* September 24, 1840, p. 62; Editor's note at end of "Petitions to Congress," *Liberator,* February 13, 1846, p. 27.

18. Williams, "Religion, Race, and Gender," 554; Wellman, "Women and Radical Reform," 121; Zaeske, *Signatures of Citizenship,* 153–64.

19. Philadelphia FASS, *Tenth Annual Report,* 10; Williams, "Religion, Race, and Gender," 554; "Intermarriage Law," *National Anti-Slavery Standard,* February 24, 1842; Deborah Bingham Van Broekhoven, "'Let Your Names Be Enrolled': Method and Ideology in Women's Antislavery Petitioning," in Yellin and Van Horne, *Abolitionist Sisterhood,* 192.

20. "The Ladies' Fair," *Genius,* November 20, 1829, p. 84.

21. "Record of the Female Anti-Slavery Society" (Lynn Museum, Lynn, MA); *Herald of Freedom,* May 16, 1835, p. 23, col. 4, May 28, 1836; Ladies' New-York City Anti-Slavery Society, *First Annual Report,* 10–11.

22. "Another F.A.S.S. at Fall River," *Liberator,* September 17, 1836, p. 150; *National Antislavery Standard,* March 10, 1842.

23. "Address of the Boston Female Anti-Slavery Society to the Women of Massachusetts," *Liberator,* October 11, 1839, p. 163; "To the Abolitionists of Rhode Island," *Liberator,* November 4, 1842, p. 571; "Eleventh Massachusetts Anti-Slavery Fair," *Liberator,* February 9, 1844; Sterling, *Ahead of Her Time,* 154.

24. "Women's Anti-Slavery Conference," *Liberator,* March 11, 1842, p. 38 (Essex County); Carolyn J. Lawes, *Women and Reform in a New England Community, 1815–1860* (Lexington: University Press of Kentucky, 2000), 59–74, 78.

25. Salem FASS, *Record Book, 1834–1846* (Salem FASS, box 1, PEM); C.H.L.C. to Maria Weston Chapman, December 20, 1844, Portsmouth, NH (BPL Ms.A.9.2.v.20.no.129); *Liberator,* January 5, 1844; Amy Post to Abby Kelley, December 4, 1843, Rochester (AKF Papers, box 1, folder 6, AASW); Nancy Hewitt, "The Social Origins of Women's Antislavery Politics in Western New York," in *Crusaders and Compromisers: Essays on the Relationship of the Antislavery Struggle to the Antebellum Party System,* ed. Alan M. Kraut (Westport, CT: Greenwood Press, 1983), 212–13; Hewitt, *Women's Activism,* 97–138.

26. "The Twelfth Annual Massachusetts Anti-Slavery Fair" *Liberator,* September 12, 1845; *Liberator,* November 14, 1845, p. 183; Evelina A. S. Smith to Mrs. Chapman, March 31, 1843, Hingham (BPL Ms.A.4.6a.1.76); Loudon Anti-Slavery Sewing Society Records (#1953-008, New Hampshire Historical Society).

27. For the antislavery societies, see Appendix Table A. For sewing societies, see *Liberator,* October 11, 1844; Lawes, *Women and Reform,* 45–82; Deborah Bingham Van Broekhoven, "'Better than a Clay Club': The Organization of Anti-Slavery Fairs, 1835–1860," *Slavery and Abolition* 19.1 (1998): 45, n. 50.

28. Van Broekhoven, "'Better than a Clay Club,'" 38; Atkin, "'When Pincushions Are Periodicals.'"

29. *Liberator,* May 4, 1849; "Anti-Slavery in Maine," *Liberator,* September 8, 1843.

30. "Notice of fair," *Liberator,* November 13, 1846; *Liberator,* November 27, 1846; "Working Parties," *Liberator,* November 13, 1846; Hallowell, *James and Lucretia Mott,* 330; Chambers-Schiller, "The Single Woman," 334–52; Karen Hansen, *A Very Social Time: Crafting Community in Antebellum New England* (Berkeley and Los Angeles: University of California Press, 1994).

31. Lawes, *Women and Reform,* 78.

32. *Liberator,* April 9, 1841; Abby Kelley Foster to Maria Weston Chapman, March 20, 1848, Worcester (BPL Ms.A.9.2.24.8); Cohen, "Clip Not Her Wings," 38.

33. *Liberator,* January 13, 1843, January 23, 1846, October 20, 1843, p. 168. See *Liberator,* September 12, 1845, for first use of "national bazaar." The fair would have multiple names for the next few years.

34. MM [Mary Moses?] to Dear Sister Abby [Kelly], August 16, 1841, Great Falls (AKF Papers, box 1, folder 4, AASW), and Hannah Wilbur to Maria W. Chapman, December 21, 1841, cited in Chambers-Schiller, "'A Good Work Among the People,'" 256; J. C. H[olley?] to [Abby Kelley], [February] 26, 1843, Farmington (AKF Papers, box 1, folder 6, AASW); Rhoda De Garmo to Maria Weston Chapman, [January] 18, 1846, Rochester (BPL Ms.A.9.22.10); Lucinda Wilmarth to Mrs. Chapman, December 20, 1842, Providence (BPL Ms.A.4.6a.1.68).

35. Charlotte Austin to Maria Weston Chapman, December 5, 1841, Nantucket (BPL Ms.A.4.6a.1.8).

36. "Cause and Effect," *Liberator,* November 13, 1846, p. 183; Van Broekhoven, "'Better than a Clay Club,'" 24–45; Soderlund, "Priorities and Power," 82–83.

37. *Herald of Freedom* article reprinted in *National Anti-Slavery Standard,* August 13, 1840, p. 38; Abby Kelley to Maria Weston Chapman, August 2, 1843, Syracuse (BPL Ms.A.9.2.19.9); Williams, as quoted in "Religion, Race, and Gender," 282 (Pennsylvania, 1855); AAS, *Annual Report, Presented at the American Anti-Slavery Society, by the Executive Committee, at the Annual Meeting, held in New York, May 7, 1856* (New York: AAS, 1856), 57–58.

38. Eighth Massachusetts Anti-Slavery Fair report, extracted from the *Liberator,* January 14, 1842, contained in Glasgow FASS, *Annual Report of the Glasgow Female Anti-Slavery Society* (Glasgow: Temperance Press, 1842), 18; Elizabeth Cady Stanton, Susan B. Anthony, and Matilda Joslyn Gage, *History of Woman Suffrage,* vol. 1, *1848–1861* (New York: Fowler and Wells, 1881), 256–57.

39. *Liberator,* May 12, 1843, July 17, 1846.

40. "Anti-Slavery Convention in Hingham," *Liberator,* November 16, 1838; *Liberator,* November 1, 1844.

41. *Liberator,* January 8, 1847, November 29, December 20, 1844, September 16, 1842; "Women's Anti-Slavery Conference," *Liberator,* August 11, 1843; "Ohio American Anti-Slavery Society," *National Anti-Slavery Standard,* December 1, 1842; "Philadelphia Fair," *National-Anti-Slavery Standard,* September 1, 1842.

42. Glasgow FASS, *Sixth Annual Report of the Glasgow Female Anti-Slavery Society* (Glasgow, 1851), 3.

43. List of articles sent by the Glasgow FASS, November 15, 1845 (BPL Ms.A.9.2.21.106); Southwick, *Reminiscences,* 36; Mrs. Chapman to Mary Welsh and Catherine Paton, January 27, 1846, Boston, as quoted in Glasgow FASS, *Fifth Annual Report of the Glasgow Female Anti-Slavery Society* (Glasgow: David Russell, 1846), 6.

44. Glasgow FASS, *Sixth Annual Report,* 4; Maria Weston Chapman to Glasgow Female Anti-Slavery Society, January 15, 1843, Boston, as quoted in Glasgow FASS, *Second Annual Report of the Glasgow Female Anti-Slavery Society* (Glasgow: Bell and Bain, 1843), 12.

45. L. H. Earle to Maria W. and Mary S. Chapman, [December] 21, 1841, Worcester (BPL Ms.A.4.6a.1.18); Maria Weston Chapman to J. B. Estlin, February 28, 1847, Boston, as quoted in Clare Taylor, *British and American Abolitionists: An Episode in Transatlantic Understanding* (Chicago: Edinburgh University Press, 1974), 250.

46. M. Welsh to Mrs. Chapman, November 17, 1846, Edinr., in Taylor, *British and American Abolitionists*, 300; Glasgow circular in ibid., 342–44; Glasgow FASS, *Sixth Annual Report*, 6; E. W. Wigham to Anne Warren Weston, [August] 30, 1850, Edinburgh (BPL Ms.A.9.2.25.p18).

47. Jane D. Carr to the Committee of the Anti-Slavery Bazaar to be held in Boston, c/o Maria Weston Chapman, [October] 30, 1846, Carlisle (BPL Ms.A.4.6a.1.110); Taylor, *British and American Abolitionists*, 247; Belfast Ladies' Anti-Slavery Association, "Address from the Committee of the Belfast Ladies' Anti-Slavery Association to the Ladies of Ulster," September 23, 1846, p. 1; Anna H. Richardson to the Ladies Connected with the Pennsylvania Anti-Slavery Society, [March] 22, 1849, Summerhill Grove [?], Newcastle on Tyne (BPL).

48. Anne Warren Weston to Maria Weston Chapman, April 2, 1849, Weymouth, Maria Weston Chapman to Anne, Debora, and Lucia, March 4, 1849, Paris (BPL Ms.A.9.2.24.70, Ms.A.9.2.24.64); Maria Weston Chapman to Lucretia Mott, Edward Davis, and Sarah Pugh, March 4, 1849, Paris (BPL Ms.A.9.2.24.65); Draft letter by Mary Grew to Anna H. Richardson, October 2, 1849, New Castle, England (HSP). Also see Taylor, *British and American Abolitionists*, 336–37, 283.

49. Rochester Ladies' Anti-Slavery Sewing Society *Circular: First Report, 1852,* 2 (RUL).

50. Ibid.

51. Rochester Ladies' Anti-Slavery Society, *Annual Reports, 1852–1854* (RUL); Rochester FASS, *Annual Reports, 1855–1856* (William L. Clements Library, University of Michigan); Rochester Ladies' Anti-Slavery Society, *Annual Reports, 1858–1859* (RUL).

52. Salem FASS, *Record Book, 1834–1846* (Salem FASS, box 1, PEM); Boston FASS, *Right and Wrong in Boston, 1835;* Philadelphia FASS, *Third Annual Report of the Philadelphia Female Anti-Slavery Society, January, 1837* (Philadelphia, 1837).

53. *National Anti-Slavery Standard,* November 26, 1840, p. 98; "Dorchester Female Anti-Slavery Society," *Liberator,* June 12, 1840, p. 95; N. S. P. Cotton to Mrs. Chapman, December 22, 1841, Boylston (BPL Ms.A.4.6a.1.20); Minutes from July 15, 1840, through December 19, 1849, Reading FASS Records (Reading Historical Commission, Reading, MA).

54. *National Anti-Slavery Standard,* November 26, 1840, p. 98, January 14, 1841, p. 127; "Weymouth and Braintree Female A. S. Society," *Liberator,* July 7, 1843, p. 106.

55. Rochester Ladies' Anti-Slavery Sewing Society, *"Circular" Second Report, 1853* (RUL); Rochester Ladies' Anti-Slavery Society, *"Circular" Seventh Annual Report, 1858* (RUL). The 1853 report notes that "auxiliary societies of Ogden and Penn Yan" worked specifically for the Canada fugitives as well. It is not clear if these were female or mixed-sex societies. *Liberator,* November 1, 1844, February 14, 1845, March 6, April 10, June 12, 1846.

56. Quarles, *Black Abolitionists,* 143–44, 150–55; Joseph A. Borome, "The Vigilant Committee of Philadelphia," *Pennsylvania Magazine of History and Biography* 92.3 (July 1968): 320–51.

57. Quarles, *Black Abolitionists,* 158.

58. Philadelphia FASS, *Ninth Annual Report of the Philadelphia Female Anti-Slavery Society, January 13, 1843* (Philadelphia: Merrihew and Thompson, 1842), 10–11; Philadelphia FASS minutes for October 8, 1846, quoted in Yee, *Black Women Abolitionists*, 99–100.

59. Philadelphia FASS minutes for October 8, 1846, quoted in Yee, *Black Women Abolitionists*, 99–100; Abby Kelley Foster to Betsy Mix Cowles, August 1, 1846, Ravenna, Ohio (Cowles Papers).

60. Frances H. Drake to Mrs. Chapman, August 6, 1843, Leominster (BPL Ms.A.4.6a.1.86); L. and S. A. Burtis to Abby Kelley, [January] 17, 1843, Rochester (AKF Papers, box 1, folder 6, AASW).

61. Yee, *Black Women Abolitionists*, 108–9, and Sterling, *We Are Your Sisters*, 117–18; Hewitt, "Social Origins," 208–9.

62. Quarles, *Black Abolitionists*, 157–59.

63. Peter D. McClelland and Richard J. Zeckhauser, *Demographic Dimensions of the New Republic: American Interregional Migration, Vital Statistics, and Manumissions, 1800–1860* (New York: Cambridge University Press, 1982), p. 88, table A-2.

64. Susan E. Gray, *The Yankee West: Community Life on the Michigan Frontier* (Chapel Hill: University of North Carolina Press, 1996), 46–47, and introduction.

65. Genevieve G. McBride, *On Wisconsin Women: Working for Their Rights from Settlement to Suffrage* (Madison: University of Wisconsin Press, 1993), 12–13.

66. Ibid.; *Free Labor Advocate and Anti-Slavery Chronicle*, October 20, December 22, 1843.

67. "Second Annual Report of the Female Anti-Slavery Society of Wayne Township, Wayne County, Indiana, [June] 12, 1843," *Free Labor Advocate and Antislavery Chronicle*, July 11, 1843 ("gloomy passage"); Peggy Brase Seigel, "Moral Champions and Public Pathfinders: Antebellum Quaker Women in Eastcentral Indiana," *Quaker History* 81.2 (1992): 96; McBride, *On Wisconsin Women*, 12–13; *Western Citizen*, April 6, November 9, 1843, January 30, 1845, cited in Mary Van Vleck Garman, "'Altered tone of expression': The Anti-Slavery Rhetoric of Illinois Women, 1837–1847" (Ph.D. diss., Northwestern University Garrett-Evangelical Theological Seminary, 1989), 113 ("befriend the outcast"), 115; "Address to the Females of Putnam County," reprinted from the *Western Citizen* in "Second Annual Report of the Female Anti-Slavery Society of Wayne Township, Wayne County, Indiana, [June] 12, 1843," *Free Labor Advocate and Antislavery Chronicle*, July 11, 1843 ("welcome the homeless wanderer").

68. Salem FASS, *Record Book, 1847–1862* (Salem FASS, box 1, PEM).

69. Julia A. Tappan to the Philadelphia Female Anti-Slavery Society, May 22, 1837, Lucy B. Williams to the Philadelphia Female Anti-Slavery Society, April 9, 1836, Brooklyn (HSP); Mary H. Watson to Maria Weston Chapman, November 14, 1857, Lakeland, Min. Ter. (BPL Ms.A.9.2.29.35).

70. Garman, "'Altered tone of expression,'" 126–27.

71. Ibid.

72. Ibid., 124–26, 128.

73. Ibid., 150–52, 155.

74. *Free Labor Advocate and Anti-Slavery Chronicle*, April 15, August 8, 1843.

75. Garman, "'Altered tone of expression,'" 140, 160–61; *Western Citizen*, March 4, 1846, cited in ibid., 163.

76. "The Ladies of Michigan," *Signal of Liberty*, September 26, 1846; *Signal of Liberty*, July 11, September 5, 1846; John W. Quist, "'The Great Majority of Our Subscribers Are Farmers': The Michigan Abolitionist Constituency of the 1840s," *Journal of the Early Republic* 14.3 (Fall 1994): 325–58.

77. Seigel, "Moral Champions," 92–98.

78. William Goodell, *Slavery and Anti-Slavery; A History of the Great Struggle in both Hemispheres, with a View of the Slavery Question in the United States* (New York: William Harned, 1852), 465.

79. Entry dated December 19, 1849, Reading FASS Records (Reading Historical Commission, Reading, MA); Chambers-Schiller, "'A Good Work Among the People,'" 270.

80. *National Anti-Slavery Standard,* January 13, May 5, 1842; Lawes, *Women and Reform,* 59–74, 78; Cohen, "Clip Not Her Wings," 30; Hewitt, *Women's Activism,* 105, 110.

81. Boston FASS, *Seventh Annual Report* (Boston: Published by the Society, 1840), 27.

82. Michael D. Pierson, "Gender and Party Ideologies: The Constitutional Thought of Women and Men in American Anti-Slavery Politics," *Slavery and Abolition* 19.3 (1998): 46–67, and "Between Antislavery and Abolition: The Politics and Rhetoric of Jane Grey Swisshelm," *Pennsylvania History* 60.3 (July 1993): 305–21; Louise M. Young, "Women's Place in American Politics: The Historical Perspective," *Journal of Politics* 38.3 (1976): 320.

Conclusion—Civil War and Emancipation, 1861–1870

1. The epigraph is from Rochester Ladies' Anti-Slavery Society, *Twelfth Annual Report* (Rochester, NY: A. Strong & Co., 1863), 3. In 1865 the society changed its name to the Rochester Ladies' Freedmen's Aid Society.

2. Salem FASS meeting, June 5, 1861, *Record Book, 1847–1862* (Salem FASS, box 1, PEM); Rochester Ladies' Anti-Slavery Society, *Tenth Annual Report, 1861* (RUL); Records of the Dover Anti-Slavery Sewing Circle, vol. 2, May 1, June 5, July 3, 1861 (Records of the Ladies' Anti-Slavery Society of Dover, #1931-9, NHHS); Philadelphia FASS, *Twenty-Seventh Annual Report* (Philadelphia: Merrihew and Thompson, 1861), 10–11; Ginzberg, *Women and the Work of Benevolence,* 133–73.

3. Elizabeth Cady Stanton, *Eighty Years and More: Reminiscences, 1815–1897* (1898; Boston: Northeastern University Press, 1993); James E. Yeatman, Rooms, Western Sanitary Commission, St. Louis, November 10, 1863, to Rev. H. D. Fisher, Chaplain Fifth Kansas Cavalry, in Salem Freedmen's Aid Society Records (Salem FASS, box 1 folder 1, PEM); Julie Roy Jeffrey, *The Great Silent Army of Abolitionism: Ordinary Women in the Antislavery Movement* (Chapel Hill: University of North Carolina Press, 1998), 223, and chap. 6.

4. Salem FASS, *Record Book, 1847–1862* and *Record Book, 1862–1866* (Salem FASS, box 1, PEM); Records of the Dover Anti-Slavery Sewing Circle, vol. 2 (Records of the Ladies' Anti-Slavery Society of Dover, #1931-9, NHHS).

5. Rochester Ladies' Anti-Slavery Society, *Twelfth Annual Report* (1863); Rochester Ladies' Anti-Slavery and Freedmen's Aid Society, *Seventeenth Annual Report* (Rochester, NY: Wm. S. Falls, 1868).

6. Philadelphia FASS, *Twenty-Seventh Annual Report,* 18–19; Rochester Ladies' Anti-Slavery Society, *Tenth Annual Report, 1861* (RUL); Wendy Hamand Venet, *Neither Ballots nor Bullets: Women Abolitionists and the Civil War* (Charlottesville: University Press of Virginia, 1991), 99–100; Philadelphia FASS, *Twenty-Sixth Annual Report* (Philadelphia: Merrihew and Thompson, 1860), 20, and *Twenty-Ninth Annual Report* (Philadelphia: Merrihew and Thompson, 1863), 15.

7. "Address of Mrs. Elizabeth Cady Stanton to the Women of the Republic," and "Call for a Meeting of the Loyal Women of the Nation," Women's National Loyal League, *Proceedings of the Meeting of the Loyal Women of the Republic, Held in New York, May 14, 1863* (New York: Phair & Co., 1863), i–iv, 3–4.

8. Ibid., 4, 19.

9. Ibid., 15.

10. Ibid., 3, 18, 25, 22.

11. Ibid., 19–20.

12. Ibid., 20–21.

13. Ibid., 24, 28. I have made minor grammatical corrections to facilitate quotation.

14. Venet, *Neither Ballots nor Bullets,* 148.

15. Rochester Ladies' Anti-Slavery Society, *Fifteenth Annual Report* (Rochester, NY: Wm. S. Falls, 1865), 4; Rochester Ladies' Anti-Slavery and Freedmen's Aid Society, *Sixteenth Annual Report* (Rochester, NY: Wm. S Falls, 1867), 3–4; Records of the Dover Anti-Slavery Sewing Circle, vol. 2 (Records of the Ladies' Anti-Slavery Society of Dover, #1931-9, NHHS).

16. Meeting, January 3, 1866, in Salem FASS, *Record Book, 1847–1862* (Salem FASS, box 1, PEM); Philadelphia FASS, *Thirty-Sixth and Final Annual Report of the Philadelphia Female Anti-Slavery Society, April 1870* (Philadelphia: Merrihew and Son, 1870), 3.

17. Philadelphia FASS, *Thirty-Sixth and Final Annual Report* (1870), 37.

18. Speicher, *Religious World of Antislavery Women.*

19. Quote from Venet, *Neither Ballots nor Bullets,* 116; Ellen DuBois, "Women's Rights and Abolition: The Nature of the Connection," in *Antislavery Reconsidered: New Perspectives on the Abolitionists,* ed. Lewis Perry and Michael Fellman (Baton Rouge: Louisiana State University Press, 1979), 238–51.

Essay on Sources

The notes for each chapter provide the best guide to the primary and secondary sources that directly influenced specific arguments. This essay highlights other works that helped shape the overall argument of this book or that provide further information on particular topics. Full citations for the works discussed below can be found in the Works Cited.

This book builds on the excellent works that preceded it. Studies that focus on specific female antislavery societies include those by Debra Gold Hansen (Boston), Carolyn Williams and Jean Soderlund (Philadelphia), Amy Swerdlow (New York City), and Sandra Petrulionis (Concord, MA). Regional networks among antislavery women have received attention from Deborah Van Broekhoven (Rhode Island), Nancy Hewitt and Judith Wellman (upstate New York), Peggy Seigel (Indiana), and Mary Van Vleck Garman (Illinois). The only specific study of antislavery women's motivations is Jane H. Pease and William H. Pease, "The Role of Women in the Antislavery Movement," which focuses on four prominent women.

Black female abolitionists have received attention from Shirley Yee, Anne Boylan, Julie Winch, and Margot Melia. Black women's incorporation of antislavery activism into broader reform organizations makes them difficult to integrate into a study of antislavery societies. However, their focus on the connections between slavery and the larger black community provided a model for many white women, which I have tried to highlight in this study.

The most comprehensive investigation of antislavery women's individual efforts against slavery is Julie Roy Jeffrey's *The Great Silent Army of Abolitionism*. While Jeffrey incorporates the activities of many female antislavery society members, she is primarily interested in a history of women, rather than a history of their associations. The best integration of antislavery women into the broader picture of reform in the nineteenth century is Lori Ginzberg's *Women and the Work of Benevolence*.

The question of "separate spheres" that weaves all through this book has been hotly debated among historians. Most agree that women in the nineteenth century faced some ideological and practical limitations on their daily activities, or at least thought they did. Few agree on where exactly those boundaries were, which makes sense since nineteenth-century women were just as confused. Some historians have begun to question the usefulness of separate spheres as an analytical concept, since the boundaries were often so gerrymandered as to make the term functionally meaningless. I am not yet convinced that we can cease to explore an issue that arose repeatedly in antislavery women's debates, arguments, and personal letters. For those interested in reading more regarding this debate, see Linda K. Kerber, "Separate Spheres, Female Worlds, Woman's Place"; Mary Kelley, "Beyond the Boundaries"; Julie Roy Jeffrey, "Permeable Boundaries"; Carol Lasser, "Beyond Separate Spheres"; Leonore Davidoff, "Regarding Some 'Old Husbands' Tales'"; and Karen Hansen, "Feminist Conceptions of Public and Private."

Historians have been less rigorous than sociologists in their study of networks. The connections among antislavery women have been called "personal associations," "social networks," and "personal networks of communication," sometimes in the same work. This study of networks focuses on the relationships among individual women and the societies to which they belonged, which resulted in the circulation of information, goods, funds, or moral support. I have drawn on the following studies as useful guides: Mary P. Ryan, "The Power of Women's Networks"; Leila J. Rupp, "Constructing Internationalism"; Lois E. Horton, "Community Organization and Social Activism"; Naomi Rosenthal, "Social Movements and Network Analysis"; Nancy A. Hewitt, *Women's Activism and Social Change;* and Lee Chambers-Schiller, "The Single Woman Reformer."

Books that focus on women's redefinition of political action have become too numerous to list. Gerda Lerner first examined the political nature of antislavery women's action in "The Political Activities of Antislavery Women." Paula Barnes made far broader claims for the fundamentally political nature of women's demands for reform in "The Domestication of Politics." Lori Ginzberg focused attention on the shift from moral suasion strategies to direct use of the political system in "Moral Suasion Is Moral Balderdash." The best overall history of antislavery politics in this era is Richard Sewell, *Ballots for Freedom.* On the Free Soil Party, see the early chapters of Eric Foner, *Free Soil, Free Labor, Free Men.* Michael D. Pierson's new book *Free Hearts and Free Homes* is a major departure in the study of antislavery politics since he sees female antislavery activities and gender as central to the party ideologies.

Recently scholars have come to accept the political nature of women's action as given and focus on the implications of their actions for the definition and meaning of citizenship. The best of these are Susan Zaeske, *Signatures of Citizenship,* Nancy Isenberg, *Sex and Citizenship in Antebellum America,* and Linda Kerber, *No Constitutional Right to Be Ladies: Women and the Obligations of Citizenship.* I have been especially influenced by Kerber's understanding of citizenship as responsibilities as well as rights, an argument made by antislavery women on a regular basis.

Works Cited

Primary Sources

NEWSPAPERS

The dates below are the years of the periodical that I examined, rather than the full print runs.

Free Labor Advocate and Anti-Slavery Chronicle, New Garden (IN). 1843.

Genius of Universal Emancipation, multiple locations and titles. 1821–1839.

Herald of Freedom, Concord (NH). 1835–1841.

Liberator, Boston (MA). 1831–1855.

National Anti-Slavery Standard, New York (NY). 1840–1850.

Signal of Liberty (MI). 1846.

ANNUAL REPORTS

The annual reports of the following societies were published as stand-alone publications in addition to appearing in excerpted form in various antislavery newspapers.

Boston Female Anti-Slavery Society

Concord (NH) Female Anti-Slavery Society

Dorchester (MA) Female Anti-Slavery Society

Glasgow (England) Female Anti-Slavery Society

Glasgow (England) Ladies' Auxiliary Emancipation Society

Ladies' New-York City Anti-Slavery Society

Massachusetts Abolition Society

Massachusetts Anti-Slavery Society

Massachusetts Female Emancipation Society

New-England Anti-Slavery Society

Philadelphia Female Anti-Slavery Society

Rochester Ladies' Anti-Slavery Society

Salem Female Anti-Slavery Society

UNPUBLISHED SOCIETY RECORDS AND COLLECTIONS
OF CORRESPONDENCE

Ashtabula County Anti-Slavery Society Records, Ms 387. Western Reserve Historical Society, Cleveland, OH.

Betsy Mix Cowles Papers. Department of Special Collections and Archives, Kent State University Libraries and Media Services, Kent, OH.

Boston Female Anti-Slavery Society Letterbook, April 9, 1834, to January 7, 1838 (Boston FASS Letterbook). Massachusetts Historical Society, Boston.

Ladies' Anti-Slavery Society of Dover, including Records of the Dover Anti-Slavery Sewing Circle and Dover Anti-Slavery and Freedmen's Aid Society, #1931–9. New Hampshire Historical Society, Concord.

Lynn Female Anti-Slavery Society Records. Lynn Museum, Lynn, MA.

Maloney/McKim/Garrison Papers, box 2, MGF 11. New York Public Library.

Pennsylvania Abolition Society Collection, reel 31, Philadelphia Female Anti-Slavery Society Records, Incoming Correspondence. Historical Society of Pennsylvania, Philadelphia.

Reading Female Anti-Slavery Society Records. Reading Historical Commission, Reading, MA.

Salem Female Anti-Slavery Society Records, mss 34. Phillips Library, Peabody Essex Museum, Salem, MA.

PUBLISHED WORKS

American Anti-Slavery Society. *Proceedings of the American Anti-Slavery Society at its Third Decade, held in the City of Philadelphia, Dec. 3d and 4th, 1863*. New York: American Anti-Slavery Society, 1864.

———. *Proceedings of the Anti-Slavery Convention, assembled at Philadelphia, December 4, 5 and 6, 1833*. New York: Dorr and Butterfield, 1833.

———. *Second Annual Report of the American Anti-Slavery Society; with the Speeches delivered at the Anniversary Meeting, held in the City of New York, on the 12th May, 1835, and the Minutes of the Meetings of the Society for Business*. New York: William S. Dorr, 1835.

———. *Sixth Annual Report of the Executive Committee of the American Anti-Slavery Society, with the Speeches delivered at the Anniversary Meeting held in the city of New-York, on the 7th of May, 1839, and the minutes of the meetings of the Society for business, held on the evening and the three following days*. New York: William S. Dorr, 1839.

Anti-Slavery Convention of American Women. *An Address to Free Colored Americans*. New York: William S. Dorr, 1837. Reprint, New York: Lost Cause Press, 1962.

———. *An Appeal to the Women of the Nominally Free States*. 2nd ed. Boston: Isaac Knapp, 1838.

———. *Proceedings of the Anti-Slavery Convention of American Women, Held in the City of New-York, May 9th, 10th, 11th, and 12th, 1837*. New York: William S. Dorr, 1837.

———. *Proceedings of the Anti-Slavery Convention of American Women, Held in Philadelphia, May 15th, 16th, 17th and 18th, 1838*. Philadelphia: Merrihew and Gunn, 1838.

———. *Proceedings of the Third Anti-Slavery Convention of American Women, Held in Philadelphia May 1st, 2d and 3d, 1839*. Philadelphia: Merrihew and Thompson, 1839.

Beecher, Edward. *Narrative of riots at Alton: in connection with the death of Rev. Elijah P. Lovejoy*. Alton, IL: G. Holton, 1838.

Boardman, Elderkin J. *Immediate Abolition Vindicated. An Address, delivered June 26, 1838 before the Randolph Female Anti-Slavery Society, at their Annual Meeting. By Elderkin J. Boardman, A.B., Pastor of the First Church in Randolph, Vt. Published by Request.* Montpelier, VT: E. P. Watson and Son, 1838.

Boston Female Anti-Slavery Society. *Right and Wrong in Boston. Report of the Boston Female Anti-Slavery Society; with a Concise Statement of Events, Previous and Subsequent to the Annual Meeting of 1835.* Boston: Published by the Society, 1836.

———. *Right and Wrong in Boston. Annual Report of the Boston Female Anti-Slavery Society, with a Sketch of the Obstacles thrown in the way of Emancipation by certain Clerical Abolitionists and Advocates for the Subjection of Woman, in 1837.* Boston: Isaac Knapp, 1837.

———. *Fifth Annual Report of the Boston Female Anti-Slavery Society.* Boston: Isaac Knapp, 1838.

———. *Seventh Annual Report.* Boston: Published by the Society, 1840.

———. *Ten Years of Experience: Ninth Annual Report of the Boston Female Anti-Slavery Society presented October 12, 1842.* Boston: Oliver Johnson, 1842.

Ceplair, Larry, ed. *The Public Years of Sarah and Angelina Grimké: Selected Writings, 1835–1839.* New York: Columbia University Press, 1989.

Chase, Elizabeth Buffum. *Anti-Slavery Reminiscences.* Central Falls, RI: E. L. Freeman and Son, 1891.

Child, Lydia Maria. *An Appeal in Favor of that class of Americans Called Africans.* Boston: Allen and Ticknor, 1833.

Concord (NH) Female Anti-Slavery Society. *First Annual Report of the Ladies' Anti-Slavery Society of Concord, December 25, 1835.* Concord, NH: Elbridge G. Chase, 1836.

Dorchester (MA) Female Anti-Slavery Society. *First Annual Report of the Dorchester Female Anti-Slavery Society, December 1837.* Boston: D. Clapp, Jr., 1838.

Dumond, Dwight L., and Gilbert H. Barnes, eds. *The Letters of Theodore Dwight Weld, Angelina Grimké Weld, and Sarah Grimké, 1822–1844.* New York: D. Appleton-Century for the American Historical Association, 1934.

Female Anti-Slavery Society of Chatham-Street Chapel. *Constitution and Address of the Female Anti-Slavery Society of Chatham Street Chapel.* New York: William S. Dorr, 1834. Reprint, Louisville: Lost Cause Press, 1965.

Garrison, William Lloyd. *Thoughts on African Colonization.* Boston: Garrison and Knapp, 1832. Reprint, New York: Arno Press, 1968.

Glasgow Female Anti-Slavery Society. *Sixth Annual Report of the Glasgow Female Anti-Slavery Society.* Glasgow, 1851.

Glasgow Ladies' Auxiliary Emancipation Society. *Three Years' Female Anti-Slavery Effort in Britain and America: Being a Report of the Proceedings of the Glasgow Ladies' Auxiliary Emancipation Society, Since its Formation in January, 1834.* Glasgow: Published by the Society, 1837.

Goodell, William. *Slavery and Anti-Slavery; A History of the Great Struggle in both Hemispheres, with a View of the Slavery Question in the United States.* New York: William Harned, 1852.

Grimké, Angelina. *Appeal to the Christian Women of America.* New York: William S. Dorr, 1836.

———. *Letters to Catherine E. Beecher, in Reply to An Essay on Slavery and Abolitionism, Addressed to A. E. Grimké. Revised by the Author.* Boston: Isaac Knapp, 1838.

————. *Slavery in America. A Reprint of An Appeal to the Christian Women of the Slave States of America. By Angelina Grimké, of Charleston, South Carolina. with Introduction, Notes, and Appendix by George Thompson. Recommended to the Special Attention of the Anti-Slavery Females of Great Britain.* Edinburgh: William Oliphant and Son, 1837.

Grimké, Sarah M. *Letters on the equality of the Sexes and the Condition of Woman, addressed to Mary S. Parker, President of the Boston Female Anti-Slavery Society.* Boston: Isaac Knapp, 1838.

Hallowell, Anna Davis, ed. *James and Lucretia Mott: Life and Letters.* 1884. Boston: Houghton, Mifflin, 1890.

Hayward, John. *A Gazetteer of Massachusetts.* Revised ed. Boston: J. P. Jewett, 1849.

Heyrick, Elizabeth. *Apology for Ladies' Anti-Slavery Associations.* London: J. Hatchard and Son, 1828.

[————]. *Appeal to the Hearts and Consciences of British Women.* Leicester: A. Cockshaw, 1828.

————. *Immediate, Not Gradual Abolition; or, An Inquiry into the Shortest, Safest, and Most Effectual Means of Getting Rid of West Indian Slavery.* London, 1824.

The History of Pennsylvania Hall, Which Was Destroyed by a Mob, on the 17th of May, 1838. 1838. New York: Negro Universities Press, 1969.

Ladies' New-York City Anti-Slavery Society. *First Annual Report of the Ladies' New-York City Anti-Slavery Society.* New York: William S. Dorr, 1836. Reprint, Louisville: Lost Cause Press, 1962.

————. *Third Annual Report of the Ladies' New-York City Anti-Slavery Society.* New York: William S. Dorr, 1838.

[Lovell, Laura H.]. *Report of a Delegate to the Anti-Slavery Convention of American Women, Held in Philadelphia, May, 1838; including an account of other meetings held in Pennsylvania Hall, and of the Riot. Addressed to the Fall River Female Anti-Slavery Society, and published by its request.* Boston: J. Knapp, 1838.

Lyman, Theodore, III, ed. *Papers relating to The Garrison Mob.* Cambridge: Welch, Bigelow, and Company, 1870.

Massachusetts Anti-Slavery Society. *Seventh Annual Report of the Board of Managers of the Mass. Anti-Slavery Society, presented January 24, 1839. With an appendix.* Boston: Isaac Knapp, 1839.

Massachusetts Female Emancipation Society. *First Annual Report of the Massachusetts Female Emancipation Society.* Boston: James Loring, 1841.

May, Samuel J. *Some Recollections of our Antislavery Conflict.* Boston: Fields, Osgood, and Co., 1869.

Meltzer, Milton, and Patricia G. Holland, eds. *Lydia Maria Child: Selected Letters, 1817–1880.* Amherst: University of Massachusetts Press, 1982.

New-England Anti-Slavery Society. *Constitution of the New-England Anti-Slavery Society with an Address to the Public.* Boston: Garrison and Knapp, 1832.

————. *Third Annual Report of the Board of Managers of the New-England Anti-Slavery Society, presented January 21, 1835.* Boston: Garrison and Knapp, 1835.

New Hampshire Anti-Slavery Convention. *Proceedings of the New Hampshire Anti-Slavery Convention, held in Concord, on the 11th and 12th of November, 1834.* Concord, NH: Eastman, Webster and Co., 1834.

Philadelphia Female Anti-Slavery Society. *Third Annual Report of the Philadelphia Female Anti-Slavery Society, January, 1837*. Philadelphia, 1837.

———. *Fourth Annual Report of the Philadelphia Female Anti-Slavery Society, Jan. 11, 1838*. Philadelphia: Merrihew and Gunn, 1838.

———. *Fifth Annual Report of the Philadelphia Female Anti-Slavery Society, January 10, 1839*. Philadelphia: Merrihew and Thompson, 1839.

———. *Ninth Annual Report of the Philadelphia Female Anti-Slavery Society, January 13, 1843*. Philadelphia: Merrihew and Thompson, 1842.

———. *Tenth Annual Report of the Philadelphia Female Anti-Slavery Society, January 11, 1844*. Philadelphia: Merrihew and Thompson, 1844.

———. *Twenty-Sixth Annual Report*. Philadelphia: Merrihew and Thompson, 1860.

———. *Twenty-Seventh Annual Report*. Philadelphia: Merrihew and Thompson, 1861.

———. *Twenty-Ninth Annual Report*. Philadelphia: Merrihew and Thompson, 1863.

———. *Thirty-Sixth and Final Annual Report of the Philadelphia Female Anti-Slavery Society, April 1870*. Philadelphia: Merrihew and Son, 1870.

Pillsbury, Parker. *Acts of the Anti-Slavery Apostles*. Concord, NH: Clague, Wegman, Schlicht, and Co., 1883.

Potter, Eli. *Remarks of Eli Potter, Esq. At the Trial of Two Individuals for A Breach of the Peace, in Disturbing a Meeting, In Which a Female Was Lecturing, Upon the Subject of Abolition*. Litchfield, CT: C. E. Moss & Co., 1840.

Rhode Island Anti-Slavery Convention. *Proceedings of the Rhode Island Anti-Slavery Convention held in Providence, on the 2d, 3d and 4th of February, 1836*. Providence: H. H. Brown, 1836.

Rochester Ladies' Anti-Slavery and Freedmen's Aid Society. *Sixteenth Annual Report*. Rochester, NY: Wm. S. Falls, 1867.

———. *Seventeenth Annual Report*. Rochester, NY: Wm. S. Falls, 1868.

Rochester Ladies' Anti-Slavery Society. *Twelfth Annual Report*. Rochester, NY: A. Strong, 1863.

———. *Thirteenth Annual Report*. Rochester, NY: Rochester Democrat Steam Printing House, 1864.

———. *Fifteenth Annual Report*. Rochester, NY: Wm. S. Falls, 1865.

Ruchames, Louis, and Walter Merrill, eds. *The Letters of William Lloyd Garrison*. Vol. 2. Cambridge, MA: Belknap Press of Harvard University Press, 1971.

Southwick, Sarah H. *Reminiscences of Early Anti-Slavery Days*. Cambridge, MA: Riverside Press, 1893.

Stanton, Elizabeth Cady. *Eighty Years and More: Reminiscences, 1815–1897*. 1898. Boston: Northeastern University Press, 1993.

Stanton, Elizabeth Cady, Susan B. Anthony, and Matilda Joslyn Gage. *History of Woman Suffrage*. Vol. 1, *1848–1861*. New York: Fowler and Wells, 1881.

Thompson, George. *Letters and Addresses by George Thompson during his Mission to the United States, from October 1, 1834, to November 27, 1835*. Boston: Isaac Knapp, 1837.

———. *Substance of an Address to the Ladies of Glasgow and its Vicinity upon the Present Aspect of the Great Question of Negro Emancipation*. Glasgow: David Robertson, 1833.

Women's National Loyal League. *Proceedings of the Meeting of the Loyal Women of the Republic, Held in New York, May 14, 1863*. New York: Phair & Co., 1863.

Works Cited

Secondary Sources

Abzug, Robert H. *Cosmos Crumbling: American Reform and the Religious Imagination.* New York: Oxford University Press, 1994.

Adams, Alice Dana. *The Neglected Period of Anti-Slavery in America, 1808–1831.* 1908. Gloucester, MA: Peter Smith, 1964.

Atkin, Andrea M. "'When Pincushions Are Periodicals': Women's Work, Race, and Material Objects in Female Abolitionism." *American Transcendental Quarterly,* n.s., 11.2 (June 1997): 93–113.

Bacon, Margaret Hope. "By Moral Force Alone: The Antislavery Women and Nonresistance." In Yellin and Van Horne, *Abolitionist Sisterhood,* 275–97.

Baker, Paula. "The Domestication of Politics: Women and American Political Society, 1780–1920." *American Historical Review* 89.3 (June 1984): 620–47.

Barnes, Gilbert. *The Antislavery Impulse, 1830–1844.* New York: Harcourt, Brace and World, 1933.

Bass, Dorothy C. "The Best Hopes of the Sexes: The Woman Question in Garrisonian Abolitionism." Ph.D. diss., Brown University, 1980.

Bloch, Ruth. "The Gendered Meanings of Virtue in Revolutionary America." *Signs: Journal of Women in Culture and Society* 13.1 (1987): 37–58.

Bogin, Ruth. "Petitioning and the New Moral Economy of Post-Revolutionary America." *William and Mary Quarterly,* 3rd ser., 45.3 (July 1988): 391–425.

Borome, Joseph A. "The Vigilant Committee of Philadelphia." *Pennsylvania Magazine of History and Biography* 92.3 (July 1968): 320–51.

Boylan, Anne M. "Benevolence and Antislavery Activity among African American Women in New York and Boston, 1820–1840." In Yellin and Van Horne, *Abolitionist Sisterhood,* 119–37.

———. *The Origins of Women's Activism: New York and Boston, 1797–1840.* Chapel Hill: University of North Carolina Press, 2002.

———. "Women and Politics in the Era before Seneca Falls." *Journal of the Early Republic* 10.3 (Fall 1990): 363–82.

Breen, T. H. "Narrative of Commercial Life: Consumption, Ideology, and Community on the Eve of the American Revolution." *William and Mary Quarterly,* 3rd ser., 50.3 (July 1993): 471–501.

Brown, Ira V. "Racism and Sexism: The Case of Pennsylvania Hall." *Phylon* 37 (June 1976): 126–36.

Chambers-Schiller, Lee. "The Cab, a Transatlantic Community: Aspects of Nineteenth Century Reform." Ph.D. diss., University of Michigan–Ann Arbor, 1977.

———. "'A Good Work Among the People': The Political Culture of the Boston Antislavery Fair." In Yellin and Van Horne, *Abolitionist Sisterhood,* 249–74.

———. "The Single Woman: Family and Vocation among Nineteenth-Century Reformers." In *Woman's Being, Woman's Place: Female Identity and Vocation in American History,* ed. Mary Kelley, 334–50. Boston: G. K. Hall, 1979.

———. "The Single Woman Reformer: Conflicts between Family and Vocation, 1830–1860." *Frontiers* 3.3 (1978): 41–48.

Cohen, Gretchen W. "Clip Not Her Wings: Female Abolitionists in Rochester, New York, 1835–1868." Master's thesis, City College of the City University of New York, 1994.

Coleman, Willie Mae. "Keeping the Faith and Disturbing the Peace: Black Women, from Anti-Slavery to Women's Suffrage." Ph.D. diss., University of California–Irvine, 1982.

Cott, Nancy F. "Young Women in the Second Great Awakening in New England." *Feminist Studies* 3 (Fall 1975): 15–29.

Cox, Stephen Lawrence. "Power, Oppression and Liberation: New Hampshire Abolitionism and the Radical Critique of Slavery, 1825–1850." Ph.D. diss., University of New Hampshire, 1980.

Davidoff, Leonore. "Regarding Some 'Old Husbands' Tales': Public and Private in Feminist History." In *Feminism, the Public and the Private,* ed. Joan B. Landes, 164–94. New York: Oxford University Press, 1998.

Dillon, Merton L. "Elizabeth Chandler and the Spread of Antislavery Sentiment in Michigan." *Michigan History* 39 (December 1955): 481–94.

Dinkin, Robert J. *Before Equal Suffrage: Women in Partisan Politics from Colonial Times to 1920.* Westport, CT: Greenwood Press, 1995.

Dorsey, Bruce. "Friends Becoming Enemies: Philadelphia Benevolence and the Neglected Era of American Quaker History." *Journal of the Early Republic* 18.3 (Fall 1998): 395–428.

Douglas, Ann. *The Feminization of American Culture.* New York: Knopf, 1977.

DuBois, Ellen. "Women's Rights and Abolition: The Nature of the Connection." In *Antislavery Reconsidered: New Perspectives on the Abolitionists,* ed. Lewis Perry and Michael Fellman, 238–51. Baton Rouge: Louisiana State University Press, 1979.

DuBois, Ellen, et al. "Politics and Culture in Women's History: A Symposium." *Feminist Studies* 6.1 (Spring 1980): 26–64.

Egerton, Douglas R. "'Its Origin Is Not a Little Curious': A New Look at the American Colonization Society." *Journal of the Early Republic* 5.4 (Winter 1985): 463–80.

Feldberg, Michael. *The Turbulent Era: Riot and Disorder in Jacksonian America.* New York: Oxford University Press, 1980.

Foner, Eric. *Free Soil, Free Labor, Free Men: The Ideology of the Republican Party before the Civil War.* New York: Oxford University Press, 1970.

Freedman, Estelle. "Separatism as Strategy: Female Institution Building and American Feminism, 1870–1930." *Feminist Studies* 5.3 (Fall 1979): 512–29.

Garman, Mary Van Vleck. "'Altered tone of expression': The Anti-Slavery Rhetoric of Illinois Women, 1837–1847." Ph.D. diss., Northwestern University Garrett-Evangelical Theological Seminary, 1989.

Ginzberg, Lori D. "'Moral Suasion Is Moral Balderdash': Women, Politics, and Social Activism in the 1850s." *Journal of American History* 73.3 (December 1986): 601–22.

———. *Women and the Work of Benevolence: Morality, Politics, and Class in the Nineteenth-Century United States.* New Haven: Yale University Press, 1990.

Gray, Susan E. *The Yankee West: Community Life on the Michigan Frontier.* Chapel Hill: University of North Carolina Press, 1996.

Grimsted, David. *American Mobbing, 1828–1861: Toward Civil War.* New York: Oxford University Press, 1998.

Halbersleben, Karen I. *Women's Participation in the British Antislavery Movement, 1824–1865.* Lewiston, ME: E. Mellen Press, 1993.

Hansen, Debra Gold. "The Boston Female Anti-Slavery Society and the Limits of Gender Politics." In Yellin and Van Horne, *Abolitionist Sisterhood,* 45–65.

———. *Strained Sisterhood: Gender and Class in the Boston Female Anti-Slavery Society.* Amherst: University of Massachusetts Press, 1993.

Hansen, Karen. "Feminist Conceptions of Public and Private: A Critical Analysis." *Berkeley Journal of Sociology* 32 (1987): 105–28.

———. *A Very Social Time: Crafting Community in Antebellum New England.* Berkeley and Los Angeles: University of California Press, 1994.

Harley, Sharon. "Northern Black Female Workers: Jacksonian Era." In *The Afro-American Woman: Struggles and Images,* ed. Sharon Harley and Rosalyn Terborg-Penn, 5–16. Port Washington, NY: Kennikat Press, 1978.

Heard, Patricia. "'One Blood All Nations': Anti-Slavery Petitions in Sandwich." *Annual Excursion of the Sandwich Historical Society* 59 (1978): 26–31.

Hersh, Blanche Glassman. *The Slavery of Sex: Feminist-Abolitionists in America.* Urbana: University of Illinois Press, 1978.

———. "To Make the World Better: Protestant Women in the Abolitionist Movement." In *Triumph over Silence: Women in Protestant History,* ed. Richard L. Greaves, 173–202. Westport, CT: Greenwood Press, 1985.

Hershberger, Mary. "Mobilizing Women, Anticipating Abolition: The Struggle against Indian Removal in the 1830s." *Journal of American History* 86.1 (June 1999): 15–40.

Hewitt, Nancy. "The Perimeters of Women's Power in American Religion." In *The Evangelical Tradition in America,* ed. Leonard I. Sweet, 233–56. 1984. Macon, GA: Mercer University Press, 1997.

———. "The Social Origins of Women's Antislavery Politics in Western New York." In *Crusaders and Compromisers: Essays on the Relationship of the Antislavery Struggle to the Antebellum Party System,* ed. Alan M. Kraut, 205–33. Westport, CT: Greenwood Press, 1983.

———. *Women's Activism and Social Change: Rochester, New York, 1822–1872.* Ithaca, NY: Cornell University Press, 1984.

Horton, James O. "Freedom's Yoke: Gender Conventions among Antebellum Free Blacks." *Feminist Studies* 12.1 (Spring 1986): 51–76.

Horton, Lois E. "Community Organization and Social Activism: Black Boston and the Antislavery Movement." *Sociological Inquiry* 55.2 (Spring 1985): 182–99.

Houchins, Sue E. *Spiritual Narratives.* New York: Oxford University Press, 1988.

Isenberg, Nancy. *Sex and Citizenship in Antebellum America.* Chapel Hill: University of North Carolina Press, 1998.

Jeffrey, Julie Roy. *The Great Silent Army of Abolitionism: Ordinary Women in the Antislavery Movement.* Chapel Hill: University of North Carolina Press, 1998.

———. "Permeable Boundaries: Abolitionist Women and Separate Spheres." *Journal of the Early Republic* 21.1 (2001): 79–93.

Kelley, Mary. "Beyond the Boundaries." *Journal of the Early Republic* 21.1 (2001): 73–78.

Kerber, Linda K. *No Constitutional Right to Be Ladies: Women and the Obligations of Citizenship.* New York: Hill and Wang, 1998.

———. "Separate Spheres, Female Worlds, Woman's Place: The Rhetoric of Women's History." *Journal of American History* 75.1 (1998): 9–39.

———. *Women of the Republic: Intellect and Ideology in Revolutionary America.* Chapel Hill: University of North Carolina, 1980.

Kraditor, Aileen S. *Means and Ends in American Abolitionism: Garrison and His Critics on Strategy and Tactics, 1834–1850.* New York: Pantheon Books, 1969.

Lapsansky, Emma. "Feminism, Freedom, and Community: Charlotte Forten and Women Activists in Nineteenth-Century Philadelphia." *Pennsylvania Magazine of History and Biography* 113.1 (January 1989): 3–19.

Lapsansky, Phillip. "Graphic Discord: Abolitionist and Antiabolitionist Images." In Yellin and Van Horne, *Abolitionist Sisterhood,* 201–30.

Lasser, Carol. "Beyond Separate Spheres: The Power of Public Opinion." *Journal of the Early Republic* 21.1 (2001): 115–23.

Lawes, Carolyn J. *Women and Reform in a New England Community, 1815–1860.* Lexington: University Press of Kentucky, 2000.

Lebsock, Suzanne. *The Free Women of Petersburg: Status and Culture in a Southern Town, 1784–1860.* New York: W. W. Norton, 1984.

Lerner, Gerda. *The Grimké Sisters from South Carolina: Rebels against Slavery.* Boston: Houghton Mifflin, 1967.

———. "The Political Activities of Antislavery Women." In *The Majority Finds Its Past: Placing Women in History,* ed. Gerda Lerner, 112–28. New York: Oxford University Press, 1979.

Lutz, Alma. *Crusade for Freedom: Women of the Antislavery Movement.* Boston: Beacon Press, 1968.

Magdol, Edward. *The Antislavery Rank and File: A Social Profile of the Abolitionists' Constituency.* Westport, CT: Greenwood Press, 1986.

———. "A Window on the Abolitionist Constituency: Antislavery Petitions, 1836–1839." In *Crusaders and Compromisers: Essays on the Relationship of the Antislavery Struggle to the Antebellum Party System,* ed. Alan M. Kraut, 45–70. Westport, CT: Greenwood Press, 1983.

Manring, Lynn, and Jack Larkin, eds. *Women, Anti-Slavery, and the Constitution in Rural New England: A Sourcebook of Interpretation.* Vol. 2. Massachusetts: Old Sturbridge Village, [1984].

Mathews, Donald G. "The Second Great Awakening as an Organizing Process, 1780–1830: An Hypothesis." *American Quarterly* 21.1 (1969): 23–43.

McBride, Genevieve G. *On Wisconsin Women: Working for Their Rights from Settlement to Suffrage.* Madison: University of Wisconsin Press, 1993.

McClelland, Peter D., and Richard J. Zeckhauser. *Demographic Dimensions of the New Republic: American Interregional Migration, Vital Statistics, and Manumissions, 1800–1860.* New York: Cambridge University Press, 1982.

McCusker, John J. *How Much Is That in Real Money? A Historical Commodity Price Index for Use as a Deflator of Money Values in the Economy of the United States.* 2nd ed. Worcester, MA: American Antiquarian Society, 2001.

McGerr, Michael. "Political Style and Women's Power, 1830–1930." *Journal of American History* 77.3 (December 1990): 864–85.

Melder, Keith E. *Beginnings of Sisterhood: The American Woman's Rights Movement, 1800–1850.* New York: Schocken Books, 1977.

Melia, Margot. "The Role of Black Garrisonian Women in Anti-Slavery and Other Reforms in the Antebellum North, 1830–1865." Ph.D. diss., University of Western Australia, 1991.

Midgley, Clare. "'Remember Those in Bonds, As Bound with Them': Women's approach to anti-slavery campaigning in Britain, 1780–1870." In *Women, Migration, and Empire,* ed. Joan Grant, 73–102. Staffordshire, England: Trentham Books, 1996.

———. "Slave Sugar Boycotts, Female Activism and the Domestic Base of British Anti-Slavery Culture." *Slavery and Abolition* 17.3 (December 1996): 137–62.

———. *Women against Slavery: The British Campaigns, 1780–1870.* London: Routledge, 1992.

Nash, Gary B., and Jean R. Soderlund. *Freedom by Degrees: Emancipation in Pennsylvania and Its Aftermath.* New York: Oxford University Press, 1991.

Newman, Richard S. *The Transformation of American Abolitionism: Fighting Slavery in the Early Republic.* Chapel Hill: University of North Carolina Press, 2002.

Nuermberger, Ruth. *The Free Produce Movement: A Quaker Protest against Slavery.* Durham, NC: Duke University Press, 1942.

Pease, Jane H., and William H. Pease. "Negro Conventions and the Problem of Black Leadership." *Journal of Black Studies* 2.1 (1971): 29–44.

———. "The Role of Women in the Antislavery Movement." In *Canadian Historical Association, Historical Papers Presented at the Annual Meeting,* ed. John P. H. Atherton and Fernand Ouellet, 167–83. Ottawa: 1967.

Petrulionis, Sandra Harbert. "'Swelling that Great Tide of Humanity': The Concord, Massachusetts, Female Anti-Slavery Society." *New England Quarterly* 74.3 (2001): 385–418.

Pierson, Michael D. "Between Antislavery and Abolition: The Politics and Rhetoric of Jane Grey Swisshelm." *Pennsylvania History* 60.3 (July 1993): 305–21.

———. *Free Hearts and Free Homes: Gender and American Antislavery Politics.* Chapel Hill: University of North Carolina Press, 2003.

———. "Gender and Party Ideologies: The Constitutional Thought of Women and Men in American Anti-Slavery Politics." *Slavery and Abolition* 19.3 (1998): 46–67.

Porter, Dorothy B. "The Organized Educational Activities of Negro Literary Societies, 1828–1846." *Journal of Negro Education* 5.4 (October 1936): 555–76.

Quarles, Benjamin. *Black Abolitionists.* New York: Oxford University Press, 1969.

———. *The Negro in the American Revolution.* Chapel Hill: University of North Carolina Press, 1961.

Quist, John W. "'The Great Majority of Our Subscribers Are Farmers': The Michigan Abolitionist Constituency of the 1840s." *Journal of the Early Republic* 14.3 (Fall 1994): 325–58.

Rice, C. Duncan. "The Anti-Slavery Mission of George Thompson to the United States, 1834–1835." *Journal of American Studies* 2.1 (April 1968): 13–31.

Richards, Leonard. *"Gentlemen of Property and Standing": Anti-Abolition Mobs in Jacksonian America.* New York: Oxford University Press, 1970.

Rosenthal, Naomi, et al. "Social Movements and Network Analysis: A Case Study of Nineteenth-Century Women's Reform in New York State." *American Journal of Sociology* 90.5 (March 1985): 1022–54.

Ruchames, Louis. "Race, Marriage, and Abolition in Massachusetts." *Journal of Negro History* 40 (1955): 250–73.

———, ed. *The Abolitionists.* New York: Putnam, 1963.

Runcie, John. "'Hunting the Nigs' in Philadelphia: The Race Riot of August 1834." *Pennsylvania History* 39 (April 1972): 187–218.

Rupp, Leila J. "Constructing Internationalism: The Case of Transnational Women's Organizations, 1888–1945." *American Historical Review* 99.5 (December 1994): 1571–1600.

Ryan, Mary P. *Cradle of the Middle Class: The Family in Oneida County, New York, 1790–1865.* Cambridge: Cambridge University Press, 1981.

———. "The Power of Women's Networks: A Case Study of Female Moral Reform in Antebellum America." *Feminist Studies* 5.1 (Spring 1979): 66–86.

———. "A Women's Awakening: Evangelical Religion and the Families of Utica, New York, 1800–1840." *American Quarterly* 30.5 (Winter 1978): 602–23.

Scott, Anne Firor. "Most Invisible of All: Black Women's Voluntary Associations." *Journal of Southern History* 56.1 (1990): 3–22.

Seigel, Peggy Brase. "Moral Champions and Public Pathfinders: Antebellum Quaker Women in Eastcentral Indiana." *Quaker History* 81.2 (1992): 87–106.

Sellers, Charles Grier. *The Market Revolution: Jacksonian America, 1815–1846.* New York: Oxford University Press, 1991.

Sewell, Richard H. *Ballots for Freedom: Antislavery Politics in the United States, 1837–1860.* New York: Oxford University Press, 1976.

Sheriff, Carol. *The Artificial River: The Erie Canal and the Paradox of Progress, 1817–1862.* New York: Hill and Wang, 1996.

Sklar, Kathryn Kish. "'Women Who Speak for an Entire Nation': American and British Women Compared at the World Anti-Slavery Convention, London, 1840." *Pacific Historical Review* 59 (November 1990): 453–99.

Smith-Rosenberg, Carroll. "The Female World of Love and Ritual: Relations between Women in Nineteenth-Century America." *Signs* 1.1 (1975): 1–30.

Soderlund, Jean R. "Priorities and Power: The Philadelphia Female Anti-Slavery Society." In Yellin and Van Horne, *Abolitionist Sisterhood,* 67–88.

Speicher, Anna M. "'Faith Which Worketh By Love': The Religious World of Female Anti-Slavery Lecturers." Ph.D. diss., George Washington University, 1996.

———. *The Religious World of Antislavery Women: Spirituality in the Lives of Five Abolitionist Lecturers.* Syracuse, NY: Syracuse University Press, 2000.

Staudenraus, Philip J. *The African Colonization Movement, 1816–1865.* New York: Columbia University Press, 1961.

Stauffer, John. *The Black Hearts of Men: Radical Abolitionists and the Transformation of Race.* Cambridge: Harvard University Press, 2002.

Sterling, Dorothy. *Ahead of Her Time: Abby Kelley and the Politics of Anti-Slavery.* New York: W. W. Norton, 1991.

———, ed. *We Are Your Sisters: Black Women in the Nineteenth Century.* New York: W. W. Norton, 1984.

Strong, Douglas M. *Perfectionist Politics: Abolitionism and the Religious Tensions of American Democracy.* Syracuse, NY: Syracuse University Press, 1999.

Sussman, Charlotte. *Consuming Anxieties: Consumer Protest, Gender, and British Slavery, 1713–1833.* Stanford, CA: Stanford University Press, 2000.

Swerdlow, Amy. "Abolition's Conservative Sisters: The Ladies' New York City Anti-Slavery Societies, 1834–1840." In Yellin and Van Horne, *Abolitionist Sisterhood,* 31–44.

Taylor, Clare. *British and American Abolitionists: An Episode in Transatlantic Understanding.* Chicago: Edinburgh University Press, 1974.

———. *Women of the Anti-Slavery Movement: The Weston Sisters.* New York: St. Martin's Press, 1995.

Tomkins, Silvan. "The Psychology of Commitment: The Constructive Role of Violence and Suffering for the Individual and for His Society." In *The Antislavery Vanguard: New Essays on the Abolitionists,* ed. Martin Duberman, 270–98. Princeton, NJ: Princeton University Press, 1965.

Truedley, Mary Bosworth. "The 'Benevolent Fair': A Study of Charitable Organization among American Women in the First Third of the Nineteenth Century." *Social Service Review* 16 (September 1940): 509–22.

Van Broekhoven, Deborah Bingham. "'Better than a Clay Club': The Organization of Anti-Slavery Fairs, 1835–1860." *Slavery and Abolition* 19.1 (1998): 24–45.

———. "'A Determination to Labor . . .': Female Antislavery Activity in Rhode Island." *Rhode Island History* 44.2 (1985): 35–44.

———. "'Let Your Names Be Enrolled': Method and Ideology in Women's Antislavery Petitioning." In Yellin and Van Horne, *Abolitionist Sisterhood*, 179–99.

Varon, Elizabeth. *We Mean to Be Counted: White Women and Politics in Antebellum Virginia*. Chapel Hill: University of North Carolina Press, 1998.

Venet, Wendy Hamand. *Neither Ballots nor Bullets: Women Abolitionists and the Civil War*. Charlottesville: University Press of Virginia, 1991.

Vorenberg, Michael. *Final Freedom: The Civil War, the Abolition of Slavery, and the Thirteenth Amendment*. New York: Cambridge University Press, 2001.

Walters, Ronald G. *The Antislavery Appeal: American Abolitionism after 1830*. Baltimore: Johns Hopkins University Press, 1976.

Watson, Harry L. *Liberty and Power: The Politics of Jacksonian America*. New York: The Noonday Press, 1990.

Wellman, Judith. "Women and Radical Reform in Antebellum Upstate New York: A Profile of Grassroots Female Abolitionists." In *Clio Was a Woman: Studies in the History of American Women*, ed. Mabel E. Deutrich and Virginia C. Purdy, 113–27. Washington, D.C.: Howard University Press, 1980.

White, Shane. *Somewhat More Independent: The End of Slavery in New York City, 1770–1810*. Athens: University of Georgia Press, 1991.

Wilkinson, Norman B. "The Philadelphia Free Produce Attack upon Slavery." *Pennsylvania Magazine of History and Biography* 64 (1942): 294–313.

Williams, Carolyn. "The Female Antislavery Movement: Fighting against Racial Prejudice and Promoting Women's Rights in Antebellum America." In Yellin and Van Horne, *Abolitionist Sisterhood*, 159–77.

———. "Religion, Race, and Gender in Antebellum American Radicalism: The Philadelphia Female Anti-Slavery Society, 1833–1870." Ph.D. diss., University of California–Los Angeles, 1991.

Winch, Julie. "'You Have Talents—Only Cultivate Them': Philadelphia's Black Female Literary Societies and the Abolitionist Crusade." In Yellin and Van Horne, *Abolitionist Sisterhood*, 101–19.

Wyatt-Brown, Bertram. "The Abolitionists' Postal Campaign of 1835." *Journal of Negro History* 50.4 (1965): 227–38.

Yee, Shirley. *Black Women Abolitionists: A Study in Activism, 1828–1860*. Knoxville: University of Tennessee Press, 1992.

Yellin, Jean Fagan, and John Van Horne, eds. *The Abolitionist Sisterhood: Women's Political Culture in Antebellum America*. Ithaca, NY: Cornell University Press, 1994.

Young, Louise M. "Women's Place in American Politics: The Historical Perspective." *Journal of Politics* 38.3 (1976): 295–335.

Zaeske, Susan. "Petitioning, Antislavery, and the Emergence of Women's Political Consciousness." Ph.D. diss., University of Wisconsin–Madison, 1997.

———. *Signatures of Citizenship: Petitioning, Antislavery, and Women's Political Identity*. Chapel Hill: University of North Carolina Press, 2003.

Zboray, Ronald J., and Mary Saracino Zboray. "Whig Women, Politics, and Culture in the Campaign of 1840: Three Perspectives from Massachusetts." *Journal of the Early Republic* 17.2 (Summer 1997): 278–315.

Zilversmit, Arthur. *The First Emancipation: The Abolition of Slavery in the North*. Chicago: University of Chicago Press, 1967.

Index

Female antislavery societies (FASS) are referred to in the index by the city and state in which they are located, e.g., Ladies' New-York City Anti-Slavery Society is addressed as "New York (NY) FASS."

Page numbers in italics refer to figures.

Ch'i, Hsi-sheng. "The Chinese Warlord System as an International System," in Kaplan, ed. (q.v.).

Chiang Chieh-shih [Chiang Kai-shek]. *Chiang wei-yuan-chang hsin-sheng-huo yün-tung chiang-yen chi* (A collection of the Generalissimo's lectures on the New Life Movement). Nanchang, 1937.

Chiang-hsi nien-chien (Kiangsi yearbook). Nanchang, 1936.

Chiang-hsi sheng-cheng-fu ho-shih pan-kung chih shih-shih (The practice of consolidating departmental offices in the Kiangsi provincial government). Kiangsi Provincial Government. Nanchang, 1935.

Chiang-su sheng nung-ts'un tiao-ch'a (Rural survey of Kiangsu province). Joint Commission on Rural Reconstruction of the Executive Yuan. Nanking, 1935.

Ch'ien Chun-tuan. "Mu-ch'ien wei-chi chung ti chung-kuo nung-min sheng-huo" (Chinese peasant life in the current crisis), *TFTC*, 32: 1 (1935).

Ch'ien Tuan-sheng. *The Government and Politics of China.* Cambridge, Mass., 1950.

——. *Min-kuo cheng-chih shih* (A history of political institutions in republican China), vol. 2. Shanghai, 1939.

China Year Book. Edited by H. G. W. Woodhead. Shanghai, 1928–38.

Chou, Shun-hsin. *The Chinese Inflation, 1937–1949.* New York, 1963.

Chuang Ch'iang-hua. "Chin-lai t'ien-fu fu-chia ti hsien-chih" (Recent restrictions on the land surtax), *Ti-cheng yüeh-k'an* (Land administration monthly), 4: 2–3 (1936).

Chung-hua min-kuo fa-kuei ta-ch'üan (Complete legal regulations of the Republic of China), vol. 2. Nanking, 1936.

Chung-hua nien-chien (China yearbook), vols. 1 and 2. Nanking, 1948.

Chung-kuo Kuo-min-tang nien-chien (Kuomintang yearbook). Nanking, 1929, 1934.

Chü Cheng. "Szu-fa tang-hua wen-t'i" (The issue of party control over the judiciary), *TFTC*, 32: 10 (1935).

Ch'ü Wei-wen. "Lan-i she yü Chung-kuo Kuo-min-tang" (The Blue Shirt Society and the Kuomintang of China), *Ch'ing-nien chün-jen* (Young soldiers), 2: 6 (1934).

Chün-shih wei-yuan-hui wei-yuan-chang hsing-ying cheng-chih kung-tso pao-kao (A report on political work by the headquarters of the chairman of the Military Council). Nanchang, 1935.

Clubb, O. Edmund. *Twentieth Century China.* New York, 1964.

Eastman, Lloyd E. "Chiang Kai-shek and the Kuomintang During the Nanking Period: An Abortive Revolution." Paper presented at the Conference of the Association for Asian Studies, Washington, D.C., March 1971.

Easton, David. *A Systems Analysis of Political Life.* New York, 1965.

Eisenstadt, S. N. "Tradition, Change, and Modernity: Reflections on the Chinese Experience," in Ho and Tsou, eds. (q.v.), bk. 2.

Fang Ch'iu-wei. "Ssu-ch'uan tsai Chung-kuo cheng-chih ti ti-wei" (Sze-chwan in Chinese politics), *Shen-pao yüeh-k'an* (*Shen-pao* monthly), 4: 12 (1935).

Fang Tung-ying. "Liu Jih shih-kuan hsi yü min-kuo cheng-t'an" (The Japan-returned Shikan Gakko Clique in the politics of the republic), *I-wen chih* (Annals of literary pursuits), nos. 54 and 55, 1970.

Fei Hsiao-t'ung. *China's Gentry.* Chicago, 1953.

———. *Peasant Life in China.* London, 1943.

———. "Peasantry and Gentry," *American Journal of Sociology*, 52: 1 (1946).

——— and Chang Chih-i. *Earthbound China.* London, 1948.

Feng Ho-fa. *Chung-kuo nung-ts'un ching-chi chu-liao* (Information on Chinese rural economics), vol. 2. Shanghai, 1935.

Fong, Hsien-ding. "Toward Economic Control in China." Data paper for the China Institute of Pacific Relations. Shanghai, 1936.

Gasster, Michael. "Reform and Revolution in China's Political Modernization," in Wright, ed. (q.v.).

Gerth, Hans H., and C. Wright Mills, eds. *From Max Weber: Essays in Sociology.* New York, 1958.

Gillin, Donald G. "Problems of Centralization in Republican China: The Case of Ch'en Ch'eng and the Kuomintang," *Journal of Asian Studies*, 29: 4 (1970).

———. *Warlord: Yen Hsi-shan in Shansi Province, 1911–1949.* Princeton, N.J., 1967.

Gray, Jack, ed. *Modern China's Search for a Political Form.* New York, 1969.

Hanwell, Norman D. "The Dragnet of Local Government in China," *Pacific Affairs*, 10: 1 (1937).

Hatano Ken'ichi. *Chugoku Kokuminto tsushi* (A general history of the Kuomintang). Tokyo, 1943.

———. *Gendai Shina no seiji to jimbutsu* (Political figures in contemporary China). Tokyo, 1937.

Hatano, Yoshihiro. "The New Armies," in Wright, ed. (q.v.).

Ho-nan sheng nung-ts'un tiao-ch'a (Rural survey of Honan province). Joint Commission on Rural Reconstruction of the Executive Yuan. Nanking, 1934.

Ho, Ping-ti, and Tang Tsou, eds. *China in Crisis.* Vol. 1: *China's Heritage and the Communist Political System*, 2 books. Chicago, 1968.

Ho Yüeh-tseng. "Lun kai-liang tang-wu kung-tso" (Essay on the improvement of party affairs), *TLPL*, no. 173, 1935.

How Chinese Officials Amass Millions. Economic Information Service of Great Britain. Hong Kong, 1948.

Hsiao Kung-chuan. *Rural China: Imperial Control in the Nineteenth Century.* Seattle, 1960.

Hsien tsu-chih fa (Organizational law of the county). Executive Yuan. Nanking, 1929.

Hsü Kao-yang, ed. *Kuo-fang nien-chien* (National defense yearbook). Hong Kong, 1969.

Hu Han-min and Sun Fo. "Hsun-cheng ta-kang t'i-an shuo-ming-shu" (An explanation of the outlined proposal for political tutelage), *Kuo-wen chou-pao* (Kuowen weekly, illustrated), 5: 13 (1931).

Hu-nan nien-chien (Hunan yearbook). Changsha, 1932, 1936.

Huang Hsü-ch'u. "Kuei chi lu-ta t'ung-hsüeh yu to-shao" (How many army college graduates are from Kwangsi?), *CC*, no. 205, 1966.

————. "Wo pei t'ui Chin-ching ts'an-chia ssu chung-ch'uan-hui ching-kuo" (My experiences at the Fourth Party Congress in Nanking), *CC*, no. 124, 1962.

Huang-p'u chien-chün san-shih nien kai-shih (A brief survey of Whampoa's thirty-year military history). Historical archives committee of the Kuomintang. Taipei, 1954.

Huang Shao-hung. *Wu-shih hui-i* (Reminiscences at fifty), vol. 2, Shanghai, 1945.

Huntington, Samuel P. "Political Development and Political Decay," *World Politics*, 17: 3 (1965).

————. *Political Order in Changing Societies*. New Haven, Conn., 1968.

I-hsün [pseud.]. *Chiang tang chen hsiang* (A true picture of Chiang's party). Hong Kong, 1949.

Isaacs, Harold R. *The Tragedy of the Chinese Revolution*, 2d rev. ed. Stanford, Calif., 1961.

Jacobitts, Suzanne D. "Political Theory and Comparative Politics: A Critique of the Political Theory of the Committee on Comparative Politics." Unpublished Ph.D. dissertation, University of Wisconsin, 1967.

Jordan, Donald A. "The Northern Expedition—A Military Victory." Unpublished Ph.D. dissertation, University of Wisconsin, 1967.

Kan-cheng shih-nien (A decade of Kiangsi administration). Nanchang, 1941.

K'ao-shih yuan kung-pao (Bulletin of the Examination Yuan), Nanking, no. 11, 1935.

Kaplan, Morton C., ed. *New Approaches to International Relations*. New York, 1968.

Kapp, Robert A. "Provincial Independence vs. National Rule: A Case Study of Szechwan in the 1920's and 1930's," *Journal of Asian Studies*, 30: 3 (1971).

Kennedy, Melville T., Jr. "The Kuomintang and Chinese Unification, 1928–1931." Unpublished Ph.D. dissertation, Harvard University, 1958.

Ko-sheng kao-chi hsing-cheng jen-yuan hui-i chi-lu (A conference record of high-level provincial administrative elites). Secretariat of the headquarters of the chairman of the Military Council. Nanchang, 1934.

"Kuang-tung t'ung-chi tsu-chih" (Kwangtung statistical organization), *Nei-cheng t'ung-chi chi-k'an* (Statistics quarterly of the Interior), no. 1, 1936.

Kung-chi Ch'en Kuo-fu hsien-sheng chi-nien ts'e (A pamphlet commemorating the public funeral of Ch'en Kuo-fu). Taipei, 1951.

Kuo-min cheng-fu chün-shih wei-yuan-hui wei-yuan-chang Nan-ch'ang hsing-ying ch'u-li chiao-fei sheng-fen cheng-chih kung-tso pao-kao mu-lu (A report by the National Military Council headquarters at Nanchang on political work in the Bandit Suppression Provinces). Nanchang, 1934.

Landis, Richard B. "The Origins of Whampoa Graduates Who Served in the Northern Expedition," *Studies on Asia*, vol. 5 (1964).

Lasswell, Harold D., and Daniel Lerner, eds. *World Revolutionary Elites.* Cambridge, Mass., 1965.

Lee, Shu-ching. "Social Implications of Farm Tenants in China." Unpublished Ph.D. dissertation, University of Chicago, 1948.

Lei Hsiao-ts'en. See Ma Wu Hsien-sheng.

Li Chien-nung. *The Political History of China, 1840–1928.* Translated by Ssu-yu Teng and Jeremy Ingalls. Princeton, N.J., 1956.

Li Chih-t'ang [Li Shi-do]. *Nankin to seifu no hisei* (A political record of the Kuomintang government). Translated into Japanese by the author. Tientsin, 1937.

Li P'u-sheng. "Hsing-cheng chi-hua ti hsing-ch'eng yü k'ao-ho" (Formulation and examination of administrative planning), *Hsing-cheng hsiao-lü* (Administrative efficiency), 2: 6 (1935).

Li Tsung-huang. "Lu-chün ssu hsiao t'ung-hsüeh hui ti chi-lu" (A record of the Four Army Schools Alumni Association), *I-wen chih* (Annals of literary pursuits), no. 47, 1969.

———. "Yun-lung feng-hu ti Pao-ting hsüeh-hsiao" (The outstanding Paoting Military Academy), *I-wen chih* (Annals of literary pursuits), no. 46, 1969.

Lipset, Seymour Martin. *The First New Nation.* New York, 1963.

Liu Chien-ch'ün. *Yin-ho i-wang* (Memories by the silver stream). Taipei, 1966.

Liu, F. F. *A Military History of Modern China, 1924–1949.* Princeton, N.J., 1956.

Liu, Kwang-ching. "Nineteenth-Century China: The Disintegration of the Old Order and the Impact of the West," in Ho and Tsou, eds. (q.v.), bk. 1.

Liu Sheng-min. "Cheng-hsüeh-hsi t'an-yuan" (In search of the origins of the Political Study Clique), *Hai-wai lun-t'an* (The overseas tribune), 2: 7, 8, and 11 (1961).

Liu, Ta-chung. *China's National Income, 1931–1936.* Washington, D.C., 1946.

Lo Tun-wei. *Wu-shih nien hui-i-lu* (Reminiscences at fifty). Taipei, 1952.

Loh, Pichon P. Y. *The Early Chiang Kai-shek: A Study of His Personality and Politics, 1887–1924.* New York, 1971.

————. "The Politics of Chiang Kai-shek," *Journal of Asian Studies*, 25: 3 (1966).

Lu-chün chün-kuan hsüeh-hsiao hsiao-shih (A history of the [Central] Military Academy), vol. 1. Taipei, 1964.

Lu-chün ta-hsüeh-hsiao t'ung-hsüeh lu (Military staff college handbook). N.p., n.d.

Lu Wei-chen. "Hsin liu sheng yü hsi-pei pien-fang ti niao-k'an" (A general look at the six new provinces and the border defense of the northwest), *TFTC*, 27: 14 (1930).

Lü P'ing-teng. *Ssu-ch'uan nung-ts'un ching-chi* (Agrarian economics of Szechwan). Shanghai, 1936.

MacFarquhar, Roderick L. "The Whampoa Military Academy," *Papers on China*, vol. 9. Cambridge, Mass., 1955.

Ma Wu Hsien-sheng. "Chung-kuo tzu-ch'an chieh-chi ti fen-hsi" (An analysis of the Chinese capitalist class), *Shih-shih yüeh-pao* (Current affairs monthly report), 7: 1 and 2 (1932).

————. *Wo-ti sheng-huo shih* (A history of my life). Taipei, 1965.

Ma Yin-ch'u. *Ching-chi lun-wen chi* (A collection of essays on economics). Shanghai, 1947.

Masutaro, Kimura. "Problems of Financial Reform and Readjustment of Public Loans in China." Data paper for the China Institute of Pacific Relations. Shanghai, 1931.

Min-kuo erh-shih-erh nien chien-she (Twenty-two years of republican reconstruction). Central Statistical Bureau of the Kuomintang. Nanking, 1934.

"Min-kuo erh-shih nien shui-tsai tsai-ch'ü ching-chi tiao-ch'a" (An economic survey of areas affected by the 1931 flood), *Chin-ning hsüeh-pao* (Nanking journal), 2: 1 (1932).

Ming Su. "Chung-yang cheng-chih hsüeh-hsiao ti hsüeh-sheng sheng-huo" (Student life at the Central Political Academy), *TLPL*, no. 186, 1935.

Moore, Barrington, Jr. *Social Origins of Dictatorship and Democracy.* Boston, 1966.

Mu, Wei-chin. "Provincial–Central Government Relations and the Problem of National Unity of Modern China." Unpublished Ph.D. dissertation, Princeton University, 1948.

Nei-cheng kung-pao (Bulletin of the Interior), Nanking, vols. 7 and 9, 1936.

Nei-cheng nien-chien (Yearbook of the Interior). Civil Affairs Section. Nanking, 1935–37.

Ni Wei-ch'ing. *Ko-chi hsing-cheng hsi-t'ung chi ch'i tsu-chih* (Various administrative systems and their organization). Nanking, 1937.

North, Robert C., and Ithiel de Sola Pool. "Kuomintang and Chinese Communist Elites," in Lasswell and Lerner, eds. (q.v.).

Paauw, Douglas S. "Chinese Public Finance During the Nanking Government." Unpublished Ph.D. dissertation, Harvard University, 1950.

————. "The Kuomintang and Economic Stagnation, 1928–1937," *Journal of Asian Studies*, 16: 2 (1957).

Payne, Robert. *Chiang Kai-shek*. New York, 1969.

P'eng Jui-fu. "Yen-cheng kai-ke yü hsin-yen-fa chih shih-shih" (Salt administration reform and the new rules in practice), *TFTC*, 32: 10 (1935).

Perleberg, Max. *Who's Who in Modern China*. New York, 1960.

Po Fen [pseud]. "Kao-k'ao chi-ke jen-yuan jcn-yung shih-lu" (A true record of appointments to those who have passed the higher examinations), *TFTC*, 32: 18 (1936).

Ran-i-sha ni kansuru chosa (An investigation of the Blue Shirt Society). Bureau of Investigation of the Japanese Foreign Ministry. Tokyo, 1937.

Report on Revenue Policy. Commission of Financial Experts, Republic of China. Nanking, 1929.

Roxby, Percy M. "China as an Entity," *Geography*, vol. 19 (March 1934).

Rush, Myron. *Political Succession in the USSR*. New York, 1963.

Salter, Arthur. "China and the Depression—Impressions of a Three Months' Visit," *China Special Series* (National Economic Council), no. 3, May 1934.

"Salvation by Assassination," *China Forum* (Shanghai), July 14, 1933.

Scott, James. "The Analysis of Corruption in Developing Nations," *Comparative Studies in Society and History*, June 1969.

————. "Corruption, Machine Politics, and Political Change," *American Political Science Review*, 62: 4 (1969).

Shang Hsi-hsien. "T'ui-hsing hsien-cheng hsiao-lü ti hsien-chüeh t'iao-chien" (Some prerequisites for promoting efficiency in county administration), *Hsing-cheng hsiao-lü* (Administrative efficiency), 2: 5 (1935).

Shen I-yün. *I-yün hui-i* (Reminiscences of Shen I-yün). Taipei, 1968.

Shen Nai-cheng. "The Local Government of China," *Chinese Social and Political Science Review*, 20: 2 (July 1936).

Shen-pao nien-chien (*Shen-pao* yearbook). Shanghai, 1933, 1936.

Sheridan, James E. *Chinese Warlord: The Career of Feng Yü-hsiang*. Stanford, Calif., 1966.

Shih Pu-chih. "P'ai-hsi tou-cheng chung Yang Yung-t'ai pei tz'u i-an" (Factional struggle and the assassination of Yang Yung-t'ai), *CC*, no. 159, 1964.

Shih Yang-ch'eng. *Chung-kuo sheng hsing-cheng chih-tu* (Administrative systems of China's provinces). Shanghai, 1946.

Shirley, James. "Control of the Kuomintang after Sun Yat-sen's Death," *Journal of Asian Studies*, 25: 1 (1965).

Shou Yü [pseud.]. "Fu-hsing nung-ts'un yü nung-min fu-tan" (Rural reconstruction and the burdens of the peasantry), *TLPL*, no. 66, 1933.

Snow, Edgar. *Red Star over China*. New York, 1961.

Sun Hsiao-ts'un. "Chung-kuo t'ien-tu ti cheng-shou" (Collection of land taxes in China), *Chung-kuo nung-ts'un* (Rural China), 1: 1 (1934).

Sun Huai-jen. *China's Financial Illness and Its Critical Analysis*. Shanghai, 1937.

Tai Yu-nung hsien-sheng nien-p'u (A brief biography of Tai Li). Bureau of Investigation of the Chinese Defense Ministry. Taipei, 1966.

T'ang Leang-li. *The Inner History of the Chinese Revolution*. New York, 1930.

Tawney, Richard Henry. *Land and Labour in China*. London, 1932.

Taylor, George. "Reconstruction after Revolution in Kiangsi Province and the Chinese Nation," *Pacific Affairs*, 8: 3 (1933).

Ti-cheng yüeh-k'an (Land administration monthly), vol. 4, nos. 2–3 (1936).

Ts'ai-cheng nien-chien (Public finance yearbook), vol. 2. Nanking, 1935.

Ts'ai Meng-ch'ien. "Wu-han shih-nien ti hui-i" (Reminiscences of ten years at Wuhan), *Chuan-chi wen-hsüeh* (Biographical literature), 18: 3 (March 1971).

Ts'ang Cho [She-ling wai-shih]. "Pao-ting chün-hsiao ts'ang-sang shih" (The turbulent history of the Paoting Military Academy), *CC*, nos. 63–71, 1960.

Tseng Shih-ying. "Chung-kuo sheng-ch'ü fan-wei" (China's provincial boundaries), *Shen-pao yüeh-k'an* (*Shen-pao* monthly), 1: 2 (1932).

Tsou Lu. *Chung-kuo Kuo-min-tang shih-kao* (Draft history of the Kuomintang), vol. 1. Chungking, 1941.

Tsou, Tang, ed. *China in Crisis*. Vol. 2: *China's Policies in Asia and America's Alternatives*. Chicago, 1968.

Van Slyke, Lyman P. *Enemies and Friends: The United Front in Chinese Communist History*. Stanford, Calif., 1967.

Wan Kuo-ting. "Chung-kuo t'ien-fu niao-k'an chi ch'i kai-ke ch'ien-t'u" (China's land tax: An overview of its present status and the prospects for reform), *Ti-cheng yüeh-k'an* (Land administration monthly), 4: 2–3 (1936).

Wang Ching-wei, Li Tsung-jen, Sun Fo, et al. *T'ao Chiang yen-lun chi* (Messages against Chiang Kai-shek). Canton, 1931.

Wang Tz'u-p'u. "Shih nien lai chih Chiang-hsi min-cheng" (Civil administration in Kiangsi in the last decade), in *Kan-cheng shih-nien* (q.v.).

Wang, Yi C. *Chinese Intellectuals and the West*. Chapel Hill, N.C., 1966.

Wang Yüan-pi. "T'ien-fu cheng-shou chih-tu ti kai-ke" (Reform of the system of land taxation), *TFTC*, 32: 7 (1935).

Whitney, Joseph B. R. *China: Area, Administration, and Nation Building*. Chicago, 1970.

Who's Who in China: Biographies of Chinese Leaders, 5th ed. Compiled by the staff of the *China Weekly Review*. Shanghai, 1936.

Wilbur, C. Martin. "Military Separatism and the Process of Reunification under the Nationalist Regime, 1922–1937," in Ho and Tsou, eds. (q.v.), bk. 1.

Wolf, Eric R. *Peasant Wars of the Twentieth Century*. New York, 1969.

Wright, Mary C. "From Revolution to Restoration: The Transformation of Kuomintang Ideology," *Far Eastern Quarterly*, 14: 4 (August 1955).

———, ed. *China in Revolution: The First Phase, 1900–1913*. New Haven, Conn., 1968.

Wu Ch'ao-shu. "So-hsiao sheng-ch'ü t'i-an li-yu-shu" (A statement on the proposal to redefine provincial boundaries), *TFTC*, 28: 8 (1931).

Yang Yung-t'ai. *Yang Yung-t'ai hsien-sheng yen-lun chi* (Lectures by Yang Yung-t'ai). Malaysia, 1963.

———. "Nan-ch'ang hsing-ying tsung-p'ing" (An overall assessment of the Nanchang headquarters), in *Kuo-min cheng-fu chün-shih wei-yuan-hui pao-kao* (q.v.).

Young, Arthur N. *China and the Helping Hand, 1937–45*. Cambridge, Mass., 1963.

———. *China's Nation-Building Effort, 1927–1937: The Financial and Economic Record*. Hoover Institution Press. Stanford, Calif., 1971.

Yü, George T. *Party Politics in Republican China*. Berkeley, Calif., 1966.

Zolberg, Aristide R. *Creating Political Order: The Party State of West Africa*. Chicago, 1966.

Index

administrative inspectorate system, 107–8, 110–11, 113

Anhwei, 5, 15, 28, 31, 50, 104, 107; finances of, 8of, 152–61 *passim*, 167, 174

bandit suppression (anti-Communist) campaigns, 5, 15, 40f, 69–70, 96–98, 101, 154, 180; and provincial finances, 155–58, 171, 173

Bandit Suppression Zones, 5, 26, 69, 76, 99, 18of; party strength in, 29, 33, 104; finances of, 82, 157–58, 171ff, 174–75; administration of, 92, 97–98, 102–14, 131–34, 138

Blue Shirt Society (Lan-i She), 3, 33, 45, 47, 53, 54–65, 71f, 178–79, 200

Bureau of Investigation and Statistics, 60, 152

Canton, 13n, 14, 29, 36, 85, 152

C.C. Clique, 3, 45, 47–52, 55, 71, 126, 157, 178f; in the provinces, 50, 132, 144; and the Blue Shirt Society, 63, 72; and the Political Study Clique, 65, 70, 149

Central Executive Committee (CEC), 11n, 12f, 17f, 27, 31–55 *passim*, 98, 116, 159, 178

Central Military Academy, 54, 56, 59, 118

Central Organization Department, 12, 33, 48, 50, 126

Central Party Affairs Academy, *see* Central Political Academy

Central Political Academy, 126–27, 132, 206

Central Political Council, *see* Political Council

Central Statistical Bureau, 50, 63

Central Supervisory Committee, 17, 27, 31, 34, 37, 48, 53

Chahar, 10, 68, 89, 156ff, 170

Chang Chia-ao, 66f

Chang Chih-chung, 54, 56

Chang Ching-chiang, 23n, 48

Chang Chün-mai, 66

Chang Ch'ün, 66ff, 71, 103f, 116n, 117

Chang Ch'ung, 200

Chang Fa-k'uei, 121

Chang Feng-hui, 116

Chang Hsüeh-liang, 28, 41n

Chang Hsün, 65, 124

Chang Huai-chih, 124

Chang Jui (Ray Chang), 24

Chang Li-sheng, 200

Chang Shao-ch'eng, 116n

Chang Tao-fan, 200

Chang Tso-lin, 14f, 109, 124

Chang Yao-ts'eng, 65

Chao Heng-t'i, 122

Chao Li-hua, 49, 51, 200

Chekiang, 5, 15, 31ff, 50, 55, 58, 93, 107, 133, 135; finances of, 8of, 152, 154f, 16of, 166f, 171, 173f

Chekiang Society of Revolutionary Comrades, 49

Chen Ch'i-ts'ai, 116n

Ch'en Chao-ying, 49, 200

Ch'en Ch'eng, 46, 53, 96

Ch'en Chi-t'ang, 28, 41n, 121, 139

Ch'en Ch'i-mei, 47, 66, 68

Ch'en Chung-ming, 12

Ch'en I, 66f, 104, 117